THE SOCIAL LIFE OF POLITICS

THE SOCIAL LIFE OF POLITICS

Ethics, Kinship, and Union Activism in Argentina

SIAN LAZAR

STANFORD UNIVERSITY PRESS
Stanford, California

Stanford University Press
Stanford, California

Printed in the United States of America on acid-free, archival-quality paper

Library of Congress Cataloging-in-Publication Data

Names: Lazar, Sian, author.
Title: The social life of politics : ethics, kinship and union activism in
    Argentina / Sian Lazar.
Description: Stanford, California : Stanford University Press, 2017. | Includes
    bibliographical references and index.
Identifiers: LCCN 2016048814| ISBN 9781503601574 (cloth : alk. paper) |
    ISBN 9781503602410 (pbk. : alk. paper) | ISBN 9781503602427 (ebook)
Subjects: LCSH: Labor unions—Political activity—Argentina. | Labor
    movement—Argentina. | Political activists—Argentina. | Political
    culture—Argentina.
Classification: LCC HD6603.5 .L39 2017 | DDC 306.20982—dc23
LC record available at https://lccn.loc.gov/2016048814

Typeset by Motto Publishing Services in 10/13.5 Minion Pro

CONTENTS

ILLUSTRATIONS

ACKNOWLEDGMENTS

This book is the result of more than ten years of work and along the way has accumulated multiple debts of gratitude. First, I thank the unionists who allowed me to interview and accompany them in their work and who welcomed my questions and thoughts each time I returned. My friends in UPCN who were instrumental in making my research happen include Antonio Montagna, Marcela Manuel, and Mariano Unamuno. I would not have been able to conduct a reasonable project there without the help of Felipe Carillo, Sabrina Rodríguez, and Andrés Rodríguez, an anthropologist by training. Omar Auton, Karina Trivisonno, and Fernando de Sa Sousa were enormously helpful at the very initial stages. In ATE-Capital, similarly crucial at the initial stage was Nelson Llano, and subsequently Gladys Sosa, Máximo Parpagnoli, Matias Cremonte, and Marina Girondo were so generous with their time, patiently ensuring that I had details correct. Lilia Saralegui shared her life story with me, as did Graciela and her mother. All these people, along with numerous others, consented very happily to be interviewed and to share their thoughts with me; they welcomed me into assemblies, training sessions, meetings, offices, press conferences, demonstrations, and cultural festivals. I am particularly thankful to the *junta interna* of the Buenos Aires Contaduría and the assembly of the workers of the Teatro Colón. Also, the UPCN delegation who allowed me to accompany them at their place of work were helpful well beyond anything one might reasonably expect: warm, welcoming, and fun to be with. They appear in the pages of this book under pseudonyms, and I have decided not to identify the ministry. So I cannot thank them by name but wish nonetheless to express my deep gratitude to everyone. Thanks go also to the tutors of the Escuela de Formación Sindical, especially Silvia.

Flavia organized me when I first lived in Buenos Aires and has continued to be a wonderful and caring friend. Dani took me to hospital when I broke my wrist and, with Flavi, has hosted me over these years. Darío and Lourdes are always there, helping me out and looking after me. Virginia Manzano, María Inés

Fernández, Julieta Gaztañaga, and Rosana Guber are unfailingly clever anthropological interlocutors, advisers, and friends. Martín Armelino was a brilliant (and overqualified) research assistant. Others also gave their time to answer my questions and orient me in this new field: Laura Perelman, Adriana Marshall, Sabina Frederic, Nicolás Diana Menéndez, and Sebastián Etchemendy. I am also very grateful to the doctoral students in a seminar I conducted at the Universidad de Buenos Aires in late 2015 and to the students and faculty there and at IDES for many fruitful interactions and the opportunity to try out my ideas.

My colleagues in Cambridge have also been important interlocutors in ways that it is almost impossible to articulate. I have discussed my ideas with them and been inspired by them; their collegiality has also enabled me to find the time to write this book. Thanks also go to my PhD students Felix Stein, Ryan Davey, Max Watson, Oliver Balch, Corinna Howard, Patrick O'Hare, and Sofia Ugarte for comments and ideas. I presented some of the material in this book at research seminars and workshops in Cambridge, Amsterdam, Halle, Oxford, Manchester, St. Andrews, London School of Economics, Goldsmiths College, University College London, Trondheim, Bergen, Zurich, Aberdeen, Kent, Essex, Brunel, Sheffield, Copenhagen, Oslo, and Liverpool. I thank those departments for giving me the opportunity to present my work and thank colleagues who attended. Undoubtedly the book is very much richer, more rigorous, and a lot clearer than it might otherwise have been because of their challenges and insights. Harri Englund and Laura Bear have been sharp, critical, and encouraging readers of parts of the book. Rupert Stasch and Jeff Juris read earlier drafts of the whole manuscript, and my gratitude goes to them and to the two anonymous readers for Stanford University Press for their insight and suggestions. Thanks to Michelle Lipinski at Stanford for being an incredibly supportive, efficient, and effective editor. This book has been greatly improved through the collaboration of all these people, but any errors of course remain my responsibility.

The fieldwork was funded by the Wenner Gren Foundation Post-PhD grant in 2008–9 and the Newnham Gibbs Travelling Fellowship in 2012–13. I was also granted a CRASSH Early Career Fellowship in 2008, which enabled me to make a start on figuring out this new field site, and a British Academy Mid-Career Fellowship in 2015, which enabled me to complete the manuscript. I am very grateful to all these funders and to the University of Cambridge; the Newton Trust; and Clare College, Cambridge, for smaller grants for travel and research assistance. I also extend thanks to the Center for Latin American Studies at UC Berkeley and to James Holston for the chance to spend some time there writing in 2013.

Finally, my love and gratitude go to my family, who have been with me all the way, and in the case of Zakk and Milo, have grown up with this book to become really cool and lovely boys. I'm looking forward to the next eleven years and beyond with the two of them, with much less trepidation than that with which I contemplated the first eleven. Finally, it's not always easy to manage parenthood and an academic career, but it would have been completely impossible without Dave. So this book is dedicated to him, my "other half" and best friend.

INTRODUCTION

La militancia tiene un gran significado en la parte social, en la
familia, los valores, que nunca debe dejar de lado.
Activism has a real significance in social life, in the family, and in
values, which should never be forgotten.

—ORALDO BRITOS

These words were spoken by a longtime activist in a video made by unionists in
metropolitan Buenos Aires and shown at their union's celebration of the Peronist Day of the Activist in November 2012.[1] In one sentence they sum up the main
themes of this book, as the speaker pithily brings together social life, family, and
values in his definition of activism. In this book, I use ethnography to investigate that combination for two groups of public-sector unionists in contemporary Argentina in a study of the intimate, personal, and family aspects of political activism.

These aspects came to the fore after the shocking result of the first round of
presidential elections on 26 October 2015. Daniel Scioli—the official Peronist candidate—won by only 2.9 percentage points, too small a margin to avoid a historic
second-round run-off against Mauricio Macri, leader of the Cambiemos (Let's
change) coalition. Just prior to the October election, most of the people I knew—
who tended to be *kirchneristas* (supporters of then-president Cristina Fernández
de Kirchner)—had expected Scioli to win fairly comfortably, certainly by more
than 3 percent. Since he had been nearly 8 percent ahead in the open primaries of
the previous August and was leading in the opinion polls, some thought he might
even avoid a second round. Instead, the unexpected first-round result created a
shift in momentum toward his right-wing opponent, as voters across the country
expressed their desire for change and their dissatisfaction with a regime widely
thought to be corrupt, cronyist, and profligate with the country's resources.

In the days following the vote, trade unionists and other opponents of Macri
told me of their shock, fear, and sadness at the result: "It's a disaster, a disaster!"
was the first thing that one general secretary said to me, rolling his eyes heaven-
ward and then launching into a lengthy analysis of how it had happened; another
unionist said that she could not leave her house for two days because she was so
depressed. Other friends posted testimonials on Facebook, describing their as-
tonishment at the result and their fear of what a win for Macri in the upcoming

run-off might mean for the country. Collectively, anti-*macristas* bemoaned what they thought would be a return to the neoliberal 1990s, an issue that seemed to be of particular concern to those who earned their living from the public sector, including academics. One Facebook post by a state-funded postdoctoral researcher circulated widely within academic circles: he announced his rates for washing dishes in the expectation that he would lose his academic job after a Macri win. The discussion rapidly moved off the pages of Facebook to offices, family gatherings, cafés, and squares, as people gathered to share their shock and anxiety and to analyze the election campaign. One particularly fervent debate that I attended took place in the office of a group of unionists in a ministry a few days after the election. Gathered around the table before a scheduled mobilization, we discussed passionately what Scioli and other official candidates had done wrong and how astonished we were that so many Argentines had voted against their interests and in favor of someone who—all agreed—would undoubtedly implement the orthodox economic policies that had caused such trauma for the country fifteen years ago. It was the first thing that everyone talked about when they met: "What happened?"

Within a couple of days at most, the mood shifted to "what now?" as groups began to convene to mobilize against Macri. University students from pro-Kirchner groups moved their booths from the faculty building onto the street to try to persuade passersby of the danger posed by Macri's neoliberal views. Meetings were called to discuss what to do. A group of artists and cultural workers convened a demonstration in the central Parque Centenario, the scene of many famous neighborhood assemblies in the early 2000s. Their slogan was "love yes, Macri no" (*amor sí, Macri no*), and thousands of people turned up on the Saturday following the election. Marches were held; posters and leaflets appeared on the streets and through the letterboxes of apartment blocks. People held deliberately loud conversations about the elections in busy streets and grocery stores in an attempt to convince those who overheard them; they argued passionately with fellow customers and other strangers. A friend told me about a retired woman who called random phone numbers in the city and asked the person who responded, "Do you know what kind of person this Macri really is?" She wanted to engage people in conversation because, she said, she was protecting the twice-yearly increase in her pension that Cristina had introduced. Groups convened to discuss and publicize all the achievements of the previous twelve years that they felt could be under threat from a Macri victory, such as higher spending on tertiary education, nationalization of strategic enterprises and pension funds, social benefits for the popular sectors and pensioners, and prosecutions of violators of human rights during the 1976–83 dictatorship.[2]

Yet, despite what one unionist described to me as "an effervescence of Peron-ist activism" in favor of Scioli, on 22 November, Macri won the second round of the presidential elections, with 51.3 percent of the vote. But the experience of the four weeks between the two rounds of the election brings to the fore several important aspects of Argentine politics. First was the role of historical memory and its contestation: Will he or won't he "return to the 1990s," and what might that mean if he does? Second, in an emotional response to political events gov-ernment supporters experienced shock, anxiety, fear, and disgust with Macri and those who voted for him (whom they perceived to be "middle class"). Third was the practice of seemingly endless and passionate discussions of how awful the situation was, many of which, we agreed, felt like a kind of group therapy. Fourth, these politically active people chose to respond to adversity with more activism to persuade others to vote for Scioli, or at least to assert the presence of a sizable opposition to Macri. Most important, they perceived the answers to political misfortune to lie in collective action, which they experienced as being drawn from a deep emotional response to that misfortune and their fear of the future.

What made that particular set of responses possible? How was it that an ad-verse election result provoked deep emotional distress followed by fervent col-lective action? How is activism understood and experienced in contemporary Argentina? In this book I explore the conditions of possibility for such mobili-zation. I also suggest that the capacity to mobilize in this way affords consider-able strength to collective organizations, even though in this particular instance they failed in their immediate political goal. That capacity lies in the intimate, personal, and family aspects of political activism, the subject of this book. Ar-gentine trade unions are unusually strong: Many of them can mobilize large numbers of workers, and they have achieved longevity in the face of repression and adverse economic change. A few key unions also hold significant power to shape politics, legislation, and employment conditions. Yet sustaining union ac-tivism in contemporary conditions is enormously challenging, as unionists are exposed to public hostility and suspicion in addition to structural and political forces that work against them on a global scale. Thus, their strength closely de-pends on the union's ability to sustain projects of collective ethical-political self-construction among its activists. For the case of public-sector unionists in par-ticular, these projects are enacted through practices of kinship and emotional connection.

In Argentina, the labor movement has been a central motor of historical and political development since the early 1900s. Unions were a prime site for active citizenship in the sense of both political participation and the distribution of so-

cial, economic, political, and even cultural rights. That situation has continued
to the present and may even be truer today than it was at the turn of this century.
Argentina has had a vigorous history of organized social movements since the
late 1800s, ranging from anarcho-syndicalism to populism in its most archetypal
form, Peronism,[3] to leftist guerrillas and revolutionaries, unemployed workers, and middle-class antigovernment protesters. The two unions I study within
this spectrum of political activism are Unión del Personal Civil de la Nación
(Union of National Civil Servants, UPCN) and Asociación Trabajadores del Estado (Association of State Workers, ATE). They represent distinct political orientations within the labor movement. UPCN is predominantly—although not exclusively—Peronist and is very disciplined and "organic," taking an "officialist"
or supportive position with regard to the government in power. This position is
easier for them to take with Peronist governments such as those of the Kirchner
regimes of 2003–15; and part of the fear generated by the most recent electoral
result comes from the fact that Mauricio Macri is avowedly non-Peronist. ATE is
more autonomous and prides itself on its democratic and horizontal approach,
answering to the assemblies of its activists rather than to any political party.[4] In
this book I explore comparatively the lived experience of both kinds of political
activism and the contrasting ways that activists from each union create themselves as particular kinds of activists and their unions as particular—and very
different—kinds of political community.

I focus on how they do so through the two interlinked processes of *militancia* and *contención*. Both are local terms. *La militancia* names the practices of
activism as well as being a group noun that describes the collective of political activists. I translate *militancia* as "militancy" or "activism" and suggest that
by studying *militancia*, we may identify how individuals create and understand
themselves and others as political actors located in a particular time, place, and
family and consisting of a particular set of values, dispositions, and orientations.
For my informants, those values included having a vocation for political action,
anger against injustice, commitment to the collectivity, and love for people and
politics. Political action was understood as membership in the labor movement,
placed in a historical narrative of anarcho-syndicalism (for some) or Peronism
(for most), resistance to military dictatorship, and mobilization against structural adjustment and neoliberalism. The values and attributes of vocation, anger,
commitment, and love were considered essential elements of individual character, almost biological. Yet they were also dispositions that could be cultivated
by individuals, passed down the generations within families, and called forth or
made stronger in pedagogical contexts, including training sessions for activists.

This cultivation, or calling forth, of values such as vocation, love, passion, and so on, happened through collective processes, which I describe ethnographically with the concept of *contención*, which means "containment" of both a psychotherapeutic and political kind. It has various dimensions (see Lazar 2013) but appears to derive in part from the concept of therapeutic containment, which originated in the work of Wilfred Bion, a British Kleinian psychoanalyst. In the therapeutic context it refers to the ability of the therapist to take on the emotions of the other and process them without being overwhelmed by them (Bion 1959; Douglas 2007: 33). More broadly, containment can be thought of as a way the group encompasses the individual, through individual therapeutic relations as well as collective activities of care and political activities of discussion and collective action, which I describe in the second part of this book. To avoid confusion with the false friend English cognate "contention," I translate the Spanish word throughout and use the term "containment." I argue that containment is an ethical process of encompassment and the creation of a collective self—the union—committed to action for the transformation of society for the better. The two unions I worked with understood the precise content of that action differently and, as a result, engaged in different acts of containment. These often boiled down to organization, but in contrasting ways. UPCN placed great weight on organizational strength and discipline and the ability to negotiate with the employers; ATE constructed its collective self as a political project of alternative unionism, summarized through its emphasis on horizontality and autonomy from governing party politics and tapping in to trends of horizontal political organization prominent in Argentina post-2001.

Both militancy and containment are ways that groups of Argentines make themselves into political subjects to participate in government and political struggle. Thus, the processes under discussion here are shaped by how the Argentine labor movement has developed in the last century, a history that is threaded throughout this book. Crucially, they are also shaped by daily life, family, and friendships. This is therefore a study of the intimate spaces of political activism within a social movement, albeit one that is now relatively unfashionable within social movement studies in the US and European academies in particular. For at least two decades, trade unions have not been a central concern for political anthropologists and social theorists outside labor studies or industrial relations departments.[5] The relative invisibility of labor politics in anthropology in particular has perhaps resulted from the dominance of theoretical framings of politics that derive from the directions in which anthropologists and others have taken Foucault. Anthropologists have tended to focus on the creation of subjecthood either as governance and resistance or as introspective care of the self.[6] In this book I investigate the relational politics of personal ethics and provide an ethnography of political relations in their fullest sense by exploring personal and collective ethics within the trade unions. Here, I first contextualize my argument within the anthropological study of social movements. I then introduce the aspects of ethics and kinship and propose that Argentine public-sector union activism is best understood as a form of collective creation of ethical selves enacted through the idioms and practices of character essence, active self-cultivation, and kinship, and revealed through the study of militancy and containment.

SOCIAL MOVEMENTS AND IDENTITY

Argentina has an especially vibrant history of organized social movements over the twentieth and twenty-first centuries. Although it would be unwise to attempt a comprehensive list, the history includes anarcho-syndicalist and reformist socialist trade unions, populism, leftist guerrillas and revolutionaries, human rights movements, popular neighborhood assemblies and organizations, unemployed workers (*piqueteros*), the workers' movement for the takeover of factories, food riots, and middle-class antigovernment demonstrations. A strong current of feminism has cross-cut all these movements, and in the northern parts of the country in particular, indigenous movements—marginalized for much of the twentieth century—are growing in significance and strength. Recent scholarship into contentious politics in the country has emphasized the mobilizations that resulted from the 2001 crisis. Scholars have focused on the popular assemblies and barter clubs of 2001–2, the *piqueteros*, the *cartoneros* (waste pickers), and the workers' movement for the takeover of factories.[7] Trade unions are not at the forefront of that analysis, despite their continuing importance for Argentine politics and collective association (see Pozzi and Nigra 2015 for an exception to this general trend). Yet the labor movement has been a central driver of historical and political development in Argentina since at least the mid-twentieth century, and today Peronism continues to be crucial to Argentine politics and citizenship action. Sebastián Etchemendy (2011) has shown that formal-sector unions even saw a revitalization under the Kirchner regimes of 2003–15, attributable to economic growth and a government-promoted resurgence in collective bargaining (see also Scolnik 2015; Arias, Menéndez, and Salgado 2015).

These developments took place in the context of strikingly neoliberal regimes in the 1990s, which were notable for a wide range of structural adjustment policies, especially the economic policy of pegging the Argentine peso to the US dollar. That period was followed by a deep recession and the debt crisis of 2001, when the country was eventually forced to default and then dramatically devalue its currency (Cohen and Gutman 2002; Blustein 2005). After this economic collapse, recovery began in about 2003, based largely on the regional commodity boom, especially resources derived from extractive industries and trade in soy with China; and the Kirchner regimes gradually returned to older distribution-ist patterns of government. They distributed state resources in the form of welfare benefits and cash transfers but, more important for my informants, also in public-sector jobs and generous wage settlements. That in turn had inflationary consequences, not least since the government could not borrow on international capital markets. By the time of the presidential election in late 2015, it was not clear how long these policies could last or what the consequences might be. Indeed, for many, it was remarkable that the distribution was able to continue for as long as it did; and newly elected President Mauricio Macri has taken a more orthodox economic approach. The relationship with the unions may very well become more conflictual over time. However, the experience of the 1990s would suggest that any change in presidential practice may not be quite as extensive as one might initially think because over the longer term the Argentine state has been largely corporatist since the 1940s, with unions and the Peronist party playing a central role in defining hegemonic forms of citizenship alongside (tragically) the military (see D. James 1988b; Torre 2012).

There is an extensive body of literature on social movements, especially from within sociology and increasingly from within anthropology.[8] Although anthropologists might have been, as Arturo Escobar says, "a late arrival to the field" (2009: 24), they are carving out an approach to social movements that is distinct from the classical sociological one to the extent that some draw a line between the latter and anthropological concerns of culture, practice, imaginaries, subjectivities, and so on (Osterweil 2014). While it would not be correct to make a very stark division between the two approaches, it would probably be fair to say that dominant sociological approaches attempt to *explain* social movements, specifically their emergence and success (or failure). They do so by resort to concepts like resource mobilization and political opportunity structures, bringing in cultural questions through notions of framing.[9] In contrast, anthropologists have focused on the internal dynamics within movements, cultures of mobilization, and more recently the development of radical imaginaries of alternative worlds, subjectivities, and possibilities.

However, the two sets of approaches do have several concerns in common, not least their emphasis on emergence and the nature of political subjects. The current focus on radical alternative imaginaries and emergent forms of activism is new to an extent but is also a reframing of an older sociological debate about the identity of the truly revolutionary political subject. This debate can principally be found in what became known as the New Social Movements

(NSM) literature, which emerged in Europe and proved highly influential in the US academy. Beginning in the 1980s, theorists—inspired by what Laurence Cox and Cristina Flesher Fominaya (2013) argue was actually a rather thin reading of Alberto Melucci and Alain Touraine—suggested that social movements had changed to become more about identity than about the structural effects of class. Thus, for them, the most potentially revolutionary protagonists were no longer the industrial proletariat but new actors mobilized on the basis of shared identity, such as ethnicity, gender, and sexuality.[10] That contributed to a perception of trade unions as an outdated phenomenon, a discursive move within scholarship and daily politics that must be understood in the context of the political convulsions in Europe and the Americas of the 1960s and 1970s,[11] as well as the increasing attacks on unions from the neoliberal Right. On the Left, the search for new political actors beyond the industrial working class was updated in the 2000s with Hardt and Negri's (2005) influential concept of the multitude. This concept is actually based on class, just not on the traditional conceptualization of the working class as industrial proletariat, since Hardt and Negri make a strong argument for new formations of labor, specifically focused on immaterial labor, as the groupings that constitute the multitude. August Carbonella and Sharryn Kasmir (2014) crucially point out the importance of understanding the mutability of class formations, arguing that it is incorrect to mistake the relative demise of one formation (Fordist working class in Europe) for the demise of class itself.

In Argentina, social movements scholars working in the context of the transition to democracy after the 1976–83 dictatorship also often focused on the new subjects of human rights activists, with special emphasis on the Madres de la Plaza de Mayo, the mothers of some of those disappeared in the so-called Dirty War (e.g., Jelin 2003; Jelin and Hershberg 1996; Brysk 1994). Subsequently, a new group of scholars emphasized the new actors of the 2001 crisis, such as the *piqueteros*. These studies contributed to the tendency of recent social movements literature to separate out newer radical activism from classical union activism, the archetypal old social movement. Yet on closer inspection, the strength of the relationship between the two becomes apparent. Some of the 2001 actors drew on their experiences in Peronist unions and factories to develop their organizations during the post-2002 period in the neighborhoods (Manzano 2013) and even in some recovered workplaces (Figari 2005). The "autonomists" often combined Peronist traditions with anarchist ones in their practices, although the latter tend to be more celebrated in the literature (Graeber 2013; Sitrin 2006, 2012). Even where they rejected Peronism, they often defined their own actions as the counterpart to it.[12] This can be seen in the emphasis of horizontality over verticality, which in Argentina is understood as a strongly Peronist organizational philosophy. In turn, the radical traditions that grew out of Argentine and global anarchism have influenced how contemporary unions imagine themselves. This is particularly so for ATE. The two traditions are interlinked in Argentina and have been since Peronism emerged in the 1940s (Munck, Galitelli, and Falcon 1987).

Theorists have retreated from some of the more extreme positions of the 1980s and 1990s, which had appeared to vacate the material aspects from all social movement practices and demands in favor of their cultural and social claims. June Nash suggests that they had "announced the 'withering away' of the class struggle" (2014: 72). In fact, from early in the debate, scholars did point out the importance of material factors, and contemporary discussions of social movements continue in this vein. Yet the concept of class has somewhat receded from view. Two contemporary developments in social movements theory illustrate this point. First, indigenous peoples in particular are seen by many as the archetypal social movement subjects today, those best placed to resist global capital, because they are and have been most affected by its ravages (Klein 2014) and because they possess "links with primordial traditions [that] provide adaptations based on collective social structures that are alternatives to those of private capitalist expropriation" (Nash 2014: 74). These represent alternative modernities, cosmologies, or, in newer framings, ontologies (Blaser 2010). For Arturo Escobar, such alternatives are "expressions of ecological and cultural attachment to place" (2009: 7). Thus, the "political ecology" of a particular location helps create the demand for alternatives to liberal democracy, capitalist development, and colonialist modernity. For some scholars, including Escobar, the mobilization in itself constitutes an enactment of these ontological alternatives (Escobar 2010; De La Cadena 2010; Nash 2014).[13]

Second, an alternative version of Escobar's definition of "political ecology" might look at the relation between people and place in the city and its effect on social mobilization (cf. Holston and Appadurai 1999). This approach has a longer pedigree in academia: In 1983 Manuel Castells was one of the earliest theorists to argue that the demands of social reproduction in the city can lead to particular kinds of neighborhood-based mobilization. In Latin America as elsewhere, this kind of mobilization usually involves a high proportion of women, who run soup kitchens or other food distribution programs and participate in church-based communities, mothers' clubs, nongovernmental organizations (NGOs), and campaigns for local infrastructure (Blondet 2002; Molyneux 2000). Argentina is no different in this general trend, and there are many social movement groups and NGOs organized in poor urban neighborhoods to provide support for social reproduction, including communal kitchens, environmental campaigning, housing, and cultural centers (Shever 2012; Auyero and Swistun 2009; Manzano 2013; Canelo 2013; Mauro and Rossi 2015). They are often linked to *piquetero* movements and even to trade unions (Manzano 2013), as well as to the increasingly organized groups of foreign migrants to Buenos Aires (Canelo 2013). Some recent work has articulated this range of issues as practices that claim the right to the city (Harvey 2012). A broader literature is also emerging that shows the importance of the desire to live a good and collective life in the city in propelling mobilization, for example, around questions of squatters' rights and the urban commons.[14]

BACK TO THE STUDY OF ORGANIZED CLASS-BASED MOVEMENTS?

Neither of these two place-based approaches (indigenous political ecology and urban right to the city) deny the very real material effects of the capitalist processes that are being resisted—indeed, quite the opposite. However, they do both have a tendency to filter out *class* as an explicit category of identity that provides the source of mobilizational energy. At one point, class was all there was for many social movements theorists and even actors.[15] But unfortunately, the understandable urge to seek alternatives to normative interpretations of political mobilization—that based on traditional institutions of political parties and trade unions—has meant that much of the *organized* class-based resistance to capitalism has slipped out of view in scholarly work and political commentary, with the exception of some work on social movement unionism.[16] Yet there are several reasons why I argue that it is a good idea to highlight class as a source of mobilization for social movements now. First, working-class identities may not have disappeared quite in the way that some would like, instead being reconfigured and respatialized in new parts of the world where traditional forms of labor organization are weak (although they need not always remain so) (Silver 2003; Kalb 2015). Second, new collective identities based on occupation (job) or the lack of one have emerged in recent years, as movements of precarious or unemployed workers have developed not only in Argentina but also in countries like Spain, even the United Kingdom. In Argentina in particular, cooperatives have become an important new form of work-based organization. The cooperative movement emerged in part from the recovered enterprises post-2002 but has developed into a broader movement for organizing workers in the "popular economy," such as waste pickers or street vendors (Faulk 2008; Fernández Álvarez 2015).

Third, and most important for this book, even middle-class identities may be a source of mobilizational force, especially in a system of global capital that increasingly favors only the hyperrich.[17] For example, many commentators regarded the 2013 protests in Brazilian cities and Istanbul to be predominantly middle class. The research presented in this book also describes how middle-class workers are organizing collectively to protect themselves and their families. Of course, an alternative possibility is also present, that the middle-class workers with whom I conducted this research are organizing not to resist capital but to maintain their privilege in an increasingly unequal economic system, and this is a tension that runs throughout my research. Whichever proves to be the case, my final general point is that most adults work in one way or another, so occupation or livelihood has significant potential to be a source for a collective identity that might lead to social and political mobilization. Refusing to recognize that potential serves only the status quo and fragments the identification of workers as a collective body with shared interests, driving wedges between young and old, formal and informal workers, men and women, peasants and manufacturing workers, the working and middle class, nationals and immigrants. As Carbonella and Kasmir (2014) point out, processes of class fragmentation have long histories, with divisions often being drawn along lines of race but also between waged and unwaged workers.

Recent discussions of the global political economy of labor have emphasized the growth of what Guy Standing has called the "precariat," a "class-in-the-making" of those in conditions of labor and income insecurity, who also lack a work-based identity (2011: 7–13). James Ferguson has also argued for refocusing understandings of development toward the politics of distribution, acknowledging that in many parts of the world, large numbers of people are not connected to the labor market but claim rights based on citizenship and political pressure (2015: 12). In this book, I take a different but complementary approach. The example of Argentina shows that labor movements retain the potential for mobilizational power, but there is little doubt that if this potential is to be fully realized, they must take into account both those who are conventionally employed and the unemployed, who make their living in ways other than through wage labor. Ideally, both activists and analysts would seek to make connections across the different camps rather than celebrate one over the other. Traditional unions will need to find ways to engage with newer actors, but we achieve nothing by ignoring the unions or accusing them of being merely part of the establishment. At the same time, there are very real power dynamics within unions and between unions and other actors, and these need to be addressed analytically and politically.[18] Furthermore, middle-class spaces have seen conditions deteriorate considerably over recent decades, as they are informalized, to use a concept from Standing's (1989) earlier work. Studying specific questions of employment conditions is central to understanding that process even in very conventional spaces like the public sector. It happens that the Argentine public-sector unions are much more able than unions elsewhere to arrest those processes, and in this book I ask why that should be.

The two unions I discuss have different political cultures, and the comparison between them is a thread that runs throughout this book. Their contrasting approaches to political action are embedded in and derive from a particular history. Yet one of their great strengths for both is the grounding of their activism in everyday life, more so than in the more spectacular moments of protest. A favorite saying of Perón's for many trade unionists is "la organización vence al tiempo" (organization defeats time). I agree and argue here that the reasons for this should be sought in the more mundane realms of everyday practice. Unions are accused by both the Left and the Right of being corrupt, bureaucratized, or co-opted, but activists continue nonetheless, and I ask why and how. This is a subjective drama with high stakes, as sustaining union activists in these conditions becomes a serious challenge. Rather than engage in a sociological explanation of movement emergence and success, I ask how practices of self-cultivation, both spectacular and day to day, such as through care, ritual, commensality or sociability (that is, containment), contribute to the development of collective and individual identities and the continuance of *militancia*. I do so in the context of an analysis of how contemporary forms relate to historical ones and to contemporary understandings of historical forms. It is here, I think, that an anthropological approach has much to contribute to how we understand social movements.

ETHICS AND POLITICAL ACTION

Maple Razsa (2013) has argued that in recent years activist practice and scholarship have taken a "subjective turn" toward questions of intimate personal experience and how to live particular kinds of lives; and one of the main themes of this book is the forms of subjectivity that are nurtured within Argentine unionism and make its particular kind of collective politics possible. Daniel James's (2000) work, especially his life history of Doña María, a lifelong Peronist activist, has shown the centrality of identity-making processes to the strength and persistence of Peronism (see also James 1988b). Javier Auyero (2003) has also explored contentious politics through the lives and memories of individual female activists. More generally, social movements of all sorts require the constructions of particular subjectivities among their adherents: activists need to be able to imagine other possible worlds, behaviors, ethical stances (Dave 2012), ways of living together (Razsa 2015), even difference itself (Heywood 2015), or become political subjects with the right to have rights (Arendt 1998). Further, as I argue here, much of the work of activism lies in building the *collective* aspect of collective subjectivities. Thus, the old social movements I discuss are shown to be just as reliant on identity and subject formation as those that seem newer.

The effervescence of activism that followed the first-round electoral result in November 2015 relied on people feeling deeply that their identity was threatened by the potential change in regime. On a more day-to-day basis, unionists persevere in the face of multiple setbacks by thinking of themselves in particular ways. This ability to keep going is, in my view, linked closely to forms of ethical-political subjectivation that are the foundation for political activity and that I explore in detail in this book. By subjectivation I refer to how unionists make themselves into particular kinds of political subjects, both individual and collective. (My approach to subjectivation is explained in greater detail in Chapter 2.) I am influenced by the work of a significant tendency within contemporary anthropology of ethics that links subjectivation to self-cultivation.[19] Drawing on Foucault's later work (especially 1988, 1990), studies of self-cultivation take various forms and have had significant implications for how we understand freedom, agency, desire, motivation, resistance, sexuality, the self, and other concepts. For Foucault, self-cultivation took place through what he identified as "technologies of the self," described as "permit[ting] individuals to effect by their own means or with the help of others a certain number of operations on their own bodies and souls, thoughts, conduct, and way of being, so as to transform themselves in order to attain a certain state of happiness, purity, wisdom, perfection, or immortality" (1988: 18).

Anthropology of personal ethics has extended beyond Foucault into more Aristotelian and Arendtian territory, exploring ethical action in "ordinary" lives (Lambek 2010; see also Dave 2012; Robbins 2013). It happens that many studies of ethical subjectivation have focused on religious aspects of life, an observation made by Fassin (2014) and Werbner (2014). In some of my earlier work I also found particular technologies of the self within evangelical churches in El Alto, Bolivia (Lazar 2008). Still, there is no reason why such processes should not be found in political life (cf. Keane 2016), and indeed among Argentine unionists I find multiple technologies of the self. For example, I demonstrate how individual unionists create themselves as particular kinds of activists, slotting themselves into a commonly understood history of action, drawing on exemplary figures for inspiration, and producing common narratives of commitment, vocation, character, and so on. They do so both in educational contexts and in daily political life. I show that theirs is an explicitly politicized self-cultivation, one that takes place in the context of a specific political economy.

Cultivation of the self is aimed not at an individual telos as Foucault's approach would suggest, but a telos imagined—if at all—as a particular kind of society. In fact, their subjectivation may not necessarily involve a clearly conceptualized end point itself but consist instead of active life within an ongoing condition of class struggle. Here I bring into my theoretical framework the notions of praxis, as theoretically informed political action on the world (Freire 1996), and hexis, as cultivated state or disposition, linked to processes of character building and subject formation (Aristotle 1988). I ask what makes it possible for unionists to continue in their struggle; what enables self-cultivation (hexis) to become action on the world to change the world (praxis)? Over the course of the book, I find the answer to lie not in reflective action understood quite as one might expect from a reading of the more religiously informed anthropology of ethics. That is, it is not understood by my informants as a matter of decision and choice. Instead, for them it has something more to do with understandings of essential character and an almost biological commitment to particular values and ways of political life. Yet those values, while part of one's being as an activist and therefore essence, can also be cultivated further or elicited through pedagogy in processes of hexis.

Militancy and containment therefore name processes of ethical and political subjectivation. Activists (*militantes*) understand themselves as committed individuals who experience their militancy as a whole-life condition. One important aspect of that is containment, an example of ethical formation occurring not simply in reflection on action but in action itself (cf. Mattingly 2014; Lambek 2010). Practices of containment ranged from forming quasi-therapeutic relationships between union delegate and individual worker-affiliate to giving people a political, social, and cultural context in which to flourish, feel cared for, and act on the world. As unionists "contain" each other, and the group encompasses the individual, they develop a collective ethical subject or self, which in turn grants them significant political strength.

Thus, I suggest, union activists cultivate their individual selves as activists (whether Peronist, unionist, or Trotskyite), but they also cultivate various collective selves and political communities—the delegation (UPCN's term) or the *junta interna* (internal council; ATE's term) at the shop-floor level; followed by the local or city-level instantiation of the union, then the national union, and finally the confederation of unions; but also they form collectives of workers in general or of public-sector workers or workers in a particular ministry or administrative body. These combine and overlap with other collective identities, such as Peronists, progressives, or residents of a particular neighborhood. I describe some of the practices through which these collective subjects are brought into being and maintained. In doing so, I recognize the relational aspect of politics and the importance of affective processes of collective self-cultivation alongside rational and material imperatives to engage in political struggle.

KINSHIP

One crucial aspect of this collectivity or relationality is kinship. If collective politics, including class politics, is a field of subjectivation, affect, ritual, practice, thought, debate, and ethics, then anthropological approaches to kinship provide an invaluable analytical language for understanding this field. Specifically, a consideration of those ethnographies of kinship that draw out the nature of kinship as relatedness and that see it coming into being through practices of commensality, care, and the circulation of substance (Carsten 2000, 2004; see also Fortes 1949) leads me to suggest that within the political field of Argentine unionism, collective politics comes into being through similar kinds of practices. What circulates in the moments of commensality and shared experience that I describe is not just substance, as Carsten describes, but also values or shared ethical dispositions, such as vocation, a desire to bring about justice or to help others, self-identification as a worker or activist, and techniques to put these kinds of values into play. So ethics are taught, shared, circulated, and crafted in the street protest, the ritual act, around the coffee table in the back room of the delegation office, and in the classroom.

Contemporary anthropologists have explored the relationships between kinship and politics through analyses of the languages of kinship in politics (e.g., nationalism) and the intimacies of governance (e.g., in colonial regimes).[20] To complement such approaches, it may now be time to return to some of the foundational works in political and legal anthropology for insight into relations between the *practices* of kinship and politics (e.g., Evans-Pritchard 1940; Gluckman 1965; Barth 1965; Bailey 1969; Fortes and Evans-Pritchard 1940). What those studies argued was that kinship connections are crucial in the *organization* of politics as well as in its more symbolic realms. Today, anthropologists recognize that kinship is more than the categorization of connectedness, and the "new kinship studies" argue for the socially and culturally constructed nature of kin relationships (Sahlins 2013: 2), kinship as "cultures of relatedness" (Carsten 2000, 2004) or "mutuality of being" (Sahlins 2013: 2). Beyond explicitly defined relationships of family, both these definitions of kinship are good descriptions of how the Argentine union comes into being as a political community, especially at the level of those who work together on a more or less daily basis. Sahlins states, "Generally considered, kinsmen are persons who belong to one another, who are parts of one another, who are co-present in each other, whose lives are joined and interdependent" (2013: 21). I hope to show this would also describe rather well the relationships between union activists.

ATE and UPCN undertake practices of "kinning" (Howell 2006) as a means of bringing their political community into being through ritual, shared cultural activities, therapeutic relationships, educational spaces, and political action. In so doing, they create political communities founded in large part in kinship or kinlike relations. This is an especially Peronist mode of kinship (see James 2000) but not peculiar to Buenos Aires, as attested by the work of Elana Shever (2012) for Neuquén, or even to Argentina, as shown by Alpa Shah (2013) for Jharkand, India. Within ATE and UPCN, the political community of the local shop-floor delegation is a common project of self-cultivation through kinning, but one that also often combines with actual family relationships, as delegates bring in their children, nieces, and nephews to jobs or to the delegation, or the making of family-like relationships ("intersubjective participations" or "mutual being" in Sahlins's terms [2013: 58, 2]) as people share time, food, political action, commitment, hardship, care, laughter, and so on.

I analyze this material specifically with respect to kinship metaphors rather than just in terms of relationality. This arose from the ethnography as people told me of their family relationships and used the language of family to describe their connections. But I also emphasize the work that goes into building these ties, the strength of the ties themselves, and the mutuality of the project of self-cultivation that happens in these spaces. That is not to say that all was harmonious—far from it—or that everyone participated equally in the spaces of mutuality. However, the fact of undertaking such a project together explains the strength of collective politics in this context in a way that a mutual agreement based on rational calculation of self-interest simply cannot. In contrast to much of the Anglo-American world, where one might argue that the latter understanding of union membership is more dominant, in Argentina unionism has continued and actually flourished, even in unlikely spaces such as among middle-class administrators and civil servants. This is something of a puzzle, given the ostensibly fierce nature of Argentine neoliberalism and international pressure toward making labor flexible. Although the legal environment within which Argentine unionists operate today is relatively favorable, that environment is constantly under threat. Further, we should note that it was won in the mid-twentieth century and shielded from the ravages of the 1970s and 1990s through the hard and often very dangerous work of political activism. That activism relied for its existence on the kinds of belonging fomented through the practices I discuss here. Despite periods of intense persecution, the unions were able to protect themselves against some of the very worst of the class warfare that has weakened unions in the United Kingdom and United States—near fatally according to many. If collective politics is going to be the only (or the predominant) way for workers to defend themselves against exploitation, I suggest that we need to look "beyond grievance" (Shah 2013) to more positive aspects of how to construct lasting collective political organizations capable of mobilizing people and keeping them mobilized. The Argentine unions, even the most "yellow" (co-opted) of them, have much to teach in this regard. This can be revealed, I suggest here, by applying some of the analytical strategies of the anthropology of kinship and of ethics to the study of these organizations.

OVERVIEW OF THE BOOK

Argentine unions are prime sites for the construction of collective ethical subjects based on a specific political agenda. Of course, any collective ethical subject should not be considered to be internally homogeneous, static, or without contestation. We know that collectivities are very fluid and require considerable and repeated work to bring into being. They shift constantly, break into smaller groupings, come together, and fragment; their members argue with each other, agree passionately, fall in and out of love, compete, and collaborate. This is what interests me here, as I explore how reflection, practice, ethical dispositions understood as essential, interaction with others, and consciously designed pedagogy all combine in different ways to construct distinct and overlapping collective ethical subjects and political actors.

This book traces that interplay through the most significant spaces of the workplace delegation, the school for unionists, and the street. In Chapter 1 I set out the context within which the unionists work, describing the organization of public-sector unionism and some of the differences between the two unions I study. I then outline some key moments in the contemporary history of state restructuring, which deeply affected public-sector workers and their unions and which framed nearly all of the discussions I had with the unionists about my research. I introduce the various histories that run throughout this book, as they are entwined with personal stories of militancy and shape projects of collective ethical self-construction and political action: histories of Peronism, the labor movement in Argentina more broadly, dictatorship, state restructuring, and neoliberalism.

Chapters 2 and 3 explore the first of the two organizing constructs of this book, *militancia* (militancy). This is a philosophy of political action and self-definition with an associated set of historical resonances and claims about character and values. Union activists often told me they had become activists because of what they considered to be their essential being: they were simply that kind of character; they joined the union because their parents had been unionists; or political activity was a biological necessity for them, an addiction or a virus. In Chapter 2, I explore the narratives of character as essence and show how militancy as subject position is deeply ethical in the sense that it has ethical consequences—for activists' life courses and for political action—because it shapes how people define and strive for the good, how they are perceived from the outside, and so on. However, it is not often reflected upon outside the research interview. Rather, according to the activists themselves, it is a process of self-cultivation that just happens and for which they are naturally predisposed. Chapter 3 demonstrates one way by which people explained that predisposition, seeing it as something inherited from their families. The character of "political activist" can be transmitted through generations by stories, childhood experience, teaching, and inherited characteristics. It is not always an easy path and does not always happen, but family loomed large in many stories that people told about their activist trajectories. Again, this is an aspect of ethical subjectivation that is considered to be part of one's essence, but it is more mutable than the character essence narrated in the previous chapter, which might be thought only to develop teleologically, by becoming stronger or weaker. In contrast, family transmission of essential ethical characteristics is more open to narration and thus to contingency, change, and variation—as siblings take very different attitudes toward politics, for example.

These two chapters present data gathered through interviews, and interview extracts have been chosen because they resonate with (or make explicit) things that were part of daily life and action but not made so explicit there. The use of quotations is also aimed at bringing polyvocality to this material, presenting the unionists through their own voices. I carried out interviews with individuals and groups throughout my research, conducting them as wide-ranging conversations that covered a broadly similar set of topics, which developed inductively as my interviewing continued and as I became more familiar with less formal and more day-to-day spaces of union life. Each interview differed according to how my research interests came into focus during the course of the project, the political context of the day, and the dynamic of the conversation. Some were more successful than others and produced a more fluid, evocative, and substantive conversation. Often interviewees chose to do the interview in a café or in their local office; and in the latter case others would jump in to the conversation, and from time to time they would engage in debate about some issue or other. So the interviews mirrored other common modes of conversational interaction, such as therapy, café conversation, and political debate in the union office. My interlocutors were familiar with the mode of a long and often therapeutic conversation between people, such that the interviews often mirrored other experiences of dialogue that are very much part of daily life.

The following chapters move the interview material to the background and focus on my experiences with the unions. Chapter 4 takes place in educational spaces run by the two unions—for the case of UPCN in the school for unionists, and for ATE in a less formal workshop structure. The chapter discusses an explicit pedagogy of construction of individual activists and the collective ethical subject of the union by examining the ways that the two unions train newly elected delegates in courses in which I participated. With the shift to a more collective register, I introduce the second organizing concept of this book, *contención* (containment). I show how the unions cultivate particular virtues among their activists, principally associated with how they orient themselves to and define the collectivity. This is a political community envisaged as vertical (for UPCN) and horizontal (for ATE), a difference that indexes the difference between political community as organism and as political project. This collective subject, and the individual selves that it comprises, is constructed through explicit exhortation by appealing to characteristics and virtues that are thought to exist already among the delegates, drawing out their predisposition to rage against injustice or feel a vocation for social action.

Chapters 5 and 6 show how the kinds of subjectivities narrated in Chapters 2 and 3, and taught in Chapter 4, are enacted in collective action and daily life. They continue my examination of the cultivation of collective ethical subjects with a more detailed discussion of the idea of containment. In Chapter 5 I discuss time I spent accompanying the UPCN delegation in an important central ministry in their daily work and explore the ways they enact collectivity in their day-to-day life. As described previously, containment is a multivalent concept that names ways that the union delegation encompasses its activists and affiliates. This can be through quasi-therapeutic relationships between activist and affiliate, as the activist seeks to resolve problems that arise in the workplace and to talk through a wider set of concerns from his or her life more broadly. But the main subject of this chapter is encompassment through practices of sociability, care, ritual, and problem solving. Like the school discussed in Chapter 4, the local delegation is a space for practices of kinning, as ethical values of vocation, will, and desire for social justice circulate alongside talk, food, and other shared concerns to build a shared collective subjectivity. Kinship also proves extremely important not merely as a mode of gathering people together but also in shaping the conditions of possibility for action and care on the part of the union.

In Chapter 6 I examine a linked but different dimension of containment: the encompassment of the political activist through the granting of spaces for self-fulfillment and political action. Shifting the focus to the ethnographic spaces of assemblies and street protests, I argue that this containment takes place for ATE activists in particular in these politicized practices of subjectivation, as unionists act on themselves and on the world: they construct themselves as a collective ethical subject and seek to transform the world for the better or prevent or mitigate its transformation for the worse. Both kinds of political ethical action take place from a particular embodied and spatialized subject position; and from that position unionists also act on the city to create it as political space. They also involve a particular relation to time, as each assembly or protest is part of a trajectory of action in history that also builds history, as well as being an experience of quotidian work that might achieve only very small but incremental improvements. Finally, they are also events where the construction of collective subjects takes place through the building of "mutuality of being" (Sahlins 2013: 2) in moments of effervescence and shared effort.

As the book progresses, I use concepts of hexis, praxis, and essence to describe different ethical modes in contemporary labor union activism in the Argentine public sector. In the Conclusion, I present this framework in more depth, examining how understandings of essential character or biological predisposition interact at both the individual and collective scales with hexis—meaning the cultivated state or disposition of political activist (drawing on Aristotle)—and then transform into praxis, or explicitly theorized political action (following Freire). The book takes the reader on a journey from essence to hexis and then praxis, introducing each concept in turn as overlapping modes of subjectivation. Throughout, I suggest that understandings and practices of kinship are central to these transformations. Thus, my contention is that the unions derive strength and longevity insofar as they are able to successfully achieve projects of collective ethical-political subjectivation, which are enacted through practices of kinning, as people become good activists and contain each other within the group. Politics is grounded in the ethical realms of the everyday, the intimate, shared values, and the family.

1

THE STATE AND THE UNIONS
IN SPACE AND TIME

It is no coincidence that "no return to the 1990s" was the slogan that summed up the opposition to Mauricio Macri's election during the period between the first and second rounds of voting in late 2015. Indeed, Argentine political history framed nearly all of the discussions I had with public-sector unionists during my research, and the 1990s were particularly prominent in that history. The nature of the Argentine state shaped their work, both as unionists and as state employees. Needless to say, the Argentine state as an entity is neither singular nor stable, and some key moments in the contemporary history of state restructuring were extremely important in shaping life for public-sector workers and in the different trajectories that ATE and UPCN took in recent decades. Those different trajectories need also to be understood in the context of longer-term histories of unionism and Peronism that stretch back into the early twentieth century.

The interplay of recent events and longer histories shapes the contemporary modes of ethical-political subjectivation that are the subject of this book. Here I introduce the two unions and describe state employment and the effects of the 1990s restructuring. I place these descriptions in the context of longer-term histories of the labor movement in Argentina and consider the class position of state workers and union activists. This is crucial context to the more microlevel analysis of the following chapters. By including this detail here, as well as threading historical resonances through the ethnographic chapters themselves, I hope both to be true to the historical consciousness of my interlocutors and to avoid some of the pitfalls of what Don Kalb describes as an anthropology that fails to "escape from its culturalist reveries and engage with the larger scales and longer terms of political economy" (2015: 10). The political economy I engage with is a product of the interaction between national and global scales but for my informants was mostly expressed in terms of national history.

UNION ORGANIZATION

Focusing on unionists—especially those at leadership levels—created a particular spatial distribution of my research field, a problem undoubtedly common to much urban anthropology. I found many of my informants in the central offices and gatherings run by the union, but they were also delegates from a workplace that consists of a distributed network of the institutions that make up the Argentine state system. The two spatial configurations overlapped. I begin by outlining the union configuration before discussing the state itself. I then address the unions in their temporal, historical dimension.

Both ATE and UPCN have national reach, but each organizes itself slightly differently. UPCN follows the structure of the federal state. It has a National Leadership Council (Consejo Directivo Nacional), under which are sectional offices (seccionales). The largest and most important sectional office, and the one that I worked with, the Section of the Federal Capital and National Public Sector Employees (Seccional Capital Federal y Empleados Públicos Nacionales [Capital Section]), is based in the city of Buenos Aires.[1] It covers all the employees of the national state and the small number of employees of the municipal government of Buenos Aires city who are members of UPCN. Andrés Rodríguez, the current general secretary of the Capital Section, is also the general secretary of the National Leadership Council, an important political interlocutor for the national and local government, and a significant figure in the leadership of the Peronist Partido Justicialista in the city of Buenos Aires.[2]

ATE organizes its affiliates on a more directly territorial basis and aims at more horizontal and autonomous forms of organization. So all those employees who work in a particular territory (e.g., the province of Buenos Aires) are members of that Provincial Leadership Council (Consejo Directivo), whether they are employed by the provincial or federal government. They also have a National Leadership Council, known as ATE-Nacional, which coordinates the actions of all the provincial councils. ATE-Capital is the council for state employees in the city of Buenos Aires, whether employed by the municipal or national government. My informants came from both ATE-Capital and ATE-Nacional.

Both UPCN and ATE organize themselves below the level of the Capital Section and ATE-Capital through internal commissions for each institution where they have enough affiliates (such as a hospital, ministry, regulatory office, or even a theater). The activists who form these internal commissions are called delegates; and the UPCN commissions are usually called delegations, while ATE activists call their commissions *juntas internas*. For both unions, each internal commission will usually include the three top positions—general secretary, adjunct secretary, and gremial secretary—but may also have secretaries of social welfare, equal opportunities, youth, culture, professionals, and other responsibilities, depending on their size.

Over the course of nine months in 2009 and shorter return trips in 2011, 2012, 2013, 2014, and 2015, I conducted extensive interviews with unionists from both ATE and UPCN in both their workplace and the union offices; attended plenaries, assemblies (at the level of the sectional offices and at the workplace), and other meetings; attended classes for new delegates run by both organizations; and attended demonstrations, press conferences, and other public events associated with union activity. In 2012 I spent two months with a UPCN delegation from an important ministry located in the center of Buenos Aires, accompanying them in daily meetings, gatherings in the delegation office, and visits. During this research my focus was initially on collective politics, through the specific example of unionism. My previous work (Lazar 2008) had explored collective politics and technologies of the self in Bolivia, and the work in Argentina became an extension of those two concerns, moving toward an interest in political activism as a problem in itself. Although I do not consider myself a political activist, I have sought to make my research consistent with a personal political interest in social movements against oppression and emancipatory education in the Freiran sense (Freire 1996). As I grew closer to my interlocutors and moved methodologically from a greater emphasis on recorded interviews to more informal methods of participation in meetings and social and educational events, I took on a position of sympathizer; some UPCN activists considered that they had managed to "Peronize" me, as over time I became more familiar with their day-to-day life. Across both ATE and UPCN, my main informants were union leaders, from union delegates at the level of the administrative unit to those with positions in the central offices of the city. This focus on the committed activists means that my study does emphasize those people who were usually relatively happy with how their union acted, although that did not mean they were entirely uncritical. Furthermore, currently, relations between these union hierarchies and their members are not on the whole characterized by the violence and antagonism that has been an important part of Argentine unionism since the mid-twentieth century (see Torre 1998; Munck, Galitelli, and Falcon 1987). At the time of my fieldwork, those union members who were dissatisfied tended not to violently confront the leadership, as has happened in the past, but simply leave the union altogether. If they were UPCN members dissatisfied with its political position, they often joined ATE, but many public-sector workers chose not to be members of any union, as it was not obligatory.

Public opinion in Argentina, particularly in the city of Buenos Aires, is often very strongly against the trade unions. Many ordinary people and rival union-ists think that the unions are corrupt, bureaucratized, and entrepreneurial, seek-ing to take advantage of their members and the workers more generally to earn money. They frequently tell murky stories of embezzlement, violence, and mis-use of power and accuse union leaders of spending all their time in union ac-tivity instead of working alongside their fellow workers. In theory, unions are financed by the 1 to 3 percent of an employee's salary that goes to pay union dues once the individual has affiliated. The precise percentage depends on num-bers of affiliates, and it is deducted from pay by the employing institution and passed on to the union account. For the associated health insurance plan, the employer pays 5 percent and individuals pay 3 percent of their salary,[3] and the retention (and disbursal) of these amounts is implemented by the national tax-ation agency, AFIP (Administración Federal de Ingresos Públicos; Federal Ad-ministration of Public Income). The government pays into a Solidarity Fund for health insurance plans in general, but according to my UPCN informants, this is for special programs, "like brain transplants," I was told jokingly. An individual can choose to pay neither health insurance nor union dues, but choosing not to pay for health insurance forfeits the employer contribution. Individuals can also choose to affiliate with more than one union. Neither employers nor the govern-ment pays money directly to the union.[4]

Union delegates are allowed a certain number of *horas gremiales*, hours of work per month that they can spend on union business, such as meetings, dem-onstrations, and negotiations, according to the Law of Union Associations (Art. 44c).[5] Precise amounts are agreed at the institutional level and on the basis of the collective bargaining agreement, but it is important that there is protection in law for workers to act on union business. For example, and in addition to the protection of time to be devoted to union business, union delegates are pro-tected by law against being dismissed while they are delegates and for a year af-ter they have finished their union mandate, under the provisions of *tutela sindi-cal*, union protection (Law of Union Associations, Sec. XII, Arts. 47–52). Leaders at higher levels of the union, such as the Capital Section and ATE-Capital offices, are granted *licencia gremial*, which is leave from their work to engage in union action. The union pays them a salary.

ATE and UPCN vary in how they define the appropriate field of struggle and suitable strategies for achieving their aims. ATE considers itself to be engaged in a broad class struggle, while UPCN is more conciliatory and seeks benefits for its affiliates through negotiation, especially within institutionalized collective bargaining. Both seek better salaries and environmental conditions and partic-ipate in campaigning and collective bargaining on measures to address workplace harassment and equality of opportunities. Both provide services to their members, and UPCN in particular considers professional training to be a core element of its activity as a union. Confrontation between civil service labor and management, when it takes place, tends to revolve around salary negotiations, pension provisions (especially with regard to how much of the salary is formally registered and therefore able to be taken into account when pensions and other benefits are calculated), and for ATE in particular the tensions around temporary and permanent contracts. Both unions seek to preserve jobs and fight situations where temporary contracts are not renewed or permanent employees are transferred to other departments (see Lazar 2016b). They do so using very different strategies and methods but share a similar understanding of what would be the best outcome for their constituency. Much of what both unions do is make themselves viable as organizations in their own right and (for ATE in particular) as a member of a broader social movement arena. UPCN and ATE are, like other unions, channels for the distribution and articulation of a wide range of political, social, and economic rights, as well as cultural life and kinship; active citizenship as made in the union is a whole-life condition, beyond specific confrontations over employment conditions.

THE ARGENTINE STATE

Any characterization of "a state" is of necessity partial and shifts according to the perspective from which one attempts such a task, and there is indeed a very well-developed literature in the anthropology of the state that explores this in depth.[6] As a foreigner in Buenos Aires, I encountered the Argentine state in multiple ways: the border guard checking my passport as I entered the country, the immigration office where I applied for a research visa, the price controls on subway and bus fares, the national museums I visited with my children, the airplanes of the privatized then renationalized Aerolineas Argentinas by which we traveled the country. Because I was a researcher studying the unions of state employees, other elements became salient, especially the institutional and political complexity of the Argentine state, the nature of formal and informal employment structures within different state entities, and some of the most important changes in the organization of the state over the course of the last couple of decades in particular. Here I consolidate those elements that are key to understanding union action and affiliation.

Argentina is a federal state, and state employment at the national (federal) level ranges over an extremely wide and complex web of institutions, from the more obvious ones such as ministries to the national parks administration, scientific research institutions, and regulatory entities. These institutions have different forms of governance and accountability and different kinds of unionization. UPCN tends to dominate the national administration and often claims to have the majority of affiliates in any given state entity. The largest UPCN delegations are to be found in agencies that reach across the country, such as ANSES (Administración Nacional de la Seguridad Social) and PAMI (Plan de Asistencia Médica Integral), respectively, the social service agency and the health insurance system for elderly people. According to UPCN leaders, they have around thirteen thousand and fourteen thousand workers, respectively; but they also have their own institution-specific unions, which compete with UPCN and ATE for affiliates. UPCN and ATE both have affiliates and delegations or *juntas internas* in ministries, secretariats, decentralized and autonomous institutions, the Congress and Senate administration, state-funded research institutions, and so on. In the past, ATE had considerable strength in the publicly owned industries, especially the dockyards. Now, few publicly owned industries remain, but those that do include the water utility, Aerolineas Argentinas, the mail service, state-owned media, and some high-technology firms. The management of the railways has remained in public hands, and YPF (the oil company, Yacimientos Petrolíferos Fiscales) is 51 percent owned by the government (as of late 2015). Neither UPCN nor ATE has significant numbers of affiliates in these industries.

It is quite remarkable to think of any union attempting to represent all the different kinds of public-sector workers that exist in any given country. In Argentina in April 2013, the executive branch of government consisted of fourteen different ministries and the presidential office, which had seven secretariats. There is also a legislative branch—the Congress and the Senate—with their associated administrative workers and the judicial branch, including the Supreme Court and two public ministries (fiscal and defense). The structure of the state is somewhat fluid, as periodic reorganizations change the composition of different ministries; for example, the Ministry of Justice was in 2009 the Ministry of Justice, Security and Human Rights but was split in 2010 into the Ministry of Justice and Human Rights and the Ministry of Security. In recent memory, the Ministry of Justice has been autonomous, connected to the Ministry of Education and part of the Ministry of the Interior.

Each ministry has a complex organogram, and some are made up of many different institutions, which have national reach and may have offices in the interior of the country or in the city of Buenos Aires. The Ministry of Health is a good example of the potential for institutional complexity. Although it no longer runs public hospitals, it is responsible for much more than just ministry administration, covering multiple institutions: ANMAT (Administración Nacional de Medicamentos, Alimentos y Tecnología Médica; National Administration of Medications, Food and Medical Technology) and its subsidiaries, the regulators of medication and of food; the national drug rehabilitation service; the national service for people with disabilities; the national transplant surgery coordinator; and the national administration of laboratories, which includes the Malbrán hospital and eight others located around the country. There are also civil servants in the ministry building itself and those entities that provide administrative service to the ministry, such as storage of materials or printing and transport services. This complexity presents obvious challenges for union organization within the Argentine state, and unionists in institutions such as the Ministry of Health were very proud that they had managed to successfully coordinate the people who worked in such a wide range of institutions, housed in locations across the city and even the country. They did so by having a nested structure consisting of a delegation in each institution, which reported to the central overall ministry delegation, which in turn consisted of delegates from across the institutions.

Not all ministries are as complex as the Health Ministry in institutional structure, while others have different kinds of complexities. For example, the very large Justice Ministry is responsible for several autonomous institutions, some of which—like the Automobile Registration institution—are effectively outsourced. The majority of the workers in such institutions are employed by a subcontracted agency and hold temporary rather than permanent contracts. For the unions, they count as state employees, but their status is blurred. This is relevant because the kinds of employment contracts operating in the public sector are of enormous importance to the unions and a key focus of their activities.

At the municipal level, especially in the city of Buenos Aires—also known as Capital Federal or CABA (Ciudad Autónoma de Buenos Aires; Autonomous City of Buenos Aires)—neither ATE nor UPCN is the majority union. That distinction belongs to the official Peronist union SUTECBA (Sindicato Unico de Trabajadores del Estado de la Ciudad de Buenos Aires; Unique Union of State Workers of the City of Buenos Aires).[7] UPCN has relatively few affiliates in the CABA government, since UPCN allied with SUTECBA after the decentralization reforms that moved most hospitals and all schools to municipal government. UPCN agreed that it would not actively seek affiliates among municipal employees and therefore did not attempt to expand affiliation in entities that had been transferred from the national to municipal government. However, a small number of municipal employees retained the membership in UPCN that they had held when their institution had been part of the national system. A similar pattern of retention of affiliation happened for ATE, but in addition there has been a subsequent process of expansion, in part because ATE presents itself as the nontraditional alternative to SUTECBA. Members of the ATE *juntas internas* in the Teatro Colón and the CABA audit office told me that the creation of greater choice among unions through the decentralization of some state functions enabled them to seek out ATE once their disillusionment with SUTECBA became too great; other CABA workers on temporary contracts found that they were not able to join either of the Peronist unions, so they affiliated with ATE. Now ATE has a significant presence in the municipal government in the city of Buenos Aires, especially hospitals, although a large majority of the members of ATE-Capital are employees of the national administration.[8]

Although not numerically majoritarian within ATE-Capital, at the time of my field research municipal employees had a higher profile than national employees in regard to political conflicts. This can be attributed to political causes, in large part because the mayor of the city of Buenos Aires from 2007 to 2015, Mauricio Macri, was a political enemy that nearly all ATE members could agree on. This in turn was important because there was an ongoing tension within ATE between *kirchneristas*—those who supported the presidencies of Néstor and Cristina Kirchner (2003–15)—and those who were more oppositional. That tension was exposed to some extent when the CTA (Central de los Trabajadores de la Argentina; Argentine Workers' Central) split in 2010–11 between the *kirchnerista* group led by Hugo Yasky (of the main teachers' union confederation) and those led by Pablo Micheli, former general secretary of ATE-Nacional. The latter group opposed the Kirchner government of the time but considered itself to be autonomous rather than necessarily anti-*kirchnerista*. Although the great majority in ATE stayed with Micheli, one or two quite prominent figures supported the Yasky faction. But after the CTA split, the autonomists appeared to gain the upper hand in leadership positions.[9]

While ATE's position in the face of the national Kirchner government was a space for internal contestation, their political positioning at the municipal level was much more straightforward, especially in 2009 when Mayor Maurico Macri pursued a number of measures that were vehemently opposed by my ATE informants. These included his attempts to reduce the numbers of Teatro Colón employees, reduce the age of criminal majority to fourteen, bring in a particular police commissioner for the city who was thought to have dubious connections to the military regimes and a violent record, close down a youth center (the Puerto Pibes) and use it for the new city police force, restructure the audit office, and continue very low salaries for hospital workers (Figure 1). All these measures provoked ATE-sponsored mobilizations at which participants attacked Macri's neoliberalism. We find a hint here about the likely consequences of his success

FIGURE 1.   Festival to protest the planned closure of the Puerto Pibes children's center

in the 2015 presidential elections. Indeed, when I talked with one UPCN unionist right after the first round, he said almost gleefully to me that "los sindicatos
somos para pelear" (we unions are here to fight). Although upset at Macri's success, he did relish the prospect of being allowed by his union hierarchy to fight
the new regime.

Furthermore, the CABA government, in common with other provincial and
municipal governments, was understood to be less well institutionalized than
the national government. Certainly, this was the opinion held by many of my informants. They pointed to examples such as a collective bargaining system that
has existed since 1999 in the national administration, based on the agreements
(convenios colectivos) of 1999—which ATE joined in 2004—and of 2006, but this
has yet to be fully achieved at the municipal level. ATE signed a collective bargaining agreement with the CABA government in 2010, but SUTECBA did not
recognize ATE's right to participate in the collective negotiations, so the CABA
government signed individual agreements with the three unions (SUTECBA,
UPCN, and ATE). ATE informants suspected that SUTECBA will in fact continue with its system of informal negotiations, about which they were in general very scathing. Across the country, negotiations at the provincial govern-

ment level are much less formal than at the national level. Agreements for wage increases in the national administration tend to set the upper limit for wage increases in municipal and provincial governments, but at the lower levels, implementation is more opaque; and many consider provincial governments to be clientelistic and highly corrupt.

Numbers

The pressure from international financial institutions (IFIs) to reduce fiscal deficits during the neoliberal period—which in Argentina was most acute in the 1990s—has meant that numbers of state employees have become a symbolic and very contentious political issue. Unions can of course assert greater pressure on their employer with larger numbers of affiliates, and there is a direct relationship between relative numbers of affiliates and the balance of power between UPCN and ATE in collective bargaining. However, Argentine governments are, like many, under pressure to be seen to reduce public-sector expenditure in an effort to keep budget deficits low. Although IFI influence was reduced since the International Monetary Fund (IMF) debt was paid off in 2005, the fact that Argentina had no access to global capital markets since the debt default of 2002 created pressure. Governments had to choose between a combination of living within their means by spending roughly what they earned through exports and taxation, adapting their financial policy to become eligible once more to borrow on international markets, or printing money to meet increasing public expenditures. As in most countries, public-sector wage bills are therefore under scrutiny from all sides. This is one of the policy fault lines exposed in the 2015 elections and one of the most important sources of dispute under Macri's presidency.

Given the complexity of the state, determining employee numbers is not entirely straightforward, and estimates vary widely. The CABA government has around 125,000 workers according to Jose Luis Matassa, general secretary of ATE-Capital in 2012, although one ATE delegate put the number at 285,000. In 2009, Felipe Carrillo, second in command at the UPCN Capital Section, told me that there were around 120,000 to 130,000 state employees at the national level, with 110,000 in the national administration covered by the SINEP (Sistema Nacional de Empleo Público; National System of Public Employment) collective bargaining agreement,[10] and Andrés Rodríguez, general secretary of UPCN, agreed; another UPCN leader estimated 100,000 workers in the national state, 50,000 of whom were covered by SINEP. An ex-UPCN delegate suggested that there were 32,000 workers in the national state. In 2012, a UPCN delegate from the Ministry of Health told me that 70,000 workers were covered by SINEP.

Understandably, estimates of union affiliation vary, and one would expect union leaders to overestimate the numbers of their members. The Labor Ministry in theory holds data about union affiliation but does not easily release the information. ATE leaders estimate their membership across the whole country at between 200,000 (Rodolfo Arrechea, 2009) and 250,000 (Pablo Micheli, 2012). Rodolfo Arrechea, general secretary of ATE-Capital in 2009, told me that 30 percent of ATE's 200,000 affiliates were in the health sector and therefore municipal or provincial employees. In a report produced by ATE-Capital (Pereira et al. 2009), around 25 percent of the nearly 19,000 affiliates of ATE-Capital in 2008 were municipal employees, and 55 percent of those were members of the health sector. However, ATE is very strong in many provincial governments, especially Buenos Aires, where Matassa told me they have around 60,000 affiliates. UPCN, which does not have a very large number of municipal/provincial employee members, estimates a total affiliation of around 250,000 to 300,000, according to Omar Auton, a key figure in the Capital Section, and Adrian Jaichenco, an ex-member of the Capital Section leadership council. Felipe Carrillo estimated (in 2009) that the Capital Section, which covers all national employees (not only those based in the city of Buenos Aires), had 38,000 affiliates, while in 2013 Auton thought this was closer to 55,000. The difference in estimates does not reflect growth in affiliation numbers, although growth is steady; rather, it reflects the difficulty of finding clear figures. Unión Personal (UP), the health insurance run by UPCN, has more than 700,000 members according to its website.[11] Affiliates of ATE and unions other than UPCN can be members of UP, but UPCN affiliates receive special discounts and assistance.

Claims around different numbers of affiliates take on a particular political cast in the case of Argentine state employment because of the way that collective bargaining is organized. In the negotiations (*paritarias*) the unions and state have equal representation, but union representation is split between UPCN and ATE at a ratio of 2:1. The word *paritaria* is used to refer both to the meetings between these representatives, on various specific commissions, and to the negotiation itself, including telephone conversations, circulation of documents by e-mail, and so on that make up the negotiation but fall outside formal meetings. The reason for the different number of representatives from UPCN and ATE is explained differently by unionists from each organization. When a count of union affiliation within the national administration was conducted in 1999, ATE had around 28 percent of the affiliation and UPCN, 70 percent,[12] hence the 1:2 ratio of representation on the *paritarias*. ATE activists mostly think that this has since changed and that they are much closer to a 2:3 ratio (ATE:UPCN), even in the SINEP. They say that UPCN does not want a recount because this would become evident and their representation ratio would then have to change. UPCN activists simply say that they are the majority union, which is a source of pride and of responsibility for them, and that the situation has not changed significantly since 1999.

Without a major count organized by the Labor Ministry, it would be impossible to say definitively who is correct, and both unions have an interest in keeping the information somewhat opaque. This is easy because the complexity of state institutionalization is reflected in a highly variable field of union affiliation. In 2009, I was shown a document detailing percentages of UPCN membership in different institutions of the SINEP and allowed to copy down some of them. The document referred to 40,000 workers in total as part of the SINEP, and UPCN affiliation ranged from 87 percent of permanent workers and 90 percent of contracted workers in the office of the National Identity Register, to 10 percent of permanent workers and 9 percent of contracted workers in the Office of the President. Curiously, UPCN had 100 percent of the permanent workers of the Secretariat for the Environment and Sustainable Development but only 34 percent of the contracted workers, while it had 52 percent of the contracted workers and only 31 percent of the permanent workers in the Tourism Secretariat. The rest of the figures did not fall into any discernible pattern, although perhaps most institutions fell into one of two groups, one of 30 to 50 percent affiliation and one of 8 to 17 percent, with little significant difference between contracted and permanent workers. But there were outliers beyond the extremes I have already referred to—for example, UPCN in CONICET (Consejo Nacional de Investigaciones Científicas y Técnicas), the national scientific research council, had 17 percent contracted workers and 71 percent of the permanent workers. However, I could not copy down the whole document and was not allowed to make a photocopy, so this identification of trends must remain tentative. And I did not note down the affiliation rates for PAMI and ANSES, two very large public institutions and UPCN delegations. However, I was surprised by the level of affiliation among contracted workers, which are a group that ATE claims to represent almost exclusively.[13]

Numbers alone will not grant power to any union, although they are of course crucial and an essential starting point. People are allowed to affiliate with more than one union, and my informants told me that this did happen sometimes, although they thought it quite rare. People may affiliate and then never participate in any union activities, perhaps until and unless they have a problem that they think the union might be able to solve. UPCN affiliates gain greater discounts with the UP health insurance, so there is probably a sizable number of UPCN members whose primary motive for affiliation is that greater discount. Beyond affiliation, union strength relies on the commitment that the union can generate among its activists and its ability to mobilize ordinary affiliates when necessary.

STATE EMPLOYEES AND CLASS

UPCN's strength in the national administration—essentially the civil servants of national ministries and state institutions—exhibited a particular class character as far as a number of my informants were concerned. Typically, they distinguished UPCN's affiliates as broadly the white-collar workers of the state, while ATE tended to be stronger among the blue-collar workers, such as hospital or lab technicians, mechanics associated with different ministries, and dock workers. This association was also made in part because of ATE's history, beginning with the workers at publicly owned shipyards in the 1920s (Calello and Parcero 2008). Although the distinction between white- and blue-collar public workers was a fairly common one, in practice different groups of workers were associated with the different unions in constellations that varied according to the state institution in question. For example, in the Malbrán institute, I was told that the laboratory technicians and professionals were generally ATE affiliates, while UPCN was based in the administrative and maintenance sectors. In the Teatro Colón, SUTECBA was much stronger among the maintenance and administration workers than ATE, whose strength lay more among the technical workers, such as stage hands. Neither had much influence among the musicians and other artists, although ATE was stronger there than SUTECBA.

Although the decision to affiliate with a union was often described to me as something that one just does on beginning a new job because of a commitment understood partly in terms of class, people did not appear to choose between ATE and UPCN on the basis of some kind of perceived class affinity. In national institutions, ATE was often thought to be the minority union, even by ATE activists. Where it had occurred, ATE's growth was attributed to very specific situations, such as particular labor conflicts as in the example of the Ministry of Justice. In another case, I was told that ATE gained a small presence in a UPCN stronghold because around one hundred jobs were opened up for ATE to fill by the Fernando de la Rua government of 1999–2001. In CABA institutions, activists told me stories of growing disillusionment with SUTECBA and hence a decision made by a few brave workers to affiliate with ATE, often under threat of aggression by SUTECBA. Affiliation, then, usually had little to do with a sense of particular class allegiance to a specific union and more to do with specific events, or in some cases preexisting political commitment.

Both ATE and UPCN might then be broadly conceived of as unions of middle-class workers. But saying that does not help a great deal in visualizing who exactly would be their constituency and affiliates. One thing that all my informants could agree on was the remarkable diversity of occupation in state employment, as explained by one leading UPCN figure:

> In our case, we have the national symphony orchestra, the national chorus, the researchers in the National Commission for Atomic Energy, in CONICET, doctors and nurses, diplomatic personnel who represent Argentina overseas. That's to say, there's a real variety of activities, which makes union life more complex.

General Secretary Rolando Arrechea of ATE-Capital in 2009 emphasized the range of state entities where ATE has affiliates:

> ATE is a union that fundamentally was born from a workers' union related to everything that was naval but that now is inserted in all of the state activities, at national, provincial, and municipal level. And our particularity is that we could represent all of the health workers, and in the national state, there is union representation in all of the areas, the technical scientific, the workers of CONICET, of atomic energy, ATE is there; the Ministries of Justice, Human Rights, the Ministry of the Interior, the Ministry of Economy, of Agriculture. That's to say, in all of the areas—in the organisms of regulation over the state, the SIGEN, the General Audit Office of the nation, the statistics institute, well, diverse areas.

The repetition of the particular figure of the atomic scientist was quite common and puzzled me until one informant connected it specifically to a film directed by Pino Solanas, called *Argentina latente* (Latent Argentina, 2007), which examines the productive potential of the Argentine state through images of the varied industries and resources in public ownership. The newly elected ATE delegate who told me this connected the diversity of state employment to questions of class, contextualizing it within a discussion of general public disdain for state employees:

> [The film] shows different state workers, who work in spaces that are key and strategic. It's not possible to say that these guys are parasites or scholarship kids, because they are really people who are doing something. . . . Those guys [the dock workers] are like the advance—really they are the vanguard of the working class, as much for the sector that they represent, which is a strategic sector, as for how they behave. Subjectively and objectively, they are the vanguard, so I have enormous respect for these *compañeros* [comrades].

The diversity of their (potential) affiliates was of particular importance to ATE and a cause for celebration: A calendar it produced for 2010 consists of photographs of state workers and has only one image of an administrative worker. The other months show a dock worker, health workers, a laboratory technician, a health worker fumigating an adobe hut in the north of the country, ballet dancers, a food inspector, miners, a municipal construction worker, a school cook, fire brigade workers, and a worker on the Patagonian Express railway.[14]

The diversity of occupation within the state was also reflected in the quite different salaries earned by various state employees, an issue that made the day-to-day work of the unions very complicated. As Ruben Mosquera, a leader in ATE-Nacional, pointed out in an interview conducted in 2009,

> Really in terms of wage claims, it's almost impossible to fight for the same salary claim for a person who is earning two thousand or fifteen hundred pesos [a month] with another person, an engineer with CONAE [the Atomic Energy commission] who is earning twenty thousand. I mean, for the CONAE engineer, ten percent is money, and for the person who earns fifteen hundred, it's nothing.

Beyond specific negotiations for salary increases, it was even more complicated when attempting to negotiate a coherent pay scale and provisions for career advancement with their employer. This is one of the most important elements of the collective bargaining agreement, which directs much of UPCN's activity.

Although state salaries are on the whole generous in comparison with minimum or average salaries in Argentina, it would be important not to imagine all UPCN and ATE activists as very well-heeled civil servants. Many, especially municipal workers (in hospitals and working for the city government), earn very low salaries, and a state salary below management level will cover the needs of a whole family with difficulty if the state employee is the only wage earner. But at the national ministry level, UPCN affiliates in particular appeared to be fairly comfortably off, as far as one can tell from clues such as clothing and housing, and salaries in the national administration are relatively good. In mid-2013, the *paritarias* agreed on an initial salary of 4,200 pesos/month (approximately US$525 at the unofficial rate, $763 at the official rate),[15] with an initial salary for professionals at 7,300 pesos/month (US$913 or $1,327), and an average salary of 8,000 pesos/month (US$1,000 or $1,455). Not all UPCN affiliates or state workers came from middle-class backgrounds, though. One day I asked members of the UPCN delegation that I worked with about their families. Out of the ten that I asked, four had parents who had been small businesspeople—selling vegetables, domestic electronics, or wholesale goods. The fathers of the others had worked as a trucker, taxi driver, railway worker, and metalworker; mothers had been a systems administrator, telephone operator, special needs teacher, social worker, and housewife. State employment may therefore be a route to social mobility, and I got the sense that this was especially the case for the older delegates, who had often come from backgrounds of manual labor (as had their families).

HISTORICAL EMPLACEMENT: "LOS 90" AND BEFORE

I have described state employment and unionization through a kind of structural-spatial modality, examining diversity, numbers of employees and affiliates, class character, and levels of government administration. However, one of the most striking elements of my interviews, and indeed of many informal conversations, was the way that both UPCN and ATE delegates sought to contextualize their contemporary action for me within a longer-term historical narrative. That is, they gave temporal as well as spatial explanations; to do them justice, I now switch to a temporal rendering of the state and unionism.

A tendency to divide the past into quite clearly defined periods was one of the most important aspects of interview data, informal conversations, and official materials produced by both unions, as well as of scholarly accounts in Argentina. These ran from the first Peronist regime in 1946–55, which was often felt to be a kind of golden period by activists from both unions; followed by resistance and 1960s radicalization; the dictatorship of 1976–83; the neoliberal period of 1989–99 (Carlos Menem's presidencies); to some extent the banking crisis of 2001–2; and the present. The period 2003–15 is gradually becoming understood as a second period of genuine Peronism under the Kirchners, which the government claimed as "La decada ganada" (the decade that was won back, a wordplay on the "lost decade" of debt crisis). A few periods stood out as most important for my interlocutors, especially 1946–55, 1976–83, and 1989–99. For many, these periods represented, respectively, a golden age in both political and economic terms; followed by the nadir of political degradation in the time of the dictatorship, when unionists and workers were targeted for political repression and a number of my informants had to operate clandestinely; then the neoliberal period, which was often viewed as one of economic degradation, where privatization policies especially affected state workers. However, in both the latter cases, economic and political degradation were not absent, just subordinate in common representations of the ills of the age.

The experience of "los 90" is crucial for understanding several aspects of contemporary public-sector unionism: first, the way that contemporary unionists view their political activism (and how ATE and UPCN evaluate each other), and second, the way that state restructuring has impacted state employment and shaped union action today. The 1990s was a time when the terms of economic citizenship—as participation in government and as distribution of rights—

shifted dramatically from a mid-twentieth-century corporatist version under state-led development to a more neoliberal model of an increasingly financialized economy and individual citizenship based on consumption (Guano 2002). That meant a significant shift in the conditions of possibility for social movements to take action in defense of a series of citizenship rights, especially economic rights (e.g., to work) and rights to social welfare. The rise of an individualist perspective also meant that collective political organizations like unions lost some of their cultural power and had to struggle against public perceptions of them as old-fashioned and bureaucratic. All this was achieved by means of the entrenchment of neoliberal, free-market economic orthodoxy in Argentine policy making under the regime of Carlos Menem. Although a Peronist, he turned his back on the classically distributive economic policy of midcentury Peronism and oversaw one of the most extreme processes of structural adjustment in the region, encouraged by the international financial institutions and the global political-economic consensus of the time. He turned Argentina into a "poster child" for the Washington Consensus, until everything collapsed at the beginning of the following decade.

Paul Blustein points out that few countries were so lionized at the time for their free-market economic policy making. For example, in 1999 the Heritage Foundation rated Argentina as tied with Chile for the best economic policies in Latin America and almost equal to Australia and Taiwan (Blustein 2005: 5). The precise details of labor flexibilization measures, privatizations, and social policy reforms are highly complex and described better elsewhere (e.g., Usami 2004; Etchemendy 2005). They were in fact not quite as thoroughgoing as was thought at the time, and Sebastián Etchemendy (2001) has done some extremely careful work to illustrate how the government made deals with established sources of power in order to partially implement restructuring and protect certain sectors from the full impact of the policy prescriptions. He argues that some "traditional rent seekers were able to protect their rents in the new market setting" because of the nature of reform as "full of midpoints, partial reforms, and economic privileges politically bestowed, be they the awarding of dominant firms in economic sectors, the negotiation of special tariff regimes, incomplete deregulation of the health system or the labor law, or an interest participation in the pension funds and other newly created markets" (Etchemendy 2001: 28). Nonetheless, the reforms were experienced by many as deeply unsettling and are still a source of controversy and passionate argument today; many of my informants, from both ATE and UPCN, thought that Menem had destroyed the Argentine state.

The 1990s saw a number of changes coming together at the same time, and the administrative reform of the state that is the focus of this discussion was undertaken alongside a reformulation of labor law, social policy, and the Peronist party itself. The thrust of these reforms was to shift influence away from the old corporatist structures of Peronism, away from the formal-sector unions, and toward more neighborhood-based forms of clientelism, incorporation, and welfare assistance (Levitsky 2003a; Auyero 2001). As Etchemendy shows, Menem was only partially successful in this aim, as the unions, particularly UPCN, managed to protect their position and that of their affiliates.

They were struggling against a series of policy prescriptions that aimed to reduce employment in public administration and increase labor flexibility. These were enacted through the laws of state reform (Ley 23.696) and economic emergency (Ley 23.697) at the beginning of Menem's government in 1989 and subsequently through emergency decrees. Martín Armelino summarizes them as follows: "The reforms suspended the employment of personnel, the stability of employees and the various salary regimes in the sector, . . . privatized state enterprises in the service sector and the military-industrial complex, transferred basic social functions (health and education) to provincial and municipal jurisdictions, and instigated administrative reform" (2015: 250). While the administrative reform was initially promoted on the basis of greater efficiency and the need to modernize the state, it rapidly became focused on reducing public expenditure and resolving the fiscal deficit to gain the confidence of international credit organizations (ibid.). This meant that, according to Armelino, the reform was quickly reduced to one of simply downsizing the number of agencies, state infrastructure, and, importantly, the number of employees (251).

The privatization of state-run enterprises particularly affected ATE, and protests quickly broke out in the defense industry in particular, where significant production facilities were due to be liquidated, including the naval dockyards (ATE's place of birth in 1925). There was also reduction in the national administrative infrastructure initially, but the numbers quickly began to grow again Etchemendy 2001; Armelino 2015). A similar pattern occurred with respect to total employment: numbers dropped dramatically with the move of health and education services from national to municipal government, leading to a drop in the numbers of ministry employees of 23.4 percent and 94.8 percent, respectively, in 1989–95 (Armelino 2015: 252). However, provincial employment rose by a broadly equivalent amount, as people simply moved between employers. Etchemendy (2001) argues that even in the most acute period of adjustment, 1989–91, public administration employment outside the Health and Education Ministries declined by only 11.5 percent and that between 1989 and 1995 overall employment reduction was only 3.7 percent. The effects of privatization on the state employment roll were more acute: employment in public enterprises declined from 236,694 in 1990 to 41,102 in 1993 (ibid.: 8).

Outside the protests organized against decentralization and the privatization of state-run industries, ATE resisted local attempts to fire significant numbers of people. Sometimes they were successful, as in the Malbrán conflict, when workers went on strike for 202 days between December 1996 and June 1997, occupying the building for 184 days. The forty-nine workers whose dismissal had provoked the mobilization were eventually reinstated and the measures lifted. The symbolic importance of the victory was great, so much so that ATE made a documentary about the protest in 2006. As one ATE member of the Malbrán *junta interna* said to me,

> [The year 1996] was paradigmatic: it was critical to break the state reform, and [the Malbrán] was the first place that said "you don't do this here" [*esto acá no se hace*]. I think that this was the longest strike in Argentine history. It was overwhelming [*contundente*], let's say. Whether you're in favor of ATE or not, this is something they did.

UPCN took a different strategy in the face of the state reforms, which were implemented through the Executive Committee for the Coordination of the Administrative Reform (CECRA), established by decree in 1990. UPCN was included on the council, but ATE was excluded. Etchemendy reports that according to one member of the CECRA, "UPCN representatives had considerable voice in redesigning the structure of state agencies, trying to protect the union's ranks" (2001: 7). Etchemendy also views the negotiations of the collective bargaining agreements as compensation from the state to UPCN in return for its participation in the reform. Most important, though, UPCN became the administrator of the new health insurance system for workers in the entire national public sector (UP). This meant a huge increase in its financial power.

UPCN leaders would take issue with this argument, and they often insisted to me that although UPCN controls UP, the union and health insurance system administration and accounts are kept separate. With respect to the administrative reforms themselves, though, UPCN leaders would not necessarily disagree with Etchemendy. On the whole, they instead argued that it was necessary for them to participate in this way. Carlos Capurro, in 2009 the gremial secretary of the Capital Section, described the reforms as a "tsunami":

> Well, at that point, in the nineties, those reforms were structural, and they were done almost like a tsunami that sweeps away a whole coast. Opposing them would have meant being swept away in the same manner, because it was a force

that just came. . . . So we had to adapt ourselves, allow ourselves to be taken, and to take advantage of this movement to put forward our needs. Not only as an organization, which is the first point—institutional strengthening. If we don't have a strong institution, we can't defend anyone; we can't make any demands if we're compromised in some way. And, differently from what people believe, at the time of Menem's government we had the fewest connections as a union organization. [In fact] the first . . . to be convened to do this reform was ATE and not us. [But] ATE had the lack of intelligence, we say, to have a demagogic attitude, [saying] "Ah, we don't want this."

It's fine, what happened happened, because ATE couldn't stop it either. The transformations came, their vision remained in critique and opposition, but they couldn't modify a single thing from that opposition. In contrast, with participation, what we achieved in that decade was [to] strengthen our organization, that's to say, respond to our reason for being [razón de ser], which was representing our affiliates; that was our strengthening. So, at the point when [the government was] rationalizing personnel, we took care that our workers, affiliated with our organization, didn't succumb to this destiny. They kept their jobs.

For him, this was the reason that UPCN was the majority union in the national administration, because it could exercise its proper function as a union, protecting its members. He felt that this was a considerable achievement given the political context of the time.

The effects of the reform were uneven, and certainly in the more administrative areas probably not as many jobs were lost as might be imagined; and some of the public-sector unions were not quite as weakened as the more radical neoliberal prophets might have wished. What is most evident is that the reforms moved people off the (national) books to other employers—mostly provincial or municipal governments or private enterprises. Crucially, they were moved to jobs where employment conditions were poorer and protections were weaker. The move from secure employment conditions to a more "flexible" and insecure employment environment gradually happened also in the more protected areas of national administration, albeit through indirect mechanisms and with variable effects.

Some administration workers remained in the higher-quality jobs through the creation in 1991 of the Sistema Nacional de la Profesión Administrativa (National System of the Administrative Profession, SINAPA), which incorporated around thirty thousand civil servants in 1990, mostly those who worked in ministries. Through their participation in the CECRA, UPCN helped design SINAPA, the system that covered the majority of their affiliates. It meant that they could protect their members from being fired; and they also took advantage of it politically by negotiating the system of collective bargaining between unions and the state. The latter was in fact the product of a law taken through Congress by Germán Abdala, a very important ATE figure. Initially, it was a source of some conflict between ATE and UPCN, as ATE felt that UPCN benefited from an unfair distribution of union representation, because the ratio of union representation was calculated on the basis of the strength of the two unions in SINAPA rather than in state employment as a whole. The conflict continued until 1998 and the count of affiliates mentioned earlier, which fixed the ratio between ATE and UPCN at 1:2. The first collective bargaining agreement was then negotiated, with ATE's participation, but ATE objected to certain elements of flexibility encoded in the agreement at a late stage and, after consulting with assemblies of their affiliates, refused to agree to it when it was sanctioned in 1999. ATE finally joined the first collective bargaining agreement in 2004 and then in 2006 agreed to its replacement, now called SINEP, or the "214."

At the same time that one group of employees was being protected through the SINAPA negotiations, there was a freezing of the *vacantes*, open job positions. This meant that when permanent state workers left their position either for another job or—more frequently—to retire, they were not replaced, at least not with another permanently employed worker. Gradually, the vacant positions were replaced by means of temporary work contracts, which took a variety of forms over the years. The most precarious is the contract for provision of services (*locación de servicios*), where the worker has the fiscal category of self-employed (*monotributista*) and where contracts usually last for a year but can have terms of six months, three months, or even one month at a time. At the other end of the spectrum is the category of the *planta transitoria*, which denotes a regime where workers have almost all of the labor rights of permanent workers without the stability. This regime is also known as Resolution 48 and was negotiated (by UPCN, according to its delegates) in 2002. Many of the most precarious contracts have by now been shifted to Resolution 48 categories, and some permanent jobs have even been unfrozen in recent years. However, new forms of contracting have also emerged, including through agreements with universities or development agencies (*pasantías*) or internships. Unionists, especially ATE activists, understand fixed-term contracts as a kind of informalization of state employment.

In many ways, the different approaches of the two unions to the question of temporarily contracted workers sum up the different approaches they take on many other issues. UPCN focuses mostly on the negotiation of improvement in the situation of contracted workers. ATE sees itself as defending contracted workers by demonstrating when they are fired (i.e., their contracts not renewed) or moved to a different job, by demonstrating more generally against precarious work, and by a legal strategy of questioning the constitutionality of such contracts in the first place. For ATE, the affiliation and defense of contracted workers have become central to its self-definition as a union, for UPCN contracted workers are more difficult to incorporate structurally, unless they are moved to more stable jobs. But both find themselves dealing with informal work for the state and seek to draw more workers from one side of an informal-formal divide to the other.[16]

TWO MODELS OF TRADE UNIONISM IN A LONGER HISTORY

The 1990s was a period when the differences between the two unions hardened, as a result largely of the different strategic decisions that ATE and UPCN made in the face of Menem's state reform. These derived from several factors: for example, the basic difference in class structure between the unions, as ATE members were concentrated in spaces that were particularly vulnerable to privatization. For ATE activists, though, the decision to differentiate themselves from UPCN and oppose the reform was a political one made as a result of their organization's autonomy from government and political parties and their democratic commitment to represent the views of their bases. They linked these in turn to a historical tradition of autonomous unionism, going back to their anarcho-syndicalist roots in the 1920s (see Martuccelli and Svampa 1997). UPCN leaders felt they had made a more sensible strategic decision and as a result had protected their bases the best they could under the circumstances. They also argued that they have made a strategic decision to work with whichever government is in power and that this stance of negotiation is more effective than taking a more combative position.

Studying the two unions thus enables a comparison between two trends of unionism within the same occupational sector, an important point because several different unions operate in the public sector with full official recognition. This is atypical for Argentine unionism, where the dominant model is a corporatist one of the monopoly of officially recognized union representation per occupational activity. Whereas UPCN is bureaucratic, Peronist, and avowedly pro-government (*oficialista*), ATE is attempting a much more social movement–like political project, which looks for inspiration to *clasista* oppositional trends of 1960s Argentina and early twentieth-century anarcho-syndicalism as much as to contemporary Latin American social movements (Atzeni and Ghighliani 2009; Martuccelli and Svampa 1997). It is a particularly Argentine version of "social-movement unionism" (Waterman 1993), including in the way that ATE activists distinguish themselves from the business or bureaucratic unionism of UPCN and linked especially to ATE's participation in the CTA.[17] Given the fact that most public-sector workers have a choice over the union they join, competition at the shop-floor level is often articulated by attributing a political position to each union and its rival, specifically differentiating between horizontality and verticalism.

This enables activists to articulate a narrative of political belonging to one of two contrastive models of unionism that have developed within the modern Argentine labor movement. Activists and academics distinguish between radical and bureaucratized unionism, each of which has been more prominent at different times since the early twentieth century. The tension is one quite common to unionism more generally (e.g., Mollona 2009) but has engendered some particularly strong divisions in Argentina, at times with fatal consequences. It continues to be important today, not least because formal-sector trade unions are still one of the most powerful social and political actors in the country. I briefly trace the development of these two contrastive trends within the labor movement and assess the role of trade unionism in the country today.

Argentine labor history has been intimately linked with the development of Peronism since the mid-twentieth century. During the late nineteenth and early twentieth centuries, anarchists were influential in the early development of the labor movement (Munck, Galitelli, and Falcon 1987; Suriano 2010; Senén González and Bosoer 2012), and some contemporary ATE activists speak with pride of the anarcho-syndicalist roots of their union (see also Calello and Parcero 2008). But with the parallel rise of the socialists and other reformist tendencies, the labor movement was split from very early in the twentieth century, and the formation of the CGT (Confederación General del Trabajo; General Confederation of Labor) in 1930 marked the beginnings of a "professional" relationship between labor unions and the state.[18] That relationship was fomented with the industrialization of the 1930s and 1940s and consolidated with Juan Perón's rise to power in the mid-1940s. Then and subsequently, the labor movement moved partially away from anarchism and socialism toward Peronism, and most unions became the "spinal column" of Peronism, a phrase still used today.

There are several studies of the relations between unions and Perón in the 1940s (e.g., Del Campo 2005; Doyon 2006), but perhaps the most thorough body of scholarly work is that of Juan Carlos Torre, and I can do little more here than scratch the surface of that remarkable work and refer the reader to it (Torre 1990, 1998, 2002, 2012). Torre traces the complex story of different interests and political conjunctures when the "old guard" of the labor movement allied with Juan

Perón in 1943 and formed the Partido Laborista (Labor Party) to help his election as president in 1946. At the time, some of the leaders wanted to maintain autonomy from Perón, but he defeated them and replaced the Partido Laborista
with his own party, the Partido Justicialista (PJ), thus establishing the corporatist state (Torre 1990, 2012; see also Doyon 2006). Torre describes this shift as follows: "From 1946 onward, the CGT had to give up its aspiration to represent the
workers to the government in order to act instead as the representative of the
government to the workers" (2012: 27).[19]

   There has been considerable debate in Argentina about the reasons for the
close relationship between the organized working classes and Juan Perón. The
sociologist Gino Germani ([1956] 2006) famously argued that Peronism initially
took hold among new migrants from the interior, largely because the more sophisticated traditional workers were not so easily duped. Revisionist scholars responded by stressing continuities between the membership of the labor movement pre- and post-Perón (e.g., Adelman 1992; Horowitz 1990; Murmis and
Portantiero 1972; Tamarin 1985; Torre 1998). They attributed the attraction of Peronism for organized labor to the concrete benefits and rights he gave to workers
in 1943–55 and to the increased political participation and a sense of themselves
as central political actors recognized as such (D. James 1988b; Torre 2012). More
recently, scholars have added to this analysis of Perón's appeal a consideration
of the cultural history of Peronism and the popular classes, exploring the interplay between state making, discourse, ritual, popular culture, and iconography
(Karush and Chamosa 2010; Adamovsky 2012). No doubt, Peronism remains the
most important political movement of the twentieth and early twenty-first centuries in Argentina. From the first Perón presidency, Peronism has profoundly
shaped Argentine politics to the extent that one could even suggest that the most
salient political and even cultural division in Argentina from the mid-twentieth
century has been that between Peronists and anti-Peronists, who are known
as *gorilas* (gorillas) among Peronist circles. Understandings of Juan Perón's regime—both inside and outside government—have shaped scholarly analyses
of populism as a mode of politics, not least because of the significance of the
Argentine experience for Ernesto Laclau's highly influential work (e.g., Laclau
2005). Non-Peronist governments—of which there have been very few that have
not been run by the military—have found it almost impossible to govern the
country because of the organizational and political strength of the movement as
much as their own incompetence. By now, more than seventy years after Perón
first rose to power, Peronism has become many things to many people and in-
corporates a wide spectrum of political approaches, both within and beyond the

PJ. But Peronism is more than the PJ and the Peronist trade unions, more than "mere" pragmatic populism. It is also a social, cultural, and political identity.

For activists from both ATE and UPCN, the first Perón government was something of a golden era (see Senén González and Bosoer 2012: 25). Informants pointed to the introduction of collective bargaining, the promotion and expansion of labor unions, introduction of labor union–based welfare schemes, Eva Perón's social assistance programs, public housing schemes, and nationalization of the railways and other enterprises.[20] All these measures brought substantive citizenship and social rights to a much broader spectrum of Argentine society than ever before, albeit still limited to male formal-sector workers and their recognized dependents (Grassi 2003). Néstor Llano, a leader with ATE-Capital, said,

> This country had ten years of happiness with Peronism—with all the differences that you can have and all the problems there were. Here, at that time, everyone had work, the grandparents had excellent retirement benefits, there was no malnutrition, none of the pests that are appearing now, that had been eradicated from Argentine—yellow fever! This didn't exist, I mean, there were prevention policies. . . . So a kid grew up, arrived [at school] fully nourished; he could think, he could study, he could play, he could, he could, and he could.

In fact, some of the positive measures that informants commonly attributed to Perón were actually established properly in later regimes—such as the health insurance schemes, which were significantly extended and granted to trade unions to administer in 1970 under General Juan Carlos Onganía (Usami 2004; Senén González and Bosoer 2012). However, there is no doubt that the period 1946–55 saw considerable strides forward for Argentine workers, and many contemporary unionists view that period of advance as one that has not been repeated.

After Perón's exile in 1955, Peronist labor unions were at the forefront of the resistance to the military regimes of the 1950s, 1960s, and 1970s. Daniel James's work (1988b, 2000) in particular has traced the deep connections between working-class identity, labor unions, and Peronism.[21] But the union movement has never been homogeneous: even during the Peronist era, a significant "pole of political autonomy" (Torre 2012: 33) existed among the higher levels of labor leaders, the "old guard" identified by Juan Carlos Torre (1990). Further, right from the beginning of the movement, there was always a split between leaders prepared to negotiate with the state and more radical elements, usually located at lower levels of union hierarchies. In the 1960s, the strategic choice to negotiate with the state was especially associated with Augusto Vandor, who as leader of the CGT attempted to create a unionism independent of Perón, known as "Peronism without Perón," which is still controversial among Peronist unionists.[22] However, after the 1966 coup, possibilities for negotiation with the state were reduced and mainstream "business unionism" declined for a while, leaving the way open to more radical leaders, known as *clasistas*, especially associated with Agustín Tosco, who led the famous uprising in Cordoba in 1969, known as the Cordobazo (Brennan 1993; Licht 2009; Carerra, Grau, and Martì 2006). The *clasista* unionists included Trotskyist elements and remnants of the early twentieth-century anarchist movement and the socialist and communist parties (Torre 1998). Later, a significant proportion of those executed, disappeared, or otherwise victimized by the notorious military regime of 1976–83 were trade unionists, although not at the upper levels of leadership, with a few exceptions. The majority were delegates, that is, those activists at the intermediary, shop-floor level, in between central leadership and ordinary affiliates (Mason 2007; Senén González and Bosoer 2012). Many of the top union leaders were prepared to cooperate with the military, policing the workers on their behalf in return for the protection of a number of institutional benefits, such as the right to continue to have representation in the workplace, as well as the principles of negotiation itself, monopoly of representation according to legal personhood, and *erga omnes* (the results of negotiations with the [single] leading union apply to all of the workers in a given sector) (Zorzoli 2015).

The loss of a generation of unionists as a result of the dictatorship is keenly felt today. The dictatorship was one of the key moments of separation between bureaucratic leaders and a more radical base, with the latter being either disappeared or moving into clandestinity. After the intervention and repression of the dictatorship, both unions underwent a process of recovery, which formed a fundamental part of older unionists' narratives and images of organization and activism. UPCN had been "intervened" during the dictatorship, which meant that a leader had been imposed on the union by the military junta, and once democracy returned, a new set of young leaders emerged from within the union. They were less tainted by associations with the military, although not necessarily completely clean, as a few had been members of the *comisión transitoria* (transitional commission) established by the military intervener to "normalize" the union as the military regimes began to weaken in the early 1980s (Zorzoli 2015).[23] Those leaders are now at the top of the union hierarchy and with some prompting will reveal bits and pieces about how they operated in semi-clandestinity during the dictatorship and in preparation for the subsequent recovery of the union.

ATE had not been intervened because its leadership was already very close to the junta: General Secretary Juan Horvath was especially connected to Admiral Emilio Massera. A group of young activists, like the UPCN activists, began to operate in clandestinity during the dictatorship. This ATE group, which focused especially around Víctor de Gennaro and Germán Abdala, formed the electoral list called ANUSATE (Agrupación Nacional Unidad y Solidaridad a ATE; National Unity and Solidarity Grouping of ATE) and fought and won the internal union elections of 1984, much to the surprise of the ATE establishment at the time. ANUSATE continues to dominate ATE, and its victory in 1984 is extremely important to them (see Martuccelli and Svampa 1997).

Subsequently, the neoliberal period of the 1990s was also highly significant for unions, most particularly for the unions of public-sector workers. Along with his structural adjustment policies, Carlos Menem oversaw the (partial) deunionization of the PJ when it began to incorporate the popular classes into political citizenship through neighborhood-based clientelistic structures rather than through the unions (Levitsky 2003a; Auyero 2001; Martuccelli and Svampa 1997). It is significant that Menem was a Peronist, because it meant that the Peronist trade unions at the time were faced with a choice. They could submit to his political program on the basis that this was a Peronist regime and obedience is owed to those higher up within Peronism. There was always the possibility that concessions could be negotiated from within the political structure. Alternatively, unions could resist, but that would require them somehow to renounce or at the very least modify their Peronist identity.

This conflict was felt most acutely in the public sector. While all the major unions of teachers broke away from the CGT as part of the resistance to Menem's reforms to form the rival CTA in 1992, public-sector workers split between the two options of obedience and resistance. ATE became one of the pillars of the CTA and has grown significantly since 1984 largely as a result of its resistance to neoliberal programs of government. UPCN participated in the Menemist reform of the state and is now one of the contemporary pillars of the (officialist) CGT. Its history is closely linked to that of Peronism: Perón had established it in 1948 as a rival to existing unions of public-sector workers, among them ATE, and he was its first member.[24]

Today, unions are not quite as central to Argentine politics and society as they were in their heyday of the 1940s–60s, but they are still highly significant social and political actors, especially with regard to the Kirchner governments (Etchemendy and Collier 2007) and especially in the public sector. Unionization there is considerably higher than in the private sector: the overall figure may have been around 64 percent in 2001 according to an estimate from Marshall and Perelman (2004: 26). In 2006, unionization was estimated to be something like 39.7 percent in the private, formal sector (Senén González, Trajtemberg, and Medwid 2009: 24). However, ILO estimates for 2009 suggest that around 50 percent of nonagricultural employment is informal (International Labour Office 2013),[25] so perhaps less than 20 percent of all private-sector workers are members of a union.

Despite the gradual increase in the size of the informal economy and the much-celebrated emergence at the turn of this century of new social and political actors such as the unemployed workers, formal-sector union membership still shapes political agency and citizenship for many Argentine citizens. This has meant that formal-sector unions (including ATE) could go one of two ways: Either they could withdraw into themselves and protect their privilege and the privilege of their members, or they could take the opportunity to create alliances with informal workers and other new social and political actors. Humberto Rodríguez (ATE) argued that the former was simply anachronistic, in a situation where structural unemployment is something like 20 percent and so few workers have registered employment. The CTA has explicitly attempted to construct a political project out of the latter strategy, which for many, like Claudio Lozano, was a project of class unity:

> If workers are unemployed, contracted, precarious, for a finite time, indefinite time, "in the white" [formally registered], illegal, self-employed, or whatever, all can affiliate to the Central; all have the right to have a collective organization that expresses them as a class. It's a search for unity, class unity, on the basis not of bringing together union structure but to organize all of the workers. . . . The exclusive organization of formal workers today breaks up class unity.

CONCLUSION

Although unions are now only one among several avenues for collective citizenship action in Argentina, they are arguably still the most powerful, whichever political strategy they choose to follow. Contemporary populist-corporatist government in Argentina is a mix of clientelistic practices, including the kind of neighborhood-based distribution of social goods examined by Auyero (2001) and union-based distribution of jobs and wages, especially in the public sector. That is not to say that public-sector unions in Argentina comply unquestioningly with the dictates of government, and indeed conflicts are common: in 2006–8, the public sector saw three times as much labor conflict as the private sector (Equipo Estudios Laborales 2010). The contemporary importance of public-sector unions is not confined to Argentina but fits in with another global trend: public-sector unionism is surprisingly vibrant today relative to the private-sector unionism in both the Americas and Europe.[26] These mobilizations demonstrate that the distribution of resources through jobs, salary increases, and other benefits in the public sector is often a conflictual process, especially in times of scarcity.

The two versions of unionism represented by ATE and UPCN differentiate themselves from each other through their assessment of (1) whether their constituency is their members or a more broad group of people (a class, or the Argentine people) and (2) how best to achieve benefit for their constituency: through direct conflict or through negotiation. Although we could say that UPCN tends to seek benefits for its members through negotiation, while ATE has a more political view of its mission and more combative tactics, actually neither union falls entirely on one side or the other of either of these axes. Different union members or leaders will argue for different positions depending on the political conjuncture and their view of what might be achievable or alternatively what they should fight for, whether achievable or not. These differences shape their political action as much as the contrasting ethical projects of militancy in which activists from each union engage, as they cultivate certain dispositions as individuals and collectives and as they seek to act on the world to transform it.

2 MILITANCIA

An Ethics and Politics of the Self

In October 2015, I was invited to the recreational facilities belonging to UPCN in San Vicente for a day-long team-building meeting organized for the union delegates of the Ministry of Economy (Economía) by the Escuela de Formación Sindical (School for Unionist Training, EFS). San Vicente is about a two-hour drive from the UPCN office in the center of Buenos Aires, depending on traffic. I traveled there in a van along with the director of the school, the facilitators who would run the day's events, and some leading figures in UPCN. Around one hundred UPCN Economía unionists made their way to the facilities either in their own cars or on the bus provided by the union.

We arrived at the car park and made our way across a green park past the sports grounds and barbecue areas to a large covered area in the center, with long tables, two enormous grills for meat, and plenty of space for people to mill around, drinking coffee, eating croissants, chatting, and greeting new arrivals. The meat for lunch was already being prepared for the grills. Once enough people had arrived, we moved on to warm-up games in a small hall. Delegates were each given a line of a song on a bit of paper and then had to find those with the lyrics from the same song and sing it at the end; we then played a raucous game where everyone put a shoe in the center of the hall that had to be retrieved faster than those in the opposing groups. The groups then moved outside and played more games together, each with a facilitator in charge. Then it was lunchtime, the most notable aspect of which for me (apart from the sheer quantity of meat available) was the moment when a young man got his guitar out and led the group in singing songs. The event organizers delayed the afternoon activities so that people could continue to enjoy this *alegría peronista* (Peronist joy). The songs ended with a rousing rendition of the *marcha peronista*, the Peronist anthem.

In the afternoon session, the delegates were organized into different groups and set training tasks to discuss where their delegation has come from and where it is going in the future. My group, of about twenty-five, went just outside the hall to sit at picnic tables and benches under the shade of the trees there. Before starting our main task, group members were asked to introduce themselves, and they were told to give their name and one word for why they had become a union delegate. The words they chose were, in the order in which they were mentioned:

> *vocación* (four people), vocation
> *ayudar*, to help
> *lealtad*, loyalty
> *convicción* (five people), conviction
> *colaborar* (two people), to collaborate
> *elección*, choice
> *me gusta* (two people), I like it
> *militancia* (three people), activism, militancy
> *compañerismo* (two people), comradeship
> *peronismo* (two people), Peronism
> *servicio*, service

It is true that the delegates who opened with the term *vocación* set the scene for the others, although clearly people felt that they could not all say exactly the same thing. Yet it is also true that the list coincides very well with interview material I have been gathering for this research. Many of the same tropes appeared in both discursive spaces, especially those of vocation, service (including collaboration and help), and conviction. They were also enacted in spoken and unspoken ways in political action, both quotidian and on special occasions.[1]

The group was then divided into three subgroups, which had to discuss the past, present, and future of the delegation in different time frames relating to speed of travel (those of astronauts, sailors, and walkers). At the end of the discussion, the synthesis the group decided on for their spokesman to present to the wider set of participants consisted of a fervently emotional speech about the importance of collective action and fellow feeling and ended with the phrase "despite all the adversities, [if we stand] together, there is no obstacle that we cannot overcome." At the plenary session itself, this sentiment received the loudest applause of all the group summaries.

This example brings together some important themes for this chapter, particularly in the delineation of the appropriate virtues of a delegate and their expression in a passionate register of emotional connection, collectivity, and commitment. In this chapter I explore how people make themselves into a particular kind of political actor within the broader political context described previously.

In the Argentine context this has a specific language, expressed in the notion of *militancia*, a concept that evokes a set of values and practices with significant local historical resonances. *Militancia* broadly refers to political activism collectively organized, and I use it here as a central organizing concept to describe activists' practices of self-cultivation in political action. It has a number of local meanings, which shifted over the course of my fieldwork. The concept of *militancia* refers both to the means and the ends of ethical self-cultivation; militancy is not a "technology of the self" per se but instead is both subject position and philosophy of action. It has ethical consequences, not least as a way to describe and cultivate the set of virtues that constitutes a good activist (Peronist or otherwise) and the values that are implicit in this kind of political action. It is also the pathway through which to cultivate oneself as a good ethical-political subject: hexis as a particular politicized disposition of the person, cultivated in the course of political action. Yet militancy also defines the scope of that political action; some forms of politics are not considered to be militancy. For example, one of the aspects of Mauricio Macri's electoral campaign that struck a number of my informants as important was that his activists called themselves "volunteers" (*voluntariados*), which was interpreted as an explicit move to distance themselves from the Peronist (and Trotskyite) "militants" behind the official candidate (see L. Álvarez 2015). This naming strategy was clearly understood as a means to claim the space of antipolitics (Ferguson 1990).

My unionist informants considered militancy to be an inherent way of being that had the consequence in their lives of a particular philosophy of action and way of life. I present these understandings mostly through the use of ethnographic interviews, which I analyze as representations of political lives and narratives of desired values. Through a discussion of different personal biographies of militancy I show how it is experienced and narrated as a kind of pathway through life. I find that much of this is articulated in terms of essential being or character, of inherent virtues, dispositions, and passions that are part of how activists understand their selfhood and consider the importance of this for how we understand ethical-political subjectivation.

MEANINGS OF *MILITANCIA*

The notion of *militancia* describes a process of self- and subject creation in a specifically political sense and evokes a set of values and practices with specific historical resonances. It is associated with collective subjecthood that is experienced as a politicized orientation to the other and to societal change, conceived in Peronist or more clearly leftist terms. At its most basic, the word describes the membership of a group and participation in the group activity. It usually has a political inflection and refers to active participation in groups such as trade unions or political parties.[2] However, I have also heard a delegate speak in passing of her militancy in an evangelical church; and others speak of *militancia social*, which describes participation in voluntary work in the neighborhood. The key is active participation as opposed to just membership. *La militancia* can also be a group noun, referring to the collective of political activists. But the word can also evoke individual pathways through a life understood as political, as people have a layered or sequential experience of activism in various organizations. For most of my informants, the trade union was the primary space of militancy in their lives.[3]

Militancy with respect to unionism must be understood in relation to Peronism, given the long-standing connection between Peronism and the organized labor movement in Argentina. However, that relation is not simple. There are plenty of self-identified Peronists in ATE, but ATE does not define itself as a Peronist union. UPCN does define itself in this way, and it does have a political wing that organizes party political activities for the PJ. Its leader, Andrés Rodríguez, is an important figure in the PJ in the city of Buenos Aires and was a key Scioli ally throughout the election campaign of 2015. However, activities associated with the PJ are very carefully separated in people's minds from those for the union, even when they are organized through the union structures.

UPCN is very keen to assert that although it is a Peronist union and the majority of the activists are Peronists, it is also pluralistic and there are plenty of spaces within the union for those who are not PJ supporters or even necessarily Peronists. For example, day-to-day discussions in the delegation office at the ministry where I spent time in 2012 exposed a wide range of political viewpoints often expressed very passionately. Most delegations had at least one self-identified Radical in a prominent leadership position,[4] and one even joked to me that he could be brought out to speak at a ceremony to display the union's pluralism. Yet he was not obliged to be a token dissenter and was happy also to refuse to take a protagonist role in a particular ritual event when he felt it would be inconsistent with his own political positioning. His party affiliation did not prevent him from being one of the most important leaders in his particular delegation.

UPCN delegates who identify more strongly with other political parties tend to take one of two paths: either they see their activism as confined to the union and do not participate in those activities that are explicitly political in favor of the PJ, or they go along with them and subordinate their political affiliation to their support for the union itself. One woman explained how this worked in her case:

We go along, even against our own thinking, because it's a commitment to the union, to the idea of the goal that the union is working toward. After that, personally speaking, each person has his ideas. I in particular don't go along with either Kirchner or his wife—I don't like them, that's the truth. But, well, sometimes I have had to be there, even contrary to what I think.

When I attended specifically political activities, such as the closing rally for Daniel Scioli's presidential campaign, it was the activists from the political wing of the union who accompanied me, and they carefully distinguished themselves from the union more generally: they were on political business, not union business, even if the two were linked. It was rare for an activity to be compulsory, so people who disagreed politically tended to absent themselves during those times when the union might seek to convene members for a rally or protest with a political objective.

In contrast, for many ATE activists, the trade union was a space for political militancy as a member of other more center-left political coalitions, such as the Frente Grande (Large Front) in the past, Proyecto Sur (Project South) in more recent elections, or the Trotskyite Partido Obrero (Workers Party). People participated in demonstrations and assemblies on behalf of their political party, distributing leaflets or pushing for a particular course of action; others mobilized for both their union and their political affiliation, and ATE emphasized its political pluralism at every opportunity in speeches at demonstrations, on posters, and in leaflets to distinguish itself from UPCN. My interviewees often told me quite complex stories of their pathways of militancy through leftist organizations, some of which I discuss later. Here I identify several trends. First, ATE activists often consisted of a group exclusively focused primarily on the union and secondarily on the CTA. These activists invested their sense of political self in those two linked projects. A second group combined a primary commitment to the ATE and CTA project with militancy at times of elections for other groups such as Proyecto Sur. A small third group felt their primary allegiance to be to the CTA rather than to ATE and participated in ATE as part of the overall CTA project. A fourth group considered their primary militancy to be in one of the small left-wing political parties and viewed the union as a space in which to enact that political project. For the remainder, their militancy in ATE grew from a less institutionalized political ideology, based on anger at injustices they saw in their workplace or other characteristics understood as personal and political.

Beyond the realm of electoral politics, the concept of *militancia* also evokes a kind of leftist political or social activism that has an important connection with Argentina's history of dictatorship. The concept is strongly associated with leftist activity in the 1970s and pro–human rights activism thereafter (Martuccelli and Svampa 1997). Early in my research, academics in Argentina at times corrected me when I used the word *militancia* in the way that my informants did to refer to activism in contemporary Peronism. For the academics, *militancia* evoked the 1960s and 1970s leftist movements, not today's PJ. And even when they did not reject the possibility of Peronist *militancia*, they pointed me to sources about the 1960s and 1970s movements when I asked if there had been any work on it as a concept or value. One particularly influential piece of work on the militancy of this time is Eduardo Anguita and Martín Caparrós's *La voluntad: Una historia de la militancia revolucionaria en la Argentina* (1997–2001). It is an astonishingly detailed history of the period 1966–78 based on the testimonies of twenty-five *montoneros* and political activists that is more than fifteen hundred pages long (over five hundred pages on the years 1976–78).[5]

Argentina has seen something of a positive reevaluation in recent years of this kind of militancy, also sometimes called *setentismo* (70s-ism). Contemporary celebration of those 1970s activists from the Juventud Peronista (Peronist Youth) and allied movements, whom Cristina Fernández de Kirchner called *jóvenes idealistas* (idealist youths), tends to evoke a figure of the activist who is easily locked into black or white categories, very much associated with the fight against dictatorship and for human rights or, from another perspective, with terrorists or guerrilla fighters. The resurgence of this particular figure of the activist was quite strongly associated with the personas of Néstor Kirchner and Cristina Fernández de Kirchner, both of whom played up their past as 1970s activists, when they were involved—albeit somewhat peripherally—in the radical Peronist youth movement in La Plata (Amato and Boyanovsky Bazán 2012).

The claim to a *setentista* heritage initially undoubtedly helped Néstor Kirchner confront accusations of too great a complicity with Carlos Menem during the neoliberal 1990s but was also extremely profound in terms of symbolic politics. As Karen Faulk (2012) has described, some of his first actions as president constituted a redrawing of the politics of memory with respect to the 1976–83 dictatorship. Specifically, he forced a change of command at the top of the military and police forces and instigated judicial reforms that removed Menem-era appointees from the Supreme Court. This led to the previous immunity laws being declared unconstitutional, and the perpetrators of the Dirty War could then be brought to trial. This shift in the state relationship to the military dictatorship was marked symbolically in March 2004 when Kirchner ordered the removal of portraits of Jorge Videla and Reynaldo Bignone (two of the principal junta leaders) from the walls of the Colegio Militar (Military College). On the same day in

March 2004, he announced an agreement to turn the most notorious detention center of the Dirty War—the ESMA (Escuela Superior de Mecánica de la Armada; Higher School of Navy Mechanics)—into a museum of memory and gave a speech allying himself with the generation of the disappeared. Cristina continued to associate herself with anti-dictatorship activism, through official pronouncements and commemorative events such as the anniversary of the coup and foundation of the Madres de la Plaza de Mayo. Jorge Videla was put on trial in 2010 and then 2012 for human rights violations and the kidnapping of children of the disappeared, and he died in prison in 2013. The human rights agenda became so closely associated with the Kirchner governments that one of the fears expressed by many of my friends about the Macri government is that he may roll back some of the advances in prosecuting human rights violators.

My sense was that between my two periods of fieldwork in 2009 and 2012, the notion of *militancia* moved from being a commonly understood description of collective mobilization to become a more prominent category in the foreground of public discourse. Two important developments had happened in the intervening years, which may help explain this. First, Néstor Kirchner died in October 2010, and in the hagiographies that followed considerable stress was placed on iconic moments such as the removal of the portraits from the wall of the Colegio Militar, in addition to the repayment of the IMF debt in 2005. Néstor Kirchner was thereby associated with a broadly leftist, pro–human rights, anti-imperialist style of militancy with symbolic roots in the 1970s. Second, Cristina moved her support base away from the traditional unions of the CGT and toward groups of young people, the most famous of which is La Cámpora. Led by their son, Máximo Kirchner, La Cámpora is a *kirchnerista* youth *agrupación* (political grouping) that took shape in 2008-9. By 2011 its leaders or very close allies had captured key political positions, as legislators at national and provincial levels, in key governmental positions (e.g., vice minister of economy), and in 2012 as CEO of the recently nationalized Aerolineas Argentinas. The rise was rapid, and in 2012, La Cámpora had a much larger presence on the political stage than even three years previously (Di Marco 2012; Natanson 2012). The discursive association of La Cámpora with the youth groups of the early 1970s—especially the Juventud Peronista—is extremely striking. One could postulate that the idiom of *militancia* became prominent along with the increase in the profile of organized youth within official Peronism. The government's adoption of this language might very well have been part of a broader project to discursively and practically ally itself with the figure of the activist and with activists themselves and even assert its association with a more bottom-up redefinition of politics and democracy.[6]

An illustrative example of the government's use of the figure of *militancia* might be found in the tweets of Alicia Kirchner, sister of Néstor and in 2013 minister for sustainable development. She regularly tweeted about the subject: for example, on 6 November 2013, "Militar es dar testimonio de compromiso, amor solidario y trabajo por el otro" (To be activist is to bear witness to commitment, love and solidarity, and work for the other). And on 30 October 2013, "Militar es jugarte por un proyecto, ¡porque siempre el héroe es colectivo! (HG Oesterheld)" (To be activist is to put yourself forward for a project, because the hero is always collective!). This quote was attached to a picture of the *eternauta*, a character from a popular series of science-fiction comics written by H. G. Oesterheld.[7] Oesterheld was thought to have joined the *montoneros* with his daughters and was disappeared in 1977. La Cámpora appropriated the figure of the *eternauta* by coining the figure of the *Nestornauta* around the time of his death and thereafter—iconically underlining the connection between *setentismo* and kirchnerism. Pictures widely available on the Internet show the famous figure of the *eternauta* with Néstor Kirchner's face superimposed into the visor of his helmet. But not everyone agreed with the focus on 1970s activism. Only a very few Argentines would today defend the dictatorship, but some political commentators expressed very low opinions of the *montoneros* and of anyone associated with them, including some members of the Kirchner governments.[8] From a different perspective, some Peronists feel that the emphasis placed on 1970s groups like the Juventud Peronista and even the *montoneros* crowds out a full acknowledgment of the earlier Peronist resistance of 1955–70.

Militancia has become a multivalent concept, in part as a result of generational changes in Argentine society. The current generation of politicians is utterly marked by the experience of dictatorship, as was the previous generation. At the time, those who are now politicians were students or had just entered work, so they are less implicated in the perpetration of state-sponsored violence, and some were its victims. They have something of a "cleaner" position politically than previous generations—who had either to comply with the dictatorship, go into exile, or risk death and torture. Meanwhile, the children of the *setentistas* are the new wave of political figures to enter important positions in government. They came of age with the demonstrations against impunity led by HIJOS (Hijos por la Identidad y la Justicia contra el Olvido y el Silencio; Sons and Daughters for Identity and Justice against Oblivion and Silence), and some of La Cámpora's leading figures are children of the disappeared. Older activists remember the experience of the Peronist resistance of 1955–70, but the politics of memory and human rights connected to the 1976–83 dictatorship marked the governing regimes of both Kirchners, and in public discourse *militancia* became very much associated with that complex of issues. Thus, the role of *militancia* in political subjectivation is intimately linked to the historical associations evoked by the concept itself: when people view themselves as activists, they do so in the light of these connotations and their reinterpretation according to contemporary politics.

PATHWAYS OF *MILITANCIA*

While the associations just described give the idea of *militancia* emotional strength in certain political contexts, its meaning is not confined to them. The valence of militancy in personal life and self-creation also has to do with more mundane meanings that refer to participation in group activity. Many of my informants had quite complicated trajectories of militancy through different organizations over the course of their political careers. These experiences shaped their political subjectivation, emphasizing elements like the collective, debate, and political commitment, such as the example that opened this chapter. *Militancia* is thus a way of living a political life (cf. Rasza 2015). Their stories combined militancy in (or sometimes just membership in) different trade unions, political parties, and other social organizations. Here, I describe some of the different trajectories that brought people to union activism in ATE or UPCN before discussing the role of choice, commitment, and personality in activism as a project of political self-creation.

Many ATE and UPCN delegates have moved through different spaces of activism as their lives developed. One common story was unsurprisingly that of trade union militancy, often a constant even when workers changed jobs. For some (if not most) informants, having a job in a particular profession naturally implied becoming a member of the relevant union. One ATE leader, Matías,[9] said to me, "I was always active [*siempre milité*] in ATE, because I always worked for the state—so therefore the union is just part of life." Javier, a newly elected UPCN delegate, described how he had initially worked for a metal works in his neighborhood so had belonged to the UOM (Unión Obrera Metalúrgica; Metalworkers Union). He had not been a delegate but had participated in demonstrations and other activities. After 2001 he was left without work but had the opportunity to work for the state, so he joined UPCN. Miguel Romero, a longtime ATE leader, had similarly come from a prior union activism, beginning in the 1960s in industrial unions—first the cobblers' union, then the mechanics' and the UOM. He was national president of the Catholic Workers' youth movement (Juventud Obrera Católica) from 1967 to 1970. So he came to ATE after a long trajectory of worker militancy.

Another common precursor to union activism in ATE and UPCN was student militancy in a university or secondary school, and informants with this background often saw union activism as a natural outgrowth of their previous activity. This tapped into a long-standing history of student and adolescent activism, especially noticeable in the late 1960s and early 1970s.[10] One example is Claudio Lozano, Congress deputy,[11] cofounder of CTA and ANUSATE, and influential in the human rights movement, having worked in the Servicio de Paz y Justicia (Service of Peace and Justice, an NGO) with the Nobel Laureate Adolfo Pérez Esquivel. He cut his teeth as an activist in the early 1970s in one of the most famous secondary schools of the country, the Colegio Nacional de Buenos Aires. He described how profoundly marked he was by his experience as a high school student at a time when "the country was a place where everything was debated"; "acá se debatió el mundo" (here, we debated the world), he said, and in his school, they debated as if they were university students. Youth activism has been consistently important after the dictatorship, too, for example, in the human rights movement related to the children of the disappeared, the carnivalesque dance protests (*murgas*) revived in the late 1990s, and the riots and popular assemblies of the early 2000s. More recently, the pro-Kirchner youth groups have come to the fore and their power acknowledged by the reduction of the voting age to sixteen.

A third pathway involved activism within a political party, and some told stories of passing through multiple spaces of militancy during their political careers. This was especially true of ATE delegates, since UPCN delegates were much more likely to speak of a longer-term militancy in Peronism. Unionists' commitment to political parties varied, with perhaps the most common involvement being participation in election campaigns. However, some narrated their participation in ATE as the culmination of or way station along a journey of political activism. One such was Gustavo Moreno, general secretary of the ATE *junta interna* in the Buenos Aires audit office. He had "militated" in the Frente Grande, a leftist coalition formed by dissident Peronists in the 1990s. Then he moved to the Communist Party but did not like the top-down methods of leadership. He said of this simply that "milité un tiempo y no milité más" (I was active for a time, and then I wasn't anymore). He went on to say that he was an admirer of Che Guevara and the Cuban revolution, and our conversation turned to other topics. He had been general secretary for over a decade by 2012 and was very active in both ATE and CTA activities. He viewed ATE-CTA as the culmination of a journey, the discovery of the most appropriate form of activism for him. At least it seemed that way at the time.

For Ernesto, one of his fellow *junta interna* members, ATE was a stop on the way through militancy. He had been active initially in the Partido Obrero but became disillusioned with the group and considered himself independent. In 2009, he was working (*militando*) in ATE "to see if it would be possible to pull a bit to the left" and talking also with members of the PTS (Partido de los Trabajadores Socialistas; Socialist Workers Party) because he felt there might be an opportunity there see "if a space to be active [*militar*] might open up." He was concentrating very much on his personal education, as a philosophy student and as a political militant. He did not see ATE as necessarily his final political home, and in fact he lost his job a year after I interviewed him and, despite ATE's support, was not reinstated.

A different trajectory was to come to ATE or UPCN as a direct outcome of a previous militancy. Carlos, a UPCN delegate, told me that he had been involved in activism for the PJ in a small town in the northern part of the province of Buenos Aires since 1993. He characterized this as territorial work, *bien de barrio* (really of the neighborhood), and told me that it consisted of multiple neighborhood activities, including assisting voters during elections by telling them where they should go to vote.[12] He then worked in the local municipality but was fired when a new candidate won, at which point he moved to provincial government, then a national institution, his position when we spoke. He followed his "political boss" (*jefe político*), who had been put in charge of the national institution; and once there he joined UPCN in search of like-minded people. He characterized his trajectory as a reverse of the expected, since people usually begin in UPCN in unionism and then go from unionism to "doing politics."

Carlos also remained more committed to his political activism in the barrio than to that within UPCN, where he was simply a delegate and not a leading member of his internal commission. His story hints at the relationship between political activity, unionism, and government jobs, as his employment was an outcome of his political activism. He explained his union activism as partly just something he did because he was a Peronist, so it was coherent with that, but also as a means of finding connections with people and a context to belong to after his move to the city of Buenos Aires. He embodied one of the links that exists between PJ political activism and UPCN activism, as he militated in both his local party *unidad básica* (basic unit of the PJ) and the party political wing of UPCN (see Levitsky 2003a for more on PJ formations). But he was not especially active on the union side of UPCN's activities in his institution and had no ambitions to be part of the upper levels of leadership there.

Marina, an ATE delegate who worked for ATE-Capital, recounted to me a quite similar move to unionism from another militancy, a move she also described as uncharacteristic, or at least unexpected. She was the daughter of a disappeared mother. On her return from exile, she got involved in HIJOS. The arrangements for the commemoration of the thirtieth anniversary of the coup were organized via meetings at the CTA, and as she tells it, that is what brought her to the CTA. She got her state job via CTA connections and, once employed, immediately began to work for ATE. She was quite open about the fact that she specifically entered her job to become a union delegate—"para militar" (to be an activist). In 2009, she articulated her militancy primarily as participation in a project linked to the CTA and in this was representative of a number of ATE delegates, especially younger ones (in their twenties) who worked at the central offices of ATE-Capital and ATE-Nacional. Subsequently, she left activism in ATE-Capital and the CTA as a result of differences of opinion and dedicated herself more to her role as a local ATE delegate at her place of work. Her story is told in more detail in the following chapter.

Another avenue for militancy was through what was sometimes understood as social work, a kind of social activism through neighborhood-based voluntary work. It was common for me to find people who participated in collective activity of this sort. Some people thought their social work had led them to unionism; others distinguished the two; and for others, participation in social activity had led to different pathways of activism. Neighborhood-based social work is a distinctive side of Argentine social life, and its prevalence points to the way that militancy is embedded in the lives of many Argentines. Especially in popular neighborhoods, many people are active members of an extremely wide range of organizations, from PJ basic units to communal kitchens, centers for old people, campaigning organizations, pro-Kirchner youth organizations, organizations of migrants, and soccer clubs. In fact, many of the latter also function as basic units, and it is probable that when ATE activists spoke of a prior militancy in social work, they were referring to activism in a Peronist-identified organization, although the connections between the organizations and the PJ are complex, as Levitsky (2003a) shows.

My informants could usually easily trace for me a trajectory of militancy throughout their lives and tell stories of the multiple individual pathways that had led them to ATE or UPCN. For some, their current union activism is the culmination of their journey, while a few saw the union as a way station. The balance of this depends of course on the staged nature of a research interview, however loosely structured it may be. When interviewed, informants tended to narrate their lives as culminating where they were at the time. Some subsequently left, and where they were possible, follow-up interviews later on helped greatly to explore the new configurations of activism.

What the stories have in common is that informants viewed militancy as something more than a status of membership in a given organization. For some it was a way of life; for most it was perhaps slightly less all-encompassing but still an activity that was at the same time an identity. Militancy is not something that one grows out of, a kind of youthful activism that recedes into the distance as middle age and family responsibilities take over. In fact, quite the opposite: it derives from (and at the same time creates) a particular sense of self and orientation toward politics. People choose their militancy according to different life circumstances, and militancy as a way of living politically changes shape and intensity at different points in the narratives of their lives.

COMMITMENT, PASSION, LOVE, STIGMA

If militancy is a pathway through life, it is also for many a commitment that is significantly demanding of resources, time, and energy. Of course, my informants were de facto those who had been able to make the commitment and had not dropped out, since I found them through the union structure itself and therefore spoke with the most committed activists. However, many told me stories of very long-term union trajectories, and the leading figures in both unions remained constant over the period of my research (2009–15). At least at the higher levels of leadership, the churn was not very great, and some of the better-established leaders were so because they had been committed unionists for more than twenty years.

In interviews, delegates from both trade unions spoke in terms of vocation, commitment, and a desire to help or change society, or they said they simply liked being in collective contexts, as in the training exercise described earlier. The repetition of the notion of vocation in particular gives an insight into interviewees' understanding of one of the most important narratives of motivation for belonging. The idea of vocation was not confined to interview material but also was constantly reiterated in the introductory training sessions run by UPCN for new delegates, both from teachers and participants. In both discursive spaces, it was often placed against the backdrop of family, friends, and colleagues not understanding and even stigmatizing their participation in trade union activity. I discuss first that stigmatization, then move to an exploration of the passion that activists often narrated to explain their continued commitment to the union and the way they connected it to embodied, essential characteristics of selfhood.

Of course, these are narrations, stories considered acceptable for "on-the-record consumption" by a foreign researcher. However, I draw on them as an ethnographic resource for two main reasons. First, despite the ways that interviews are performances, common understandings can and do emerge. One way this occurred was when once particular ideas had been repeatedly offered up by different interviewees in answer to general inquiries, I gradually moved into more specific questions, a methodological practice derived from "grounded theory" approaches (Glaser and Strauss 1967). A good example of this was the case of stigma—after several interviewees brought up and discussed at length the public disparagement of unionists and public-sector workers, and I heard it repeated in training sessions and saw it in action in conversation with nonunionist friends and acquaintances, I began asking delegates how they continued in the face of negative external valuation of their work. The rationale for highlighting interviews in these sections is also related in part to how I negotiated research access, which was complicated and therefore a determining factor of my methodology, especially at the beginning of my research. People were initially more ready to be interviewed and did not understand my desire to accompany them in participant observation. Furthermore, I found that my interlocutors were familiar with the mode of a long conversation between people, such that the interviews often mirrored other experiences of dialogue that are very much part of daily life. To keep this methodological approach rigorous, I use the grounded theory approach and emphasize only interview material that recurred and that resonated with what I observed ethnographically in less formal settings.

Second, it seems to me that in this instance it is neither entirely necessary nor realistic to seek to probe deeper behind some narrative that is imagined to be operating at only a surface level to try to ascertain what the "real" motivations of my informants are. The reason is partly that many Argentines, especially middle-class *porteños* (residents of Buenos Aires), have a well-embedded tradition of quasi-therapeutic discussions of motivations and of politics related to the strength of the psychoanalytical tradition there (Lazar 2013; Plotkin 2001). Long discussions over mate, cigarettes, or coffee are part of the daily life of unionists, and my most informative interviews had something of this quality to them. Furthermore, the "surface" performance of self is in any case something that matters for the practice of political action and belonging, as people develop common narratives to explain their participation in the group, and those narratives then shape that belonging. Conversely, they articulate narratives against which they want to present themselves as more moral beings. For example, the stigmatization of unionism is very much associated with corruption, so one important aspect of the commonly held narrative that I encountered was the claim that, in contrast to this view of unionists that was thought to be so prevalent in society, the speaker had the best of motivations. In this kind of material we can determine which are the acceptable or desired values without taking a position on whether they are a true description of an individual's motivation or action.

Then, some of the "below-surface" motivations can be detected in the interstitial spaces between "acceptable" utterances, for example, emerging as an ambivalent relationship to motivations that are not stated in interviews but that might instead surface during less formal interactions. An example here is the idea that someone has entered the union to gain individual benefit, especially through the corrupt distribution of resources. Interviewees accused others of entering the union for these kinds of reasons, or they emphasized what they considered to be more acceptable motivations, but no one admitted to this as his or her main reason for joining the union and becoming a leader. Yet people I knew did of course gain individual benefit as a union delegate, albeit not always in ways that they understood to be corrupt. Acknowledgment of these kinds of motivation might happen through denunciations of others but also in joking asides during training sessions and daily interactions or through sideways glances to me as someone articulated a more cynical position, one that we all knew to be "incorrect." Very occasionally, I witnessed people gaining individual benefit from their activism, or my informants admitted to me practices that they felt could be misconstrued by their rivals and asked me to hold these *en reserva*, off the record. So the narrative of passionate—and implicitly selfless—commitment should be taken with some skepticism; it is a hegemonic narrative that requires repeated assertion to maintain its dominance. However, it would be equally naïve merely to reproduce the cynical narrative of unionist corruption and self-interest that is hegemonic outside the union.

Ethical projects are made evident, then, not only in the kinds of moral decisions that people make in practice or in the exemplary narratives produced by moral theorists but also in the narratives and performances of ethical subjects themselves. James Faubion's (2011) work shows this with respect primarily to two particular individuals (or composite individuals), as he discusses his relationship with a Portuguese aristocrat and a millenarian from Waco, Texas. My research follows specific individuals in less depth than his but seeks instead to draw out common elements and preoccupations over a broader group of people, to get a sense of the generally understood characteristics of the activist as (ideal-)type against which individuals constructed their personal senses of political selfhood and thus engaged in practices of subjectivation.

Throughout this book I use the term "subjectivation" in its sense as the translation of *assujettissement*, a concept that appears in volume 2 of Foucault's *History of Sexuality* (1992). Foucault used *assujettissement* ambiguously, and some earlier texts translated it as "subjection" or "subjugation" rather than "subjectivation."[13] The tension lies between an understanding of what Foucault called the *mode d'assujettissement* as either subjugation to a moral code or set of power relations or a slightly more active process of the individual in relation to that authority. The most authoritative translation is that of the Penguin edition, where Robert Hurley translated *mode d'assujettissement* first as "mode of subjection . . . : the way in which the individual establishes his relation to the rule and recognizes himself as obliged to put it into practice" (ibid.: 27). However, he then changed the translation to "subjectivation," in a passage that describes the key distinction within morality as that between "codes of behaviour and forms of subjectivation" (29). Foucault argued that

> for an action to be "moral" it must not be reducible to an act or a series of acts conforming to a rule, a law, or a value. Of course all moral action involves a relationship with the reality in which it is carried out, and a relationship with the self. The latter is not simply "self-awareness" but self-formation as an "ethical subject," a process in which the individual delimits that part of himself that will form the object of his moral practice, defines his position relative to the precept he will follow, and decides on a certain mode of being that will serve as his moral goal. And this requires him to act upon himself, to monitor, test, improve and transform himself. There is no specific moral action that does not refer to a unified moral conduct; no moral conduct that does not call for the forming of oneself as an ethical subject; and no forming of the ethical subject without "modes of subjectivation" and an "ascetics" or "practices of the self" that support them. (28)

For Foucauldian anthropologists of ethics, one of the most important implications here is the nature and extent of freedom that subjects have in relation to moral codes. Laidlaw argues that although subjectivation refers to "how subjects are formed in power relations," the crucial insight is that it includes *but is not exhausted by* processes of subjection, or "mechanical processes of 'interpellation' into structures." Instead, subjectivation includes "active processes of reflective self-formation" (2014: 101).

The curious aspect of my material is that although I would argue very strongly that my interlocutors were forming themselves as identifiable ethical subjects within a clearly understood set of power relations, much of their talk about these processes of subjectivation focused on essential aspects of their being or character and downplayed the role of reflection. Somewhat paradoxically they often did so in a context that was eminently reflective—an interview with a researcher who had asked them to reflect on their activism. While the realm of the ethical might require some kind of reflection on action and evaluation according to criteria of the good (Robbins 2013), at the very least we can say that reflection often does not occur at the same time as a given action. It may not even occur at all, constituting instead what Jarret Zigon (2008) describes as morality, dispositions that orient moral life. This can be remarkably unreflective, even when in practice these kinds of dispositions demand very strong commitment, as in the case of labor movement activists. Furthermore, it is possible that the ethical nature of any given action or set of actions might become evident—in the sense of becoming appropriate for ethical reflection—only due to the intervention of the researcher. By explicitly asking people to reflect on their modes of subjectivation, I was inevitably prompting further subjectivation.

One of the suggestions in this book is that it is not possible to reduce the ethical solely to moments when people have made a conscious choice to do one thing rather than another. We need space in our analysis for actions that "just are," things that you do because that is who you are, or who you understand your self to be, or that are represented as such. Nonetheless, the fact that a set of actions or dispositions is understood to be essential does not preclude their cultivation—indeed, quite the opposite.

Stigma and Difficulties

I was and remain perplexed at how union delegates managed to continue in a position for years even though defeat or simply being ignored by government and employer was so common, for ATE unionists in particular. I have discussed elsewhere how unionists live a kind of "attritional time" of repetitive political activity and mobilization with seemingly little resolution in sight (Lazar 2014: 91). UPCN activists had perhaps more experience of resolution because they focused, for example, on individual problems or the negotiation of a specific salary increase. In contrast, many if not most ATE activists wanted to refound the state and society and were able to find the energy to demonstrate and mobilize repeatedly to that end. They did so in part by viewing themselves as a small part of a larger narrative, a longer tradition of struggle—la lucha, in its strongest and most political sense (Lazar 2014). Activists from both unions also maintained their commitment in the face of strong societal stigmatization of them, as both civil servants and unionists. This was crucial to how they understood themselves as political subjects.

Public-sector employment is often negatively viewed in wider society, as civil servants are thought to be corrupt, lazy, and rude. Given the opportunity, many "ordinary" Argentines fume at the figure of the ñoqui, the state employee who

turns up at his or her office only at the end of the month when families traditionally eat gnocchi and salaries are paid. Informants pointed me to a popular
sketch show that features the recurring character *la empleada pública* (the civil
servant). The comedian Antonio Gasalla plays the role of a state employee who
sits with her colleague at the same desk and plans ways to get money from the
public. There is always a queue of waiting petitioners who come to hand over
their forms and pay the charge. When they leave, the two employees divide up
the money, and Gasalla leans over the wastepaper bin to rip up the forms and
throw them away.[14] The stigmatization of the supposedly bureaucratic and in-
efficient state employee was particularly acute at the time of the state reforms in
the 1990s, when politicians and media figures alike often blamed the crisis of the
state on the state workers. This was largely functional in prefiguring and making
acceptable the worsening of labor conditions for many such people, and it was a
powerful discursive trope. In a DVD that brings together some of Germán Abdala's TV appearances in the 1990s, it is evident that even this leading ATE figure felt it necessary to participate in the discourse of (state) crisis, albeit arguing for the need to debureaucratize rather than reduce the number of employees.

Unionists are even more stigmatized than public officials, although this may
be particularly acute in metropolitan Buenos Aires, especially in middle- and
upper-class areas. I had innumerable informal conversations with taxi drivers
and friends not directly associated with my research where my description of my
project was met with exclamations of horror followed by stories of the wealth,
corruption, and criminality of unionists. One particularly lurid one was from a
hairdresser, who recounted to me how one of her clients had separated from her
unionist partner but knew that she could not get together with another man because he would be killed. She exclaimed, "You don't know the impunity these
guys have. . . . For me, it's a complete mafia . . . these guys are millionaires, and
yet they came from nothing." It was rare to find a taxi driver who would defend
the unions when I mentioned what I was studying. Lest it be thought that I am
falling into the all-too-common trap of equating taxi drivers and hairdressers
with the vox populi, I point out that almost all of my informants thought that
the general public had a very low opinion of unionists. It was of particular concern for ATE activists, because they were very keen to distinguish themselves
and the unionism of the CTA from UPCN/SUTECBA and the unionism of the
CGT. However, for most ordinary people, there was little to no distinction between unions and their different central organizations.

Some of my ATE interviewees told detailed stories about their rivals' corruption, suggesting that UPCN and SUTECBA leaders were extremely wealthy, with

fancy houses and SUVs, and pointing to Andrés Rodríguez's ownership of race-horses to indicate personal wealth, gathered in implicitly dubious ways. They contrasted this picture with their own situation or that of individual ATE and CTA leaders—especially Víctor de Gennaro—and argued that their lifestyle remained well within that of an ordinary state employee. Others dismissed other union leaders as outright thieves and criminals, and one of the most common associations was between the enrichment of unions and individual leaders and union control over the health insurance companies. This happened repeatedly, in on-the-record interviews as well as informal conversations, public speeches, and interventions in assemblies. Some suggested that such actions were a result of the corrupting nature of managing considerable "economic power" as a union leader. For Miguel Romero (from ATE), only some could remain "faithful," while others "han hecho buenos negocios" (have done good business) and become multimillionaires. In his opinion, this has meant that in general, the public and union affiliates do not trust union leaders. As a result, as one UPCN delegate also said, family and friends did not always understand these activists engaged in unionist activity.

Commitment must be maintained not only because of societal stigma and rumors of corruption but also because union work can often be very hard. Informants attributed health problems to the stress of unionist activity; for example, one UPCN general secretary said that listening to all the problems that affiliates and other workers brought to him was traumatic and in the end detrimental to his health: "Te entran las cosas y me gané un infarto" (These things enter you, and I earned a heart attack). His colleague had also had health problems and agreed that the stress was very difficult because the delegation office is "a place where people offload things, and you absorb them, whether you want to or not."[15] For an ATE delegate, the need to maintain affiliates "calm and united" was very demanding and meant that you risked heart, cholesterol, or gastric problems. But, she said in a matter-of-fact tone, "It's a job—a job that you take on [que uno asume]."

Interviewees also at times mentioned the damaging effects that union activism at a high level could have on family life. I have no means of verifying this: I knew delegates who were divorced, separated, or on their second or third marriage, but I also knew delegates with long-standing and apparently happy partnerships. Some told me that they had been forced to "forget their family a little bit" at moments of particularly acute conflict, but of course it is not possible to say whether the relationship breakdowns that I knew of had happened because of union activity or for other reasons. I can testify that delegates and leaders at the central offices often work very long hours and many weekends and that almost all of those I knew who were parents either had teenage children or a partner who was the primary carer.

More radically, it is not so long ago that unionism led to more than stress-related health problems but was a highly dangerous activity, as some of the older leaders in both unions know very well. They told stories of operating clandestinely during the late 1970s and early 1980s, of participation in anti-dictatorship demonstrations, and of recovering the union after 1983. Outright persecution of union delegates appears to have ended with the dictatorship in 1983, but police repression of demonstrations does continue and from time to time results in deaths of demonstrators. Furthermore, interunion rivalries can also occasionally become violent, as stories of *la patota* attest. *La patota* is a group of young men armed with sticks and very occasionally even guns who are sent by shady union leaders to influence workers, affiliates, or rival unions. Even from ATE this accusation was applied only to what they saw as extremist elements, and UPCN leaders strenuously denied that they used the tactic of *la patota*. But it was a common topic of discussion. During a strike in one local government office, the rumor went round that the CGT-affiliated union SUTECBA was about to send in *la patota*. Such a rumor in itself evokes all sorts of unsaid accusations of violence and corruption and reinforces the discursive universe that delegitimizes the activities of a particular union. It also taps into the popular view of unionist leaders as at best corrupt and at worst, violently criminal. The balance between truth and rumor is obviously very delicate when it comes to the use of *la patota*, but as one delegate said with respect to her own institution, which had a significant history of aggressive unionism in the past, "You have to put your body on the front line [*ponerle el cuerpo*]; it's like that, very physical, because sometimes there are fights, discussions" (on *poner el cuerpo*; see Sutton 2010).

Passion

The previous section may very well tell as much about *why* activists maintain their commitment to the union as it provides reasons *despite which* the activists maintain commitment. That is, the challenge and excitement may be part of the attraction. But when I asked interviewees why they continued in the face of stigma and hardship, they gave explanations that were often very visceral, relating to how they understood their own essence: in terms of personality, passion, conviction, and vocation. Later I offer additional social explanations for unionists' commitment and passion, but here I focus in particular on these common discourses of activism and political subjecthood. These notions were remarkably dominant, articulated most explicitly in interviews but also operating as a background understanding of daily political life and commitment. If people really do not subscribe to these hegemonic notions, then their response is usually to slip away from the highly committed political activism; they just stop coming to the union office. They can seek political activism elsewhere or can stop activism altogether. On a daily basis, for most of the people I know, their activism is experienced as work that they enjoy doing, with people that they like. At times they justify it according to the narratives of militancy—which are remarkably consistent internally—but it is also the case that they can live that life of activism in both a passionate register and a mundane one. And people really do reproduce these passionate narratives in daily life, for example, in ceremonial acts, street protests, or Facebook posts, as well as in the more or less staged space of the interview. Yet there is not quite the same kind of compulsion that one might find in other ethical communities, such as very pious religious ones, and people can slip in and out of commitment without very serious consequences.[16]

A number of interviewees spoke passionately about their militancy. Nestor Llano, who had come to ATE in the early 1970s, said that he "fell in love" with ATE during the process of recovery of union democracy after the dictatorship in 1984. That love and conviction, which he held in common with many *compañeros*, was the reason for him that ATE could achieve everything it has managed to achieve since then. And Pablo Micheli, former general secretary of ATE-Nacional, and from 2010 head of one of the two rival CTAs, spoke in similar terms in an interview in 2011. After telling me about a very serious illness that he had suffered the previous year, he said,

> I am in love with this cause, and that produces in me a conviction that makes me live. I am happy, do you understand? I am very happy. I mean, it's not that I'm happy fighting with the bosses, but I have dignity [*soy digno*]; I feel that I am doing something just and that I haven't enriched myself by being a union leader. . . . What keeps us going is the freedom of conscience. What can I say to you? There isn't perhaps a rational explanation; there's an explanation that has to do with *la mística*. When I say to you that I am in love with this cause, in love with the CTA, I definitely feel a profound love for what I do, for this thing we do; I feel very happy with my *compañeros*, each thing we do. . . . I enjoy it.

Micheli is a very experienced politician, used to giving interviews and speeches, so one should probably take some of his more passionate declarations with a pinch of salt. However, his reference to the *mística* of being a unionist is reflective of a wider point. It is not a coincidence that he uses a word that is very closely associated with the cultural activities of the MST (Movimiento dos Trabalhadores

Rurais Sem Terra; Landless Rural Workers' Movement) in Brazil, where there is a well-known philosophy of the *mística* as what Daniela Issa describes as "love for a cause, solidarity experienced in collectivity, and belief in change" (2007: 125), imparted through a collective pedagogy of artistic and theatrical events.

Further, he took the opportunity of this particular answer to emphasize the extent of his commitment to a particular moral project, in contrast to the figure of the unionist who uses his position to enrich himself, by going on to tell the story of the general secretary of UPCN in the province of Buenos Aires who was caught on the ferry to Montevideo with a bag containing forty-five thousand US dollars, destined, he said, for spending in the casino:

> He's leader of the state workers of the province of Buenos Aires, where their monthly salary is a miserable two thousand pesos [about three hundred US dollars at the time]. This guy took forty-five thousand dollars to play in a casino! Son of a whore, you imagine what they must have—no?—if he took that just for one week. I've never seen forty-five thousand dollars together in my life!

Such stories of the corruption of others were common in my interviews (see Martuccelli and Svampa 1997), often being stories of my informants' own personal morality. The point is not whether this is an accurate reflection of Micheli's own feelings, although I have no reason to assume that he was lying. Rather, the connections he made between coherence, morality, freedom of conscience, the political project of the CTA, and a personal passion for all those aspects, including that of simply being with his *compañeros*, are recurrent themes in unionists' self-presentation as moral political actors.

Others said more simply that they liked being a unionist. One ATE lawyer said that she "[se fue] enganchando con el derecho de trabajo" (became hooked on labor law), but that it was also her vocation in a more professional sense. For her, being "on the side of the workers" made her happy in her work. A UPCN member felt similarly. He found union work highly demanding but spoke of it as very exciting and something he liked a lot because "you know that whoever is on the other side has needs or has interests that you like to defend, and you're part of that."

As he pointed out, the work and the questions "involved people," and this was another dominant theme, as unionists quite often identified their connection with "the people" as one of the most meaningful or gratifying parts of their activism, one woman calling it "una inyección de vida" (an injection of life). Julio Fuentes, general secretary of ATE-Nacional since 2011 (at the time of interview in 2009 he was adjunct secretary), felt that his love for his work and the gratification it brought him came from a connection to a particular political project and, specifically, the people involved, the workers. He placed great emphasis on the personal satisfaction that he derived from fighting for those who are subject to injustice and oppression.

UPCN leaders also emphasized the day-to-day relationship with the worker and the satisfaction that comes from being able to change things for the better. Andrés Rodríguez, the national general secretary, was fairly matter-of-fact about it, pointing to the importance of having a permanent connection to "reality," by which he meant the workers, whose experience was for him mediated by his connection with the union delegates. He liked being a union leader, he said, because "generating a whole mechanism of transformation, so that people live better, or have greater justice or defend their own interests . . . perhaps that's our mission." His colleague, Fernando de Sa Sousa, at the time head of communications at UPCN Capital Section, argued that working for a labor collective was much more gratifying than working for any other employer, especially because of the daily relationship with the worker. They both emphasized the importance of a face-to-face relationship with the delegates, important especially for them as leaders of the central UPCN Capital Section, who could perhaps be accused of being rather distant from the everyday experience of civil servants.

Beyond the seemingly artificial proclamations of selflessness in the relatively formal setting of an interview, it was evident to me that in daily life the most successful union leaders did enjoy "being with people." In social and political events held by the unions, from training sessions to protests, they thrived on conversation, drawing people in to circles of debate, greeting all those they knew, and sharing jokes and laughter. Most of the work of the unionists I knew consisted of social interaction—such as meetings, discussions, shared moments of commensality, ceremonial acts, and phone calls. It was their job, and the way that politics is practiced in Argentina requires those in positions of power to enjoy and be good at gathering in friends, clients, and employees. Union leaders, especially those who were middle aged or older, held their positions largely because of their ability to develop and maintain social networks, and in many ways that was the nature of their work on a day-to-day basis. They had built up their prestige by pulling people into their circle so were often very appealing people, able to create a following because they thrived on the kind of expansive, incorporative, and avuncular sociability that was indispensable to their work.[17]

Articulating this as a passion for the political project of unionism was the other side of the coin of the day-to-day enjoyment of activism itself. That passion was in turn often described in visceral, almost biological terms: as part of their personality or something that they could not get away from, like a virus or addiction, as one UPCN delegate said. Miguel Romero explained his political activism as something innate, a kind of priesthood, or vocation for service. A SUTECBA delegate at the Teatro Colón took a similar position and said that even when he had tried to leave unionism, he could not do it. It was for him a question of nature, personality. When I asked him what it was about his nature that meant he could not leave union activism, he pointed to what he felt to be an inherent, natural reaction against oppression, another attribute that union- ists commonly described as part of their character. He explained his vocation in terms of class sentiment and rage against injustice that was part of his nature and to which there were only two responses: submission or fight. This left him, he said, no alternative but to confront the bosses.

Some activists explained their militancy as an outcome of their personal- ity without using the term "vocation," linking it more simply to just a desire to do things. José Piazza (ATE–Teatro Colón) said that he hadn't intended to be- come a unionist, but it happened because he was working and "I see that night is coming, and well, something has to be done. And how? Well, one's a man of ac- tion; you don't stay quiet." Raúl Benítez, UPCN delegate at PAMI, was similarly matter-of-fact: "My nature is not so much going into the union for the sake of the union but in going in and grappling with [*hacerme carne con*] the problems."

As dictionary definitions show, vocation is both a calling from outside (from God) and something innate.[18] It is an active choice, dependent on answering the call, but is also something that can be inculcated and strengthened through con- viction and repetition. At the same time, it is understood to be innate, part of your personality, and somehow unavoidable. "Con eso se nace," said Romero. "You're born with it." With this, he evoked an idiom of membership that is of- ten used with reference to Peronism, when people say "el peronismo no se hace, se nace" (Peronism is not made but born), which has familial implications, the topic of the following chapter.

CONSTRUCTING PARTICULAR *POLITICAL* SELVES

As the previous discussion indicates, interviewees' discussions of their subject- hood as founded on an essential, innate proclivity toward political activism of- ten ran parallel to passionate defense of the specific political project in which activists were involved. This was especially true for ATE activists, who in part constructed their sense of political self through the language of militancy. The idea of *militancia* both describes and creates particular kinds of political actors and thus is a performative concept (Butler 1990; Callon 2007; Austin 1962). De- scription thus becomes prescription, and in complex ways. ATE delegates were very self-consciously constructing a political project that they viewed as an alternative to the mainstream. For them, militancy required a critical stance toward government, the traditional trade unions, and most political parties, among other actors (see also Martuccelli and Svampa 1997).

So, for Marina Girondo in 2009, participation in UPCN in particular did not really qualify as militancy per se. I asked her why it might be difficult to talk of officialist militancy in UPCN, and she responded:

Well, it's just that I don't know if they see themselves as activists [*militantes*]. Some yes, but I don't know if in UPCN they see themselves as activists. Well, let's see, why ATE? . . . In ATE you are an activist, and you're an activist in the sense that you don't discuss only career progression and salary. . . . The majority see themselves as unionist activists and social activists. And the relation between CTA and ATE is very strong . . . [and] the Central [CTA] has a very big territorial construction and a very big social militancy. The CGT, no; it's completely unionist [*sindical*]. So if a delegate from UPCN doesn't work in his neighborhood or isn't in his district PJ, I don't know if he sees himself as activist, because it's very connected to that which is purely and specifically unionist [*gremial*].

Here, she is making a strong connection between the political project of ATE and the CTA and what she called *militancia social* (territorially based social work). She further explained the difference between ATE and UPCN by turning to the distinction between *gremialismo* and politics. The former refers to the kind of trade unionism that provides a service to union members: protecting them, negotiating with the employer on their behalf, providing social assistance, and so on. Many ATE activists accused UPCN of confining themselves only to this aspect of being a trade union, avoiding the broader political project of constructing a better society. This distinction is rather long-standing, being present also in Martuccelli and Svampa's (1997) study, as well as being a widespread critique of bureaucratic unions globally, dating back to the nineteenth century (Fairbrother 2008; Fantasia and Voss 2004; Haidar 2015; Moody 1997; Phelan 2009; Turner and Hurd 2001; Anderson 2005). The accusation is probably a little unfair. Although not as overtly combative and political as ATE, UPCN activists do tend to see their participation in the union as at the very least part of the broader political project represented by Peronism. For many of them, unionism itself is a political project of betterment for workers, as it was for some ATE activists.

However, ATE activists were frequently very emphatic about how their participation in ATE-CTA constituted a political project for a better society. Pablo Sanseverino made a similar distinction between *gremialismo* and politics, the latter being for him necessarily transformative—of both self and society: "We also say that we are not union leaders [*dirigentes gremiales*]; we are political leaders in a social movement; there's a difference. Our objective is not to be only union delegates but to change society. . . . Every ATE activist . . . rapidly becomes a political activist."

One young lawyer for ATE-Nacional also saw his participation in the union as participation in a transformative political project, which changed society (the system) but also became *una razon de ser* (a way of being) for him, something that gave sense to his life that he did from both necessity and conviction and for the satisfaction of being part of such a collective and of gradually achieving change for the better. Thus, he combined his understanding of praxis as transformative political action with a personal ethical project of the self. His colleague had a similarly Marxist analysis of capitalism and the necessity for workers' movements, and she explained her political commitment to ATE as arising out of a conviction that it was necessary because if there were no unions to struggle for rights, then the workers would be "dispossessed, exploited, discriminated against, and marginalized."

ATE activists tended to see themselves as participating in a specific kind of unionism, which Julio Fuentes described as revolutionary. This kind of revolutionary syndicalism was one where activists specifically aimed to change society rather than simply concern themselves with wage scales and the like. He sought to distinguish ATE's form of syndicalism from the kind that was seen so negatively in society by arguing that it was about committed people, young and old, who had decided that they could resolve their problems only by changing their reality collectively.

This conceptualization of revolutionary syndicalism was a significant part of many ATE activists' narratives of political action and has been a consistent aspect of ATE's identity project since at least the mid-1990s (Martuccelli and Svampa 1997). In this sense, ATE activists of this stripe were much more closely connected than UPCN delegates to a notion of militancy as leftist political activity and selfhood especially associated with the 1970s. For them, militancy ranged much more broadly than merely participation in a political party or even the union. It was a way of life, at work, in the neighborhood, and in the CTA. They thus placed themselves in a history of the labor movement that was also a history of democracy in Argentina. Marina Girondo articulated this by describing the recovery of the union after the dictatorship and the founding of the CTA, as a "backpack" that each ATE activist takes on, a "genetic inheritance." As told by her and other ATE-CTA activists, the labor movement history referred to is one of two competing models of unionism: the orthodox Peronist versus more radical trends, of anarcho-syndicalism, *clasismo*, and autonomous unionism represented by the CTA (Armelino 2005; Lazar 2013).

This division structured much of the ATE activists' self-representation, for example, in formal interviews and less formal interactions, in assemblies, meetings, conversations, training materials, and publications. The distinction was articulated by both ATE and UPCN informants through debates about organizational practice. It was manifest also in the presentations and cultivations of self, particularly by ATE activists, as they asserted their emplacement in a long history of political struggle. The word *militancia* itself suggests such an emplacement, although its appropriation by the official governmental apparatus of 2009–15 destabilized an easy equivalence between *setentismo* and antiestablishment politics. Under the post-2015 regime, the situation is settling back into cleaner rhetorical and discursive distinctions between government and activists.

CONCLUSION

Although some of the material presented here is based on interviews, which are undoubtedly public presentations of self, we should take seriously the explanations that people gave me for their desire to participate in the union and to keep participating given the stigma and misunderstanding they faced from wider society, and even sometimes from family and friends. Some common themes emerged in those narratives: For example, the advocacy of the CTA project was remarkably consistently expressed by the ATE activists; and the issue of the stigmatization of unionism was also very consistent across both unions and in wider society. Crucially also, the theme of a kind of innate proclivity to activism deriving from a specific set of personal characteristics was also consistent among interlocutors from both ATE and UPCN.

Paying attention to recurrent tropes even in the dialogical context of a set of interviews enables a comprehension of the ways that militancy and related concepts (such as vocation) are ethics of creation of the self and of political subjectivity that can be explored further through more conventional ethnographic methods. One aspect of this was the sense in which people's experience and creation of their own militancy is cross-cut by individuality and collectivity, because militancy is expressed as individual will or political conviction, or with a strong component of basic and interior identity, but it is in practice experienced as part of a collective and for some explicitly defined as such, as in the Oesterheld quote tweeted by Alicia Kirchner. Informants' expressed desire to change society or the state, their need to "do something," was crucially linked to a conviction that the impetus for change must come through collective organization.[19]

Militancia is, then, an ethics of activism that is about an affective attachment to either a particular politics as described in this chapter or to an organization or group of people, an issue I explore in greater detail later. It is about the interior lives of activists but is enacted collectively through the union. It is not presented as purely an individual choice, yet considerable rhetorical emphasis is placed on individual will, articulated along a spectrum that ranges from passionate commitment to a specific political project to a liking for union activity that cannot be explained. This is complemented by an understanding of essence, a biological narrative of inherent characteristics, or militancy as virus or addiction. For all these reasons, unionists say they can continue in the face of stigma, health problems, or other job difficulties.

This dynamic relation between essence and will is another important aspect of how activists create themselves, as out of this relation individual commitment is thought to grow. It is important that people chose not to narrate their commitment to me as a pragmatic decision reached after rational contemplation of their best interests. Instead, they spoke of discovering unionism, of finding a passion for it, of unionist activity as the culmination of a political pathway that they were drawn to out of a liking for politics, a rage against injustice, and an innate orientation toward the other.

Of course, keeping them on that pathway is no easy task, since trade unionist activity is attritional and often thankless. It exposes the individual to disparagement and suspicion, even from family and friends; it can be very hard work and draining, emotionally and physically. Partly for these reasons, some activists do pull back from committed activism at different points in their lives, and the very passionate articulation of total commitment is likely to be one of the mechanisms by which people keep themselves in place. On the other hand, activism can also be enjoyable. I later take a perhaps more classically (social) anthropological orientation and discuss some of the practices of activism that help maintain allegiance: the buzz and adrenaline of participating in a demonstration, the togetherness of the union delegation, the inculcation of specific ideology. The next chapter examines the question of individual essence further by exploring the role of kinship relations in helping the kind of political orientation or natural personality characteristics described by informants here to emerge and consolidate.

I have presented my informants' explanations of their activism as both inherent to them and a choice they have taken. Their explanations for that choice show the power of political philosophies in self-representations and self-constructions: UPCN delegates view their militancy as a relationship between unionism and Peronism, while ATE activists articulate a different story of an alternative unionism and political project for society. Allegiance to both these philosophies is a complex dynamic of belonging, reflection, experience, and embodiment. The varied projects of ethical-political subjectivation summed up in the term "militancy" challenge dominant Foucauldian analyses of ethical self-cultivation as a matter for the individual engaged in reflection on action and self-conscious cultivation of particular ways of being (albeit "with the help of others"; Foucault 1988: 4). Yet they are not the outcome of unthinking habitus in Bourdieu's (1977) sense. Instead, they lie somewhere in between these different understandings of social action or even entirely outside that dichotomy. The fact that unionists are able to navigate between the two shows that the different understandings are not incompatible in daily life. People do cultivate particular virtues and dispositions, and if asked, they can describe the virtues of an activist, but those virtues are often understood as essential characteristics, albeit ones that might be best recognized through narration. One of the most important that emerged both in narrative form during interviews and in ethnographically observable action is the desire to act collectively and not individually. That desire has much to do with a long history of collective organization in Argentina. Thus, for activists from both unions, essence—both biological and historical—becomes the foundation for self-cultivation to produce a particular disposition toward the world, which in turn is the grounds from which militancy can become transformative action on the world.

3 FAMILY AND INTERGENERATIONAL

TRANSMISSION OF *MILITANCIA*

One of the common phrases I heard from informants and colleagues in Argentina about Peronism was that a Peronist "se nace no se hace" (is born and not made). Of course, the Peronists I knew had come to Peronism via multiple trajectories, and many of them had indeed "made" themselves and continued to do so. However, the phrase points to the importance of understandings and practices of Peronist militancy in particular, and militancy more generally, that stress its grounding in family. The familial in this sense is an extension of the biological metaphors discussed in the previous chapter, but biological essence should not be understood as absolute and deterministic. Here I continue the theme of the analytical intertwining of the moral self-making undertaken by the individual with a more collective subjectivation that operates within and through a series of networks and relationships. The relationships that I explore are intergenerational ones: between children and their parents, aunts and uncles, or grandparents, and between different generations of activists. In fact, the latter emerged as a concern during my discussions with unionists as they interpreted my questions on intergenerational transmission of militancy rather more broadly than I had initially intended them to be. This chapter includes stories gleaned from interviews and ordinary conversations. Where I use quotes from interviews, I do so because they represent ideas or tropes that were especially common across both more formal research settings and the quotidian interactions I had with unionists over the course of my fieldwork.

Initially, the question of family had emerged as I asked people to tell me their personal trajectories toward becoming a unionist. Both ATE and UPCN delegates would often begin their stories by mentioning that their father or mother had been a unionist—or a Peronist, Maoist, Trotskyist, communist, socialist, anarchist, or some combination of those. In doing so, they often meant simply to indicate that this was why they joined the union when they started in their job;

for them, the two just went hand in hand, and this is in large part a reflection of the highly organized nature of Argentine society. Once in the union they had decided to become active, they said. Others had found their job through a parental connection with the union. Some felt that activism was an inherited quality, consisting of a concern for the other or an orientation toward charitable activity, which they sometimes attributed to parental example and often attempted to inculcate in their own children. For others, their militancy was a rebellion against a family that was either uninterested in politics or very anti-Peronist. They had discovered Peronism in school or university, via friends and books. So there was a wide range of stories, but family featured regularly, unsurprisingly, as state employment and politics are often quite familial in nature.

I begin by exploring how Peronism in particular is thought to be rooted in family. My informants often explained their Peronism through metaphors of blood, inheritance, and family experience, especially storytelling; but their stories also spoke to larger political histories of proscription, resistance, and resurgence. I then continue the discussion of the emotional and embodied nature of Peronism by telling the family story of three activists, two from UPCN and one from ATE. Kinship and politics intertwine in these stories to shape the intergenerational transmission of activism within families. I use quotes from interviews and group discussions to give a sense of the activists' voices as they narrated to me their personal and familial commitment. Finally, I examine these processes with respect to the relations between different generations of activists within the unions. Again, it brings out the importance of political history in shaping collective self-making and intergenerational transmission of political agency. I have introduced the concept of the ethical as the "just is" that derives from essential character but is cultivatable through activism. Here I examine how that essential character can be derived from kinship relations, which are experienced as both biological and social, product both of inheritance and experience in childhood and early infancy. But essential does not mean immutable or even predictable: none of these processes will automatically create a particular kind of activist, and the kinship stories I present here show how this subjectivation can have multiple outcomes.

PERONISMO: UN ESTILO DE VIDA

Many considered Peronism to be particularly familial, a characteristic that was narrated both as internal to the family and in the context of historical memory. They described Peronism using metaphors of biology and early infancy but also through the narration of Peronist feeling and family stories located in political history. The two intermingled, but I begin with the former and then move to discuss the latter. My analysis echoes some of the insights presented briefly in Martuccelli and Svampa, whose study from the mid-1990s also found allusions to the familial nature of Peronist militancy (1997: 154). Those authors did not discuss the quotes about family at length, preferring instead to give them as evidence for the ways that Peronism was described by its activists as either a natural destiny or alternatively a calling from "History," but in both cases as something that was inevitable (1997: 153–56).

For my interlocutors, family Peronism was both essential and cultivated through experience. I was told often that one is "peronista de corazon" (Peronist of the heart), "uno nace peronista" (you are born Peronist), "lo llevas en la sangre" (you carry it in your blood), both in interviews and as passing comments and informal conversations. Once in a workshop in the UPCN school for new delegates, I said that I had been impressed by how Peronism was "sanguinario," meaning "bloodthirsty." I was quickly corrected, as I should have said "sanguineo" (of the blood). My mistake caused much amusement, along with general agreement that once I had made the correct word choice, I had understood how people felt about Peronism.

In addition to metaphors of blood, other common metaphors referred to early infancy. People said that one was a Peronist "de cuna" (from the cradle) or, very often, "uno lo mama," meaning that you absorb it from a very young age. *Mamar* is the verb that means "to feed at the breast," and baby bottles are called *mamaderas*. Ariel Negrete, a thirty-five-year-old general secretary of the ANSES UPCN delegation, combined these various tropes in an interview:

> One is a Peronist from the cradle. My father was general secretary of the Leatherworkers' Union, of the Argentine Federation of Leatherworkers, and, well, you carry that. I always say, I played the drums in a union before I said "mamá"! You carry it in your blood. . . . I think you absorb it from the home [*Creo que lo mama desde la casa*].

Miguel Romero, a leader with ATE with a long trajectory of activism and now in his sixties, said something similar:

> This vocation for unionism, you see, it comes from Peronist militancy. My family was Peronist, and so . . . you are born in an environment where you hear all about Peronism, its good aspects—and unionism is very linked to Peronism. That's to say, it was very favored by the state. So from childhood one absorbs [*uno mama*] its symbols—the *marcha peronista* [a song], what your parents tell you. . . . And these are the signals that you feel from your home.

So Peronism can be transmitted, or taken on, through experiences in the home when the person is very young, and even through breast milk.

Aside from this kind of physical incorporation, the cradle and breast-feeding were often linked to storytelling. So one of the most important mechanisms of transmission at this stage appeared to be the stories that parents and grandparents told babies and very young children. In a discussion with a group run by UPCN in the southern Buenos Aires neighborhood of Parque Patricios, two older activists demonstrated precisely this:

> A: It's as though Peronism is everything for us because we've absorbed it [*lo hemos mamado*] as children and because it gave us a whole load of things, and because really he was the only person who thought about humble people. . . . I lived the Perón of Peronism. . . . I come from a Peronist cradle, my first toy— although you won't believe this—is when Perón and Evita passed through a city where I lived, one hundred kilometers away; they passed through in the presidential train and in the station, Perón and Evita gave me my first doll, and my brother's first football as well. [But] it wasn't just because of what he gave you, but because of what he did for all of us and for the country.
>
> B: I'm also from a Peronist cradle; my father also was a Peronist leader; I lived it from when I was born. But I have a memory, and I'm going to tell it to you: on Caseros Street . . . one day I went with my grandmother to run an errand, and the lady from the meat shop [*fiambreria*] said, "Stay here because Evita is going to come to bring a sewing machine"—it makes me want to cry when I think about it—"she's going to bring a sewing machine, that some people in a tenement building asked her for." I was a little girl, but I've never in my life forgotten it. Evita's car arrived, Evita got out—she got out—they got the sewing machine, she went into the tenement building, then she left, greeted everyone, got into the car, and went, with her guards. It's one of the small things that stays with me here [indicating her heart].
>
> A: That's why you absorbed it [*lo mamó*] as a girl.
>
> B: My mother's first freezer was from that period.

As is evident in this exchange, Evita featured heavily in these stories, as did a sense of the golden era of 1946–55, when Perón delivered for the *gente humilde* (humble people), and the period then and afterward, when the unions enjoyed their heyday. Julio Fuentes—at the time of the interview adjunct leader of ATE-Nacional, later general secretary—linked this personal experience to a commitment to syndicalism and the transmission of that commitment to subsequent generations:

I think that this is through transmission from our parents, our grandparents. They taught us this. If you are a worker, you have to have a union; you can't be anywhere else. A worker cannot not be in his union. I think that this is a transmission that they have done from generation to generation, and also because the best times that our class remembers have to do with the unions.

Personal things. I went on holiday as a child to the union hotels. My father was an oil worker, so during the holidays we went to the hotels that belonged to the oil workers' union. That's to say, all our good memories have to do with this organization that they made. I was brought up in a house that belonged to a workers' cooperative, also oil workers. The union helped to form cooperatives, and this permitted the workers to make a living. So this becomes part of you [*te va metiendo*], and you transmit it to your own children. That's to say, you start a job and the first thing you do is affiliate to the union, because you have to affiliate to the union, you have to be in the union.

Another activist from the UPCN group in Parque Patricios said that he was also from a Peronist cradle, as his father was a leader of the cobblers' union:

Yes, this you absorb as a child [*lo va mamando de chico*], but also afterward you realize that in the reality of this country, all of the governments that have been— in reality no government did as much as Peronism for people of the lower and working classes. You see how from 1945 . . . the social change that there was in the country. At that point there were no paid vacations, no Christmas bonus— and so from there began the dignifying of people who worked, and this is very strong for us. And until today, all of the governments we've had, including some of the democratic ones prior to this government, have dedicated themselves to destroying all of the achievements of Peronism. So, we're Peronists because of a question of conscience, conviction, and because in reality we are all workers; we come from [a] worker's family that thanks to Peronism—for example, I could study. Peronism opened the doors for the working class to go to university and do a mountain of things that before were only for a few privileged people.

Scholars commonly recognize now that the Perón presidency was the first to incorporate the workers as political subject through very material means, extending rights and benefits hitherto unknown (D. James 1988b; Torre 2002; Elena 2011). The previous quotes show the ramifications in a passionate commitment to the political grouping nearly seventy years later. As Daniel Presas said, after the group discussion at Parque Patricios, "People say that it's an inexplicable passion, something that you feel, but the explanation has to do with what [the activists] relate, of reality, that's to say, these were realities." Thus, they combined the spiritual and affective stories of allegiance with a discourse about the material and political benefits Peronism brought to the country and to their class. Such tropes emerged frequently in different utterances outside the more formal space of the interview, such as in posters, placards at demonstrations, images circulating on Facebook, and status updates.

The other storytelling figure that emerged was an uncle or aunt who coached his or her niece or nephew in politics, perhaps Peronist or more generally in terms of class consciousness. In a group discussion with delegates at the UPCN school for unionists, on the theme of family, one activist said that the only person with whom he could talk politics was a Marxist-communist uncle who had lived for a while in Europe.[1] He related that he is now playing this politicizing role for his three-year-old nephew, whom he had taught to sing the *marcha peronista* and who had—he said—requested to hear that song on YouTube precisely on the anniversary of Peron's first presidency, even without knowing the relevance of the date. He felt that he had a special connection with this nephew, mediated through politics and football. The other night his nephew asked to be allowed to sleep in the Independiente soccer team T-shirt that he had received as a present from his uncle: "You see, we have this connection that I can't explain," and after some jokes from the others, he responded, "Well, there's no choice when it comes to football and politics." By this, he was making an equivalence between allegiances to political groupings and to football teams as a means of emphasizing the strength of the political belonging. Everyone knows how strong loyalties are to a football team (Archetti 1999). This same trope can be found in some of the material in Martuccelli and Svampa's study (1997: 158, 161).

People deploy these everyday ideas to explain their political trajectories and to emphasize the strongly spiritual or affective character of their activist pathway. This is a kind of belonging (to Peronism) that just is—it does not become or get chosen; it exists as part of one's essence. Yet, as in the notion of vocation, the combination of essential character or disposition toward a particular calling and the calling itself is crucial. The calling is quasi-divine, as can be seen in the ways that Juan and Evita Perón are often talked about as almost divine figures, for example. It is transmitted within the family through storytelling and physical incorporation. Thus, an aspect of essential being is called forth and cultivated, a process of hexis, to use Aristotelian language. Hexis is summarized by the philosopher Joseph Malikail as "a compound product of nature, habit and reason, achieved by an appropriate disposing of personal inclinations and qualities" (2003: 14). For Aristotle, hexis was a state or disposition of the person that might be cultivated through habituation. Habit or habituation should be understood as a conscious process of cultivation, not an automatic adherence to specific social mores or "the inculcation of bodily reflexes" (Laidlaw 2014: 75). Aristotle did not distinguish between hexis as cultivated and a kind of essential moral disposition, since he thought that those virtues that would be cultivated were already present and that reflection was intrinsic to action. But for my informants, although they had chosen Peronism—in the sense that things could have gone in a different direction and they could have turned away from the movement—the choice itself was often experienced as somehow inevitable; at least it was narrated as such. As mentioned previously, their calling was not necessarily amenable to reflection until the intervention of the researcher.

This feeling of essential being, the "just is" of moral and ethical choices that are not really choices, is encapsulated within another prominent symbolic trope of Peronism, the *marcha peronista*. Composed during Peron's first presidency, the origins of this song are uncertain, but by 1956 it was so popular that it was banned by decree after Perón was deposed by the military. Its title is "Los muchachos de Perón," Perón's boys. It is an encomium to Perón himself: the chorus repeats Perón's name, calling him the first worker, and the verses speak of his achievements and personal greatness.[2] As in the previous story and in the quote from Miguel Romero, it is one of the symbols of allegiance to Peronism that recurred frequently in interviews and discussions (see Martuccelli and Svampa 1997: 177). It was also a living song: People frequently broke into the *marcha* at ritual events, meetings of the UPCN school for unionists, and demonstrations, singing it with great passion and gusto. In informal and formal situations they repeatedly used it to symbolize Peronism and underline their loyalty to Perón.

The following lengthy quote combines a number of the themes described here, with a sense of both the quotidian nature of Peronist practice and the affective charge that the singing of the *marcha peronista* evokes. I asked Sabrina Rodríguez, daughter of Andrés Rodríguez, to explain Peronism to me:

It's very confusing for everyone to understand Peronism—describing it and understanding it have taken years. And I think that the best way to describe it is that Peronism is a way of life [*estilo de vida*]—and this is a Peronist of the heart talking to you, no?—so, Peronism is a way of life. . . . I always say that Peronism is a feeling [*sentimiento*]; it's a way of life. Why do I say that? My dad is Peronist, my grandfather was Peronist, do you understand? You'll meet Peronists, and they will say to you, "My child is Peronist," "my father was Peronist," "in my house we sang the *marcha* on Sundays," "because my grandfather was Peronist," "because in the [1940s] Evita gave my grandmother a sewing machine." That's to say, there's a concept that has to do with the family, with the social, with what Evita was as well, within Peronism. Not only Juan Perón, the figure of Evita was very strong, perhaps in social work, and that's stayed in the retinas and in the minds of many Peronists, who recount emotionally how their grandparents had their first hospital thanks to Evita, or they had the first sewing machine—which is a true anecdote. Thanks to Evita and to this, the mother could help her family. So, as I say, one is *born Peronist*; you don't have a choice, because it's a question of family, of the environment where you grow up , and it's a really strong feeling, so much so that it's hard to think in any other way; it's very difficult. You sing the *marcha* for the millionth time, and you get goose bumps; you've sung it six million times, and you get emotional with each word. So, I insist, I will add to the confusion about Peronism, because I live it as a feeling and a question of family, especially of family. . . . But I don't know if I can help you describe Peronism. I'll say it again, because I live it very emotionally and sentimentally, I'm not a political scientist. It's a question of family and feeling. Absolutely. (emphasis in original)

The power of some of these stories and practices, such as the singing of the *marcha peronista*, was undoubtedly made more acute by the experience of proscription immediately after the first coup against Perón in September 1955. In March 1956 President Pedro Eugenio Aramburu's government prohibited the mention of Perón's name, as well as various other elements of "afirmación ideológica o de propaganda peronista" (ideological affirmation or Peronist propaganda), including the *marcha* (Decreto-ley 4161, 5 March 1956;[3] see also Seveso 2010). People told me stories about how their parents had to hide any Peronist materials they possessed—books, postcards, and so on—under floorboards and in secret holes in the wall, in case the police raided their houses. In the face of such proscription, resistance was enacted through quotidian memory. So, as people hid their Peronist "propaganda," they also refused to keep quiet and continued their earlier practices. For example, the Ciudad Evita neighborhood in La Matanza was renamed officially in 1955 (and again in 1976) but remained Ciudad Evita in everyday talk. Others engaged in direct resistance, such as sabotage activities and clandestine meetings, as Lilia Saralegui described to me (also see D. James 1988b, 2000; Martuccelli and Svampa 1997).

In later years, Peronism could again be articulated publicly, and the experience of bringing Perón back from Madrid in 1973 was a formative one for some of my informants' parents and for a few of the older delegates as well. The subsequent 1976–83 Dirty War featured more obliquely in informants' stories of militancy as offered to me: a story of a young aunt who was taken away for a few weeks and returned only because of remote family connections with the military; a personal experience of imprisonment because of mistaken identity as the military were searching for another woman of the same name; a distant cousin involved in the Uruguayan guerrilla movement; or more abstract discussions of the loss of a generation of activists. Generally, these discussions did not happen within recorded interviews; rather, they emerged as fragments in day-to-day interactions.

Disentangling the influence of repression in the continual production and reproduction of a commitment to Peronism is beyond the scope of this book (but see D. James 1988b). But perhaps in response to the movement's relationship to recent Argentine history, and also as a result of day-to-day practices described later, that commitment is felt very passionately by my Peronist informants. As in the quote from Sabrina Rodríguez, they often described Peronism as both a *sentimiento* and an *estilo de vida*. The English translations do not convey the depth of emotion involved in these phrases. For example, the translation of *estilo de vida* as "lifestyle" has some of the sense of a choice of lifestyle that can be put on and taken off at will, such as the lifestyle found in magazines, with the consequent ring of inauthenticity. But Sabrina and my other interlocutors were not using it in this sense. Rather, they meant something more like a way of life, as I have translated it previously. Peronism is for some of its most committed activists an ethical project, but one not exactly actively chosen as a result of rational contemplation leading to a decision to engage. Rather, it is deeply affective—*un sentimiento* in the fullest sense—and embedded both in the arc of Argentine history and in daily life in the family and at work. Martuccelli and Svampa's 1990s Peronist informants also called Peronism *un sentimiento* and stressed what the authors describe as Peronism's "esoteric" nature. For Martuccelli and Svampa, this is a "construction" that is peculiar to Peronism and that enables Peronists to claim that what is in reality an utterly political link between activist and party is instead prepolitical. It is just as constructed as are alternative discourses that emphasize the rational adherence of activist to party or movement (1997: 161–63). This does not mean that by virtue of being "constructed" such feelings are not deeply felt. Indeed, the activists I knew would not have been very happy with such a description. They have chosen Peronist militancy because not all of the children of Peronists are Peronists themselves, by any means; but they also live it as something essential, inherent to their person, as an individual and in the context of family life.

THREE STORIES

For some, that family context was especially consequential. Here, I tell three stories of growing up in a political or activist family. They are not the most representative of stories—in part I chose them for the particular storytelling ability of a given person or the connection that I developed with the person while researching other aspects of militancy. They do, however, give a more fleshed-out sense of the variety of family trajectories of activism and the varied intergenerational responses to it, whether fiercely Peronist or not. They also draw out some of the effects of the 1970s on the longer-term arc of Peronist militancy, as well as speak to broader questions of gender, domesticity, family, and personal development in times characterized by political upheaval.

Mariano

Mariano was general secretary of an important ministry delegation and an especially charismatic and vibrant UPCN leader. Like some of the other delegates in UPCN, he comes from a family connected to noted Peronist politicians. His father, Miguel Unamuno, was heavily involved in the post-1955 Peronist resistance, a leader of the Union of Bank Workers, the PJ, and later a member of the Council of Buenos Aires and Isabel Perón's last minister of labor for just under two months in 1976 before the 24 March coup. After the dictatorship, he served as national deputy for the PJ; ambassador to Ecuador nominated by his friend Carlos Menem; and then director of the National Archives, a position he kept under the presidencies of Eduardo Duhalde and Néstor Kirchner. He served at least three terms in prison in 1955, 1959, and 1976 and had more close shaves, especially during the early period of the resistance. He retired in 2006 and died in 2009. Mariano's mother, Lilia Saralegui, whom I knew as Sara, accompanied her husband through his militancy while bringing up their six children. Once they were old enough, she began a more active trajectory of militancy in her own right, based very much in neighborhood organizing. She broke from the official PJ in the early 1990s to join Chacho Alvarez in the Frente Grande and FREPASO;[4] and she became one of the legislators for the city of Buenos Aires in the first legislature after it became autonomous in 1995. She helped organize the first national *encuentro de mujeres* (women's encounter) and continues her militancy today in feminism and cultural politics. She and Miguel divorced when her youngest, Mariano, was twenty years old, and Miguel remarried and had three more children. I interviewed both Mariano and his mother about their experiences and spent time with Mariano during several research trips.

Mariano's paternal grandfather, Juan Unamuno, was a socialist who worked for the *Diario crítica*. Mariano explained to me that this was a fairly sensationalist newspaper, something like the UK newspapers *News of the World* and the *Sun*, but it employed intellectuals as reporters, including famous literary writers such as Jorge Luis Borges and Roberto Arlt to report on crime stories or horse racing. Mariano said that Juan Unamuno became disillusioned with the socialists for "having lost the reason for which they had become socialists. That is to say, they ended up working for power and not for the popular sectors." Along with many other socialists, as well as radicals, conservatives, and so on, he moved into Peronism in the 1930s and 1940s and participated in the first Perón government. Juan and his son Miguel were both imprisoned in 1955, and when Miguel was released, he joined the Peronist resistance. With Mariano's uncle (his mother's brother), they were known as *los vasquitos* because of their Basque ancestry. According to Mariano, his uncle "opted for a more direct road [than Miguel]" and participated in armed resistance in Santiago del Estero.

Sara told me of her first experience of the resistance. Newly married, she had a small infant, Pablo, and was pregnant with her second child. She and her husband were involved in an attempted revolution headed by General Juan Jose Valle in 1956; her husband's role was to print leaflets for distribution along one of the railway lines. They had recently moved into a small house, organized by the Plan Eva Perón, which "had its stove, its hearth, its parquet floor—beautiful." It was small but full of people working a large mimeograph machine all night. Having risen early one morning, she heard on the radio that the uprising had been aborted, that a state of siege had been declared, so she ran to wake everyone up so they could escape. Before leaving, her husband buried the machine in the foundations of the house. That was the first time that the "civilian commandos" came to her house. She said they weren't even the police, because they were civilian, but they were more like terrorists, "who killed Peronists as if they were out hunting." Someone warned her husband as he was about to get off the bus when he returned to the neighborhood later. The neighbor had seen the commotion as the commandos entered her house, kicking down the door and hitting her, "to frighten me, no?" Afterward, and as her husband became more and more active in his union, each time there was a strike, the police would come to her house, and Miguel would be taken to prison, including one time to the prison of La Pampa, where she visited while pregnant with her fourth child. Then, when Perón eventually returned in the early 1970s, she said that life improved, although the climate was also stressful, especially after the murder of José Ignacio Rucci in September 1973:[5] "I don't know how to describe it; you never knew where the shot would come from." Yet "life went on, with these comings and goings." At the time of the 1976 coup, Miguel was imprisoned with the other leading members of Isabel's government and released to house arrest after just over a year.

Throughout, the "comings and goings" (*vaivenes*) were not only political but also personal. I asked Sara if she had ever thought to question her husband why they continued when things were so dangerous, and she said never; on the contrary, at times she kept him going. She liked politics, and she was also impressed with his ability to do politics.

> I encouraged him [*yo lo incentivaba*]. . . . I'm not going to make out like I'm a hero; there were times when things got too much for me, especially with the children; it was really hard. But deep down, I envied him; I envied the capacity he had to do politics. And the truth is that I sustained him, when—because there aren't heroes, you see? There are men who seem to be very strong, but there are moments when they fall, you see? And in his case, especially when he was a prisoner and older, he was a bit depressed, and so I got his friends together; every weekend we made a barbecue to lift his spirits and keep him going. And after, I had a custom: I got up early and read the newspaper, and he got up later than me to drink mate and whatever, and I recounted the paper to him. And there I accentuated the things that I liked, what I didn't like, and I talked politics with him.

The small details of domestic life in partnership, like the barbecue with friends or the daily discussion of the newspaper, were important in maintaining Miguel Unamuno's political career and keeping him going.

At the same time, Sara was conducting her own militancy in their neighborhood, taking her children to the local basic unit once things had started to normalize a bit and it was possible to be an active Peronist. There, she said, "I could combine private life, family life, with militancy. There has always been this double function in me—I could never disentangle myself from the family nor could I dedicate myself exclusively to politics either." Social work at the neighborhood level is a kind of urban mobilization based around the means of social reproduction. That mobilization is gendered in Argentina as well as elsewhere in Latin America (Molyneux 2000; Blondet 2002). Participation in social organizations, in which women are very often the protagonists, is intimately linked to the conditions for survival in the city, as Javier Auyero's (2001) work on local Peronist brokers and Elana Shever's (2012) work on a communal kitchen in the city of Buenos Aires both highlight. For women like Sara, this kind of militancy was a form of active citizenship that transformed into a politics that operated at a larger scale. She said that even when a legislator in the late 1990s, she saw it as a means to seek improvements for her local district and the surrounding area; and she linked her political activities very much to her local militancy.

When her youngest, Mariano, began kindergarten at the age of three (in 1966), she entered the University of Buenos Aires to study sociology, where she also participated in what she called a kind of "Peronization" of the university until 1973. But the coup of 1976 stopped her militancy. She had begun to teach on some of the university degrees as an assistant, but

> in no time at all the coup came, and you see everything stopped. . . . Yes, there the thing was really hard, and you had to take refuge and stay put. Those of us who were free, we took refuge in our houses, above all with a lot of fear for the children. My kids were adolescents; my husband was imprisoned again. Well, there was a lapse, where I stayed put in my house, like the majority of Argentineans. Which was what they [the soldiers] wanted, that people did not participate.

As things relaxed toward the end of the dictatorship, she rejuvenated her militancy and began her own political career, with FREPASO and the city legislature of Buenos Aires. She is most proud of her involvement in the renovation of the Casa Marco del Pont, a cultural center in her neighborhood, and in her continuing militancy in favor of her neighborhood and the city. She is a remarkable woman.

Mariano's story focused more on the actions of his father—his *viejo* (old man)—and he also gave a sense of the tensions of life in a political family in such times:

> They were [times of] constant interventions in my house, the police arrived, my old man had to go, the police entered [the house], a disaster. My old woman [mother—affectionate term], was an impressive person [*una persona bastante tana*] to cope and put up with these things. But this generated a climate in which, in its time, my family has always dedicated itself to politics. . . . It's like, in general, in political families, politics takes over everything, and even more so in a situation like what we lived in those times. I mean, each time you had to leave your house because the police were coming, well, your old woman set you moving, with a rucksack [*tu vieja te mandaba a mudar, con una mochilita*].

He suggested that these kinds of experiences create in you a *sentimiento*, an allegiance to Peronism that is experienced prior to reading about it, prior to ideological commitment, rational choice, and active militancy. To illustrate this point, he told the story of his father asking Perón to be godfather to Mariano's sister, who was born in 1960. At the time, Perón was in exile and supposedly excommunicated at the instigation of the Argentine church, so she was baptized with Perón's representative present and was thus Perón's first godchild while in exile. The event caused a huge scandal in the newspapers according to Mariano, for the church "hated" Perón. Mariano said of experiences like this, that such a politicization of everyday family life colors your life. . . . It has to do with affect, obviously, with what you have lived, have debated since you were very little; you discussed politics without knowing anything, but you debated from the stupid little things you heard in the house. And yes, in secondary school, you begin to debate and to read a little more and give it a foundation.

Crucial for him was the fact that in his family, he said, they discussed politics all the time, especially on Sundays, the archetypal family day, and often at length, at high volume, and very passionately; "the neighbors must have thought we were killing each other."

He remembers family life as also difficult, somewhat isolated from the rest of the people he knew in the neighborhood, who had more "normal" lives. His family discussed books and politics, whereas his friends from the neighborhood were involved in football. He thinks that he and most of his siblings have tried not to pass on this experience in quite such an extreme way to their children:

> I think we've all passed on the fact that it's not a good life. And that was our ex-perience because I think there was no other choice, but you say no, for your chil-dren, no. . . . I mean, I think it's a passion that can be transmitted, and I don't disagree when people do that. What I know is that it is also complicated. It's complicated, and it exposes you to a situation that isn't normal, in my view. For us it hasn't been normal. So, it's not good that your children don't have a normal life; I want to have a normal life. We lived it as brothers and sisters, like a sect as we said, because there were six of us. I think that the external aggression gener-ated this, so that we all got together and became a clan. In its turn it also gener-ated in us a mechanism to say, "Okay, we're not going to be like our parents [*los viejos*].

His oldest brother, Pablo, was a leading *montonero*, spokesman for Mario Fir-menich, and according to Mariano he retained something of the twenty-four-hour commitment to politics and intellectual life that characterized their par-ents. But the rest of his siblings have not had such active political lives. Of course, a key factor shaping Mariano's parents' militancy, and making family life "ab-normal," was what Mariano called "external aggression." He is grateful that this is not the case today and that his militancy in UPCN—which is quite committed by most people's reckoning—can be conducted separately from his family life.

According to Sara, today her children's politics range across the spectrum: Mariano was a "passionate defender" of Cristina's government, while Pablo, her oldest, was totally the opposite and hated Cristina. Her other son, Miguel, was somewhere in the middle, a Peronist lawyer who has worked for the state but is not especially active: "He's a Peronist, and he supports them, but he's not an activist" (*es peronista y acompaña, pero no milita*). One of her daughters defended Macri, while another lived in Italy and was broadly progressive, and another daughter was very *cristinista*, that is, in favor of Cristina. She did not expect any of them to follow in their father's footsteps and become conventional politicians. Yet I am assured that the vibrant political discussions at Sunday mealtimes continue, albeit in a less charged atmosphere.

This provides a hint of the fact that although political allegiances are felt very deeply, they do not trump family. It's something like football: people are able to support different teams passionately but also be very close to rival fans. Family—and Peronism and the union delegation—is a kind of grouping that has the capacity to encompass strong and passionately held difference. That may emerge in friendly debate or in situations where siblings do not really talk very much. But the difference itself is not considered to be a problem for any of the competing groups. Family can coexist along with wildly differing politics. In a different context, a friend of mine, a Cuban-born and ex-Maoist academic married to an Argentine, told me once about a friend of his in-laws who supported the Argentine military dictatorship, which he found despicable. But, he said, you just inherit these kinds of family friends, and there is not much you can do about it. There is no need for Mariano, his siblings, or his mother to discipline those among them who do not cleave to the family inheritance of political activism, and they do not feel the need to bring anyone back to the fold. Passionate debate based on different political positions is actually inherent to their self-perception as a family. As it is, indeed, to the self-perception of Peronism itself: a frequently cited quote from Perón describes Peronists as like cats: when they seem to be fighting, they are actually mating.

Marina

Marina's militancy was directly shaped by her family's experience during the 1976–83 dictatorship, since she is the daughter of a disappeared mother. Neither of her parents came from especially political families. Her father was from a family with "mucho apellido y barrio norte" (a good surname, from the north of the city), and her mother was the daughter of a doctor, "also upper middle class, comfortable, Christian, Catholic, religious school, all that." They met in a political grouping (*agrupación*) called the *descamisados* (the shirtless ones, a phrase popularized by Eva Perón), in Munroe in the northern part of the city, that combined Peronism with liberation theology. Gradually, that grouping became the northern branch of the *montoneros*.

She's not clear precisely what constituted her mother and father's militancy, since her father does not speak much about it and her mother was taken when she was very small, but she knows that they had some kind of relationship with the unionist arm of the *montoneros*. She thinks that her mother was more of a "militante de base" (base-level activist) who worked in the neighborhoods, but she was also at some point part of a group that falsified documents, specifically identity papers and passports. Then, "bueno, en el 76 nace mi hermano, en el 77 mi mama desaparece, mi papá está en la ESMA un año y medio, cuando sale se va a Francia—y yo y mi hermano también" (well, in seventy-six my brother was born, in seventy-seven my mother disappeared; my father was in the ESMA a year and a half; when he got out, he went to France—and I and my brother as well).

Marina did not want to spend a lot of time discussing the specifics of her parents' situation. She was only four years old when her mother disappeared, and she lived with her grandparents in the countryside while her father was imprisoned. They died when she was an adolescent, and her father does not talk about those times. Nor did Mariano's father. Mariano, who was a teenager in the late 1970s, describes people like his father as having an "alma tumbera" (literally, tomb soul):

> Since my old man had a tradition of being detained, he never spoke of it. . . . There was a sector of Peronism that was constantly detained, in prison; they had this *alma tumbera*. The prison was called the tomb [*la tumba*]; they were guys very linked to the prisons so never said anything. Never told any stories, but one supposes that it couldn't have gone well for him. Why? Because there were others that did tell what happened, and it didn't go well.

For Marina's father, the period of militancy was clandestine, and if he was interned in the ESMA, he was tortured, so it was evident that neither is a comfortable topic of conversation. Although I found Marina to be a very open interviewee on the occasions that we met, I also assume that she did not want to talk about these questions in detail with me. Indeed, a conversation in a café is probably not an appropriate space to explore such individually traumatic experiences. While politically it is important to remember those experiences, ethnographically we must acknowledge silences and respect that some paragraphs begin but are broken off at the level of bald facts and before the detail can emerge, such as her discussion of her mother's disappearance, her father's imprisonment, and move to France ("bueno, en el 76 nace mi hermano, en el 77 mi mama desaparece, mi papá está en la ESMA un año y medio, cuando sale se va a Francia—y yo y mi hermano también"). We can find complementary information about the details of these kinds of experiences in fiction and the testimonies collated in the Nunca Más report published in 1984 and in comparable reports from other countries in the region (see Nouzeilles and Montaldo 2002).[6]

So I asked about the experience of being in exile in France, and Marina told me that the exile of the parents and of the children is different because as a child you end up missing that which you never really knew, so you create a fantasy of what it was like. She felt that she was never really French, but neither was she fully Argentine. She was the only one of her family to return to Argentina. From the end of the dictatorship and until 1989, her father still ran the risk of being prosecuted, so he could not even visit before then. In France, he had also remarried and had two more children.

At the age of twenty-one, Marina returned to Argentina definitively. She had wanted to become a social worker in France, and passed the exams easily enough, but disclosed her family history in the interview with a psychologist and failed that part of the test. While waiting a year to retake the test, she and her parents decided that she would go to Argentina and see what happened. After a few months, she decided to stay. She lived with family members and friends until she received her compensation money. Her father had begun the process of applying for this for her and for her brother while she was still a minor. So the bureaucratic procedure was already in process when she arrived in 1995, and when she was twenty-five years old, she received the money and bought herself a house. Some of her friends received more money and managed to buy two or three apartments, but she had nothing left after buying and renovating her house and paying off her debts.

From the time of her arrival in Argentina, Marina had been active in HIJOS. The acronym spells out the Spanish word for children, and it is formed by children of parents disappeared during the dictatorship of 1976–83. Its website tells us that this group was formed originally by some architecture students at the Universidad Nacional La Plata in 1995 to "get together, reclaim the struggle of our fathers, mothers, and their *compañeros*, seek our brothers and sisters who have been stolen [*apropiados*], and struggle against impunity. . . . We continue to struggle for prison sentences in civilian prisons, that is, perpetual [i.e., life term] and effective for all the genocides of the last civilian-military dictatorship, their accomplices, instigators, and beneficiaries."[7] They are especially known for the tactic of *escraches*, which are creative protests that denounce the presence of military, doctors, priests, and other participants in the torture centers in residential areas; through graffiti and demonstrations letting their neighbors know that they have a criminal living near them; and demanding justice (Benegas 2013; Kaiser 2002; Lessa and Levey 2015).

HIJOS was a very heterogeneous organization, where the personal was the political and political differences were very stark; according to Marina, "cada uno pensaba lo que se le cantaba" (everyone thought what he sang). One member might think that the most important thing was to mourn his or her disappeared parent; another wanted to "do the revolution now: 'all right, give me the machine gun.'" After much discussion, and gradually, HIJOS moved from being a human rights organization into more of a political grouping, she thought, and there was an important moment when people started to articulate a position that was more about generational heritage than specific personal stories. So, "it wasn't about the fact that we are all children of the disappeared, in the generational aspect; we are all a generation that lives and is politically active [*milita*] because of the consequences of what happened." However, she personally moved away from HIJOS. She describes her trajectory as one of a developing class consciousness via militancy at the CTA, which had grown out of her HIJOS militancy. Then, as a result of her CTA connections she got a state job through ATE and chose union militancy over militancy with HIJOS. She felt that for her the two forms of militancy were incompatible, even contradictory.

Nonetheless, she also described her militancy in HIJOS and in the 1990s as invigorating, a very different experience from contemporary youth militancy. They were a small group of activists. "We knew each other; there was no way that you hadn't crossed paths during a march, in a meeting, a party, a tent—[we were] a separate social sector [*una capa social aparte*], a microclimate, a ghetto." They had no money, so from the beginning of deciding on an action they had to raise the money to do it and go out at night to graffiti walls, for example. It was an apprenticeship, where she learned that "whatever thing we could think of we could do," even if it seemed crazy at first. The main difference between the 1990s and now for Marina is that in the 1990s militancy came from resistance to the government and the system, whereas contemporary youth militancy is *kirchnerista*. This makes it strange to her: at that time, going out to distribute leaflets or to paint walls was a necessity, whereas now it is somehow part of a training course one might do to qualify for militancy. She worried that what was lacking was a specifically political training, which she distinguished from theoretical training, but which for her revolved around class consciousness. Younger generations do not conceive of themselves as workers, she said. This is a change, which derives from a failure of political transmission between generations, somewhere between the generation of her parents and that of young people in their twenties today. She worried that if her parents' generation "didn't create a political transmission of their experience, what they lived and did," then what will the current generation of young people be able to teach their own children "of solidarity, of life"?

Graciela

Graciela, a UPCN delegate and tutor at its school for delegates, also made a distinction between particular kinds of militancy now and in the past. She was born in 1975 into a Peronist family. She remembers at the age of four carrying the coffee while her parents graffitied walls: "In that way, militancy comes inside of me, and I take it as something natural, something completely my own." She loves activism and says she does not do it for money, as you can see today where someone demands money for painting the walls.[8] Her mother, with whom I also talked, agreed that the "militancia de antes" (militancy of old) was different from today's militancy:

> We all went as a family; it's not as though we only went on our own. So she took part in everything from when she was a girl, and we all went out to work, to preach—as if it were a religion, but instead of a religion it's a political party. That's all I can tell you. We went out to paint [graffiti]; now the kids don't go out to paint; *la militancia* don't go out to paint; they don't get themselves dirty. But we did; we froze our socks off [*chupábamos frío*], but we returned happy; sometimes we caused an uproar among groups, but that doesn't happen now. Now we talk about football games; in that time [among] *militancias políticas* the same happened.

Graciela's parents were both workers, and her father was an activist with Saul Ubaldini, a prominent leader of the CGT. They knew each other in the meatpacking plant Lisandro de la Torre, in the neighborhood of Mataderos, before it was privatized in 1959. Graciela said that her family life was always one of politics; she went to the Peronist basic unit and demonstrations from when she was small. She told a story about attending a demonstration and her mother telling her that the shots she could hear were fireworks: "They took me running from one side to another; I also remember the water cannons, with the color."[9] When we talked about this later with her mother, Graciela described watching a particular demonstration on the television to see if her father was there:

> G: I remember we were watching television; I don't remember what struggle [*revuelta*] it was, there were water trucks, and we watched to see if he was there—when they broke the window of Modart [a clothing store].
> MOTHER: Yes, and he came back with only one shoe.

G: I went to the front door to pray and to cry so that he returned alive.

MOTHER: He lost his shoe.

G: But that was the only time he went on his own [to a demonstration].

MOTHER: No, but he left work and found himself in this mess [*ese lío*].

As is evident in this exchange, her mother wanted to play down the dramatic nature of her political experience, and she said simply that there was a lot of politics in the meatpacking plant at the time they worked there. A lot of people were involved, not only Peronists but also communists and Radicals. Because of the politics, she said, "that's the reason they fought us, and that's why they closed the meatpacking plant, because of politics." Once it was privatized, the workers went in different directions, but one group joined together in a basic unit with Graciela's godfather, who was at the time a Peronist deputy. They had known each other before he became a deputy and when he was simply a worker in the meatpacking plant.

Graciela's mother attributed her own Peronism to two sources: the nuns in her school who told them to pray for Perón in the early 1940s; and her grandfather, who also always told her that Perón would save the nation. She recounted that he had had a rebellious son (her uncle) who repeatedly deserted from military service and who had sent out a letter with a friend insulting the soldiers. As a result he was sent to the island prison of Martín Garcia, "and in those times I'm telling you about, people who went there never returned. It was a desert island, and they never came back." So her grandfather wrote a poem to Perón, and when Perón thanked him and asked what he wanted, her grandfather replied, "'I need you to save my son,' and he [Perón] said, 'You're asking me this?! He insulted the army, and you come to me to ask for this? I'm a soldier,' and he [Perón] saved him [her uncle]." She continued, "That's how [Peronism] comes from the cradle." This was clearly a well-worn story, an example of the kinds of stories told by Peronists to their children, grandchildren, nieces, and nephews, passing on the personal connection and commitment.

When the basic unit met after the meatpacking plant closed, they "did politics" even in the time of the military dictatorships. What was not possible, she said, was singing the *marcha peronista*, but otherwise, they met and talked politics: "We got together, made a barbecue, sausage, and we all went with our families." This meant that they were all known to each other, so their group could not be infiltrated by the security forces. The group came out of a neighborhood that had been constructed by Evita, so, according to Graciela, "they were all the same people, the same class—workers—the same class thankful for the apartment that Evita had given them; so it was different from people of another class or social level." At the same time, her father was involved in the clandestine meetings to bring Perón back from exile, although he was just a kid who ran errands. Later, he and her godfather were the first to arrive after Rucci died, and they covered his face with a handkerchief.

During the 1970s dictatorship, militancy also had to happen within the family, as Graciela's mother explained in contrast to the present:

> But equally, we never made a fuss [*nunca hicimos lío*]; we were a group of people—calm, family, you see, it's different when all the young kids [*la muchachada*] go, but we were all family. One of us brought the yerba [mate], the other the sugar, the other the cookies [*masitas*]. We took everything to the basic unit, from what we were going to eat to the toilet paper. And everything is different now, when the young kids get together, and that's when they make a fuss. We were all families.

All through the period when Graciela's father was active politically, meetings were often held in their house. Graciela said, "Here it just filled up with people; when he was alive, it filled up with people because 'let's do a barbecue'; 'well, come over.' He was the king of the grill [*el dueño de la parrilla*]; nobody touched his grill." These meetings included figures politically active now, such as Daniel Scioli (according to Graciela's mother).

In the 1980s, it was much freer, and they "did politics" for the PJ representatives in the elections. Now Graciela's mother continues her activism, but it is more of a social militancy (*militancia social*); she was very emphatic that she does not do politics in her center for retired people, which is located in her front room. Like Lilia Saralegui, she had a vigorous social militancy, but unlike Sara, that neighborhood-based social work had not translated into politics as such, and she was very clear that the two were different. She has to treat the pensioners all the same so avoids political discussions: "They know my ideas, and they respect that, and I know their ideas." She organizes yoga, computing classes, massages, discussions of folklore, crafts, memory development, games, excursions, and celebrations on national holidays. She also helps with bureaucratic procedures, for example, if they need to go to PAMI for their social security. Graciela explained how her mother's center contains the old people:

> They get together every day in the center, and they talk about their worries, and they contain each other [*y se contienen*]; it's super important. They sit in a circle and tell each other what's happening, and between everyone they help each other and don't let them fall. If one's depressed, the other helps her, and it's like that. Or they organize excursions if someone's depressed.

For Graciela's mother, militancy both political and social took place in the home; it was and continues to be about family and friends. This was all that Graciela, an only child, knew, and by living her own life of militancy for UPCN, she is continuing the intergenerational transmission of militancy to her children. Her ten-year-old daughter has apparently been particularly receptive. Although Graciela does not take her daughter on street demonstrations, she takes her to mobilizations within the office building; and her children have grown up with her trade union militancy and their grandmother's social militancy. Her nineteen-year-old son is not as committed as her daughter seems to be, at least right now. For example, her daughter wants to be a general secretary when she grows up.

> So, it's as though she's already immersed in the world of trade unionism, whether I like it or not. I don't even need to say to her "sing the *marcha peronista*." She was born like that; it happened with her the same as with me; she was born and lived it all from the womb. So it's as though she's going to take her militancy as a question of life, not something to take on [*incorporar*].

Graciela also attributes this to an inherited rebelliousness, a desire to stick up for herself and for others. She is already very passionate and will be worse than Graciela: "She's in fifth grade, and she's always worrying—say, the teacher said something to her and [she tells me] 'why? I've got to go and talk with the principal.'" When she recounted this story in our group discussion, Maria, another very committed UPCN leader, said, to general agreement, "Yes, because then you'll find that they are fourteen and they're delegates in the school center." Her children, she said, also "grew up in the middle of the chaos [*quilombo*]," as she took them to all the marches and demonstrations.

Graciela's story and that of her mother combine a number of themes that run through these individual stories and others I heard from activists: the nexus between Catholicism and Peronism, from the nuns in Graciela's mother's school to her description of politics as like religion; the family aspect of meetings over barbecues; children accompanying parents to marches, meetings, demonstrations, and so on; the symbolic operation of the *marcha peronista* as definitive of a commitment to Peronism—suppressed after the first coup against Perón but also an indication of the ten-year-old girl's commitment, as she doesn't even need to be told to sing it; and the relationship between political activism and state repression, combined with a reluctance to talk in too much detail about the experience of the late 1970s, when people had to retreat into their houses, as Lilia Saralegui explained. Graciela's family also shows just how far into Buenos Aires society Peronism went: a very ordinary Peronist family, ex-meatpacking workers, one (Graciela's mother) granddaughter of an indigenous Argentine and a French immigrant, but who came to know through her activism a Congress deputy and one of the most important political figures in Argentina, Saúl Ubaldini, and who held barbecues hosting figures later to become politicians at the highest levels of government. Times are less stressful now, less dangerous, but through interpersonal histories of militancy, the lives of very ordinary people are connected to key moments and characters in political history.

INTERGENERATIONAL TRANSMISSION
AND CUTS IN TRANSMISSION

Thus, commitment to political activism is built in the context of and through family life, experienced as driven by stories, blood, debates over the dinner table, accompanying parents on marches or graffiti sessions, or simply as something that just is. This is not to say that it is not thought through or abstracted as well, but often people described this rationalization as coming after the more essential aspects of allegiance. How, then, to pass this kind of commitment and what Marina called *formación política* (political training) to younger generations? This is experienced by some as something of a problem, by which I do not mean a question that needs a solution but as an analytical concern that invites discussion. The issue is that there have been some very important intergenerational cuts or breaks, which became a topic of debate as I began to ask people specifically to discuss intergenerational transmission of militancy.

The first "cut" is a rhetorical one and involves a cut that some felt to be characteristic of the younger pro-government activists in the early 2010s. One of my interlocutors described it as though Peronism had "jumped straight from the 1970s to 2003." He was pointing to the Cámpora-style rhetorical reclaiming of 1970s activism described earlier, where the *kirchneristas* (and sometimes their opponents) sought to make connections between Néstor and Cristina and the Juventud Peronista and allied movements, if not directly with the *montonero* wing. This has had two effects: First, it downplays the role of the Peronist resistance of 1955–73, which as the stories of the mothers of both Graciela and Mariano show was remarkably vibrant and dangerous and which has clearly shaped contemporary Peronism in very complex ways. Second, this rhetoric does not acknowledge the struggle of Peronism in the 1980s and 1990s, downplaying that period of activism as well. This is difficult for contemporary Peronists, many of whom are embarrassed to acknowledge that they supported Carlos Menem's neoliberalism in the 1990s. The relationship with the 1990s is a difficult one, especially for UPCN delegates, given their union's complicity with his program of structural adjustment and administrative reform. The 1990s were in addition a moment of intergenerational cutting in a different way, as neoliberalism and the 1:1 parity between the peso and the dollar are thought by many to have led to a kind of de-politicization of Argentine society, as it became more and more consumerist and individualist (Guano 2002).

However, the most dramatic intergenerational cut was that of the 1976–83 Dirty War. Again and again, my informants told me that a whole generation of political activists and union leaders—mostly at shop-floor level—was simply wiped out (see Martuccelli and Svampa 1997). So many were disappeared or exiled that, they said, you would find it hard to locate very many unionists of about fifty-five to sixty-five years old in 2009–12. Those I knew around that age, at the higher levels of UPCN leadership in particular, had mostly been schoolchildren in the mid-1970s, coming of age toward the end of the dictatorship when they began their union activism clandestinely and then, from 1983 onward, openly, with their first objective the recovery of union democracy. One had been "saved" in 1975 by his military service, in the sense that although it was a horrible experience for him, it removed him from the activist circles he had been frequenting in the university at the time and probably thereby saved his life.

Other families retreated into their houses, and I sensed that many also retreated from politics in a less literal way. Many of those 1970s activists who survived did not talk about their experiences with their children—some of them were perhaps *almas tumberas*, as Mariano described his father, or perhaps they wanted their children to have a more normal life, as Mariano did for his children. Antonius Robben (2007) has explored in detail the effects of trauma on Argentine life after the transition to democracy, and there is a considerable literature on the public ritualization of memories of the Dirty War (e.g., Jelin 2003; Kaiser 2011; Taylor 2003; Guglielmucci 2013). Yet at a personal level it is probable that repression was as much a feature of the posttraumatic experience as was the need to remember.

In the 1980s and 1990s, political activism in Argentina tended to take one of what we might characterize as two main routes, which were by no means mutually exclusive and often overlapped: pro-democracy and human rights; and anti-neoliberalism. In 2003–15 the scenario was more complicated and the villain less clear. The Kirchner governments were explicitly Peronist and managed to appropriate much of the pro–human rights and anti-neoliberal discourse, linking the two together very effectively.[10] The regime even managed to create an extremely vibrant and very passionately *kirchnerista* youth movement. The unionists, many of whom in both ATE and UPCN were broadly supportive of the national government, found themselves in an odd position, without a clear enemy at this level. The *very* neoliberal mayor of Buenos Aires, Mauricio Macri, was much more self-evidently an enemy for activists in both ATE and UPCN. Their response to the lack of a clear antagonist in the national government until 2015 was to develop and articulate a political discourse that focused on the gremial, that is, the order of business that is specifically unionist and relates to workers' rights. For ATE, this required an autonomous political position, critical of the government and of UPCN. For UPCN, it tended to take the form of a conceptual separation between its Peronism and its unionism, rather like for Graciela's mother, when she insisted that her social militancy with the retirees was distinct from her political positioning.

Both unions can be seen as contemporary intergenerational spaces for *formación política*. Although generally led by men and women in their fifties, there are plenty of younger activists. Activism is transmitted through the generations in day-to-day life during political discussions in the delegation or *junta interna* office and in training sessions and workshops. Some of the group sessions that formed part of my research also turned into spaces where older activists educated the younger ones on their political heritage, for example, through telling stories of their family activism and sharing ideas about how to educate their own children. All these are ways of kinning through the circulation of stories and values, a concept I explore in more depth in the following chapter. They are means for contemporary unionists to attempt to recover from the intergenerational cuts administered during the periods of dictatorship and neoliberalism.

CONCLUSION

Initially, the intergenerational transmission of militancy had appeared to me to be something relatively straightforward: fathers and mothers passed on to their children either a specific political orientation or a more general disposition toward political activism, and the key for me would be to find out how. This seemed to be the case for many of the activists who mentioned their family histories and allegiances, and a number of the metaphors they used stressed the biological nature of their activism, Peronism in particular. Hence, Peronism was "from the cradle," often mediated by stories especially about Evita but also Perón, as in the case of Graciela's mother. Or the explanations for how activists came to join their union stressed its automatic nature—their parents were members, so they joined up when they got their first job.

However, when I explored the question in more depth, it became clear that there were multiple responses to these modes of transmission: not all children became equally activist, and a politicized family could just as well lead to children rejecting politics completely, especially if they felt that their parents' activism had not granted them the normal life they craved. Thus, the essential nature of a predisposition to political militancy both just is and is mutable. Still others turned to Peronism against the grain of their family politics, discovering it in universities through friends and books. Others turned away from strongly Peronist families to a more leftist politics. Political activism as ethical project must therefore be a choice *as well as* derive from essential being, but for very many of my informants it was predominantly the latter, even when they chose it. They felt they had chosen activism *because of* an essential characteristic of their being. Thus, activism itself is a hexis that derives from the cultivation of an already existing ethical character, an emotional response as well as intellectual choice.[11]

Kinship nonetheless remained central to how activists articulated their militancy, both in practice and when describing it to me. So, they might tell an obviously well-rehearsed story—about burying the mimeograph in the foundations of the house, or about Perón saving a rebellious child, Evita providing their first toy or their mother's first freezer, and in that performance of the story we can see a version of the retelling to children that passes on the political disposition or hexis. They might take their children to demonstrations and meetings, engage in political barbecues or activism in the home or basic unit. They might include their children in the charitable acts carried out by their political group on key dates—as recounted to me by an anonymous delegate who explained how he gets his children involved in handing out gifts to the children of the neighborhood on the annual Day of the Child. In such ways, children live their parents' militancy; they "grow up in the middle of the chaos." Mothers may even take their children to visit their father in prison; or the mother might be absent and the rest of the family in exile because of parents' militancy. Thus, ordinary life is imbued with political activism, and kinship is infused with politics, and vice versa.

The relationship also works at less ordinary moments, as kinship ceremonies become infused with political meaning. So the story that Mariano recounted of his sister's baptism, with the exiled and possibly even excommunicated Perón as her godfather, both attaches his family firmly and personally to Perón through a kinship relation and in the story's retelling decades later underlines his family's commitment to the cause. Another friend told me once that he and his wife decided to marry in the Church of Santa Cruz in the middle of the dictatorship. He had not been especially bothered about having a religious ceremony but agreed to it when they decided to make it a politically symbolic act. This was the church where the infamous intelligence agent Alfredo Astíz, known as the Angel of Death, infiltrated the Mothers of the Plaza de Mayo and was involved in the kidnapping of human rights activists, including two French nuns. With activist friends and the agreement of the priest, in the homily the priest prayed for the political prisoners and the disappeared, infuriating my friend's brother, who was a soldier. For my friend it was a way to resist the dictatorship and to locate himself politically. Religion, kinship, and politics thus intertwined in consciously symbolic acts.

This is a kind of politics that lies "beyond grievance" (Shah 2013) and beyond rational contemplation of interests; it is a politics of activism as hexis and way of life. The imbrication of life, kinship, biologically understood disposition, self-cultivation, and political commitment as lived by my activist friends is complex, enacted in times both of relative peace and of state repression and in the context of stories they tell themselves—and researchers—about political and intimate history. In multiple ways these elements combine to form activists as ethical subjects and to transmit activism and political consciousness across generations. Ethical-political subjectivation takes place across generations and through family relations; militancy comes into being through kinship; and family histories intertwine with national histories to produce political commitment and subjecthood.

4 PEDAGOGY AND

POLITICAL COMMUNITY

Previous chapters have focused on more individual senses of activism as an ethical project, even when located in a familial context. This chapter shifts toward the collective, with an exploration of the contrasting and often rival political projects of unionism represented by ATE and UPCN. I explore how these are reflected in formal educational processes, since education is one of the spaces where each union constructs a dominant narrative of who it is and what it does and through which each brings its members together. In the process, the unions construct themselves as a collective ethical subject.

This collective focus introduces the second main organizing concept of this book, *contención*. To avoid confusion with the false cognate "contention," I translate it as "containment" and use that English term throughout. The concept originated in the work of Wilfred Bion, a Kleinian psychoanalyst (Douglas 2007; Hinshelwood 1989; Bion 1959). For Bion, the first container-contained relationship is that between the mother and infant, but in therapy that relationship is then replicated with the therapist being the container, whose responsibility is to "receive and understand the emotional communication of another [the contained] without being overwhelmed by it, process it and then communicate understanding and recognition back" (Douglas 2007: 33; see also Bion 1959; Hinshelwood 1989). That process should "restore the capacity to think in the other person" (Douglas 2007: 33). The word itself appeared quite frequently in the everyday talk of my interlocutors, although not as frequently as the concept of *militancia*. For example, when activists said that their health suffered because they "took on" all of the problems that workers brought to them, they were in part describing that process of receiving and understanding emotional communication. More explicitly, Graciela said of her mother's group of retirees that they "contain each other." People often used the word to refer to collective help—for example, Sara told me that she had a "lot of containment" from her family to help her look after her children while she and her husband were politically active. The following chapters discuss the multiple meanings of containment more explicitly, but as I move to more collective ethnographic material, containment starts to become important as a category that describes how the group encompasses the individual. It is an active process by which individuals make the collective as well as a means of describing how they feel part of a collective political project.

Explicit pedagogy is important for that process in the case of both ATE and UPCN. Both unions conducted training sessions for newly elected delegates. ATE did so through a two-day workshop, while UPCN ran the Escuela de Formación Sindical (EFS). For both organizations, the educational spaces were explicitly understood as spaces of collective self-formation, and much care was taken to consider both the content and method of how they wanted to shape participants. They are conscious and collective forms of hexis as self-cultivation. The formal side of pedagogical imperatives combined with less formal processes of community building and kinning, as participants in the workshops shared time together; broke for conversations, coffee, and cigarettes; discussed their workplace concerns; and just got to know each other. In the process of both formal and informal pedagogies, the unions also transmitted their particular vision of how to act on the world to transform it, that is, their praxis. In Latin America, the concept of praxis is indelibly linked to Paulo Freire's work, and his philosophy of popular education informs almost all forms of adult education. So it is unsurprising to find a kind of praxis in these educational contexts. What I illustrate here is how the different philosophies of praxis are articulated through contrasting philosophies of organization, which are at the same time forms of collective subjectivation. Specifically, for UPCN activists, their political community was characterized by "verticalism" and a conception of their movement as an organism; while ATE delegates saw themselves as enacting a more "horizontal" ethic, consonant with the more anarchist philosophies of contemporary alter-globalization activists in Europe and the Americas (Juris 2008; Graeber 2013; Maeckelbergh 2009; Sitrin 2012; Flesher Fominaya 2014; Juris and Khasnabish 2013).

POLITICAL COMMUNITY AS ORGANISM:
UPCN TRAINING SESSIONS

The EFS, a relatively new initiative, is modeled to some extent on the Escuela Superior Peronista (Peronist Further Education School), one of Perón's own projects in the early 1950s (Camusso and Santiago 2008). It is thus an important place where well-thought-through practices of organization operate to instantiate the political logic of Peronism in the everyday. After a pilot project in 2007,

FIGURE 2.   EFS session, 2013 (students)

UPCN established the EFS in 2008. By 2015, it had developed a wide range of courses and workshops. For example, in 2013 these consisted of a cycle of training for new delegates that comprised two two-month introductory courses covering the nature of the union, public-sector employment, collective bargaining and related questions, as well as complementary workshops on oral and written communication, negotiation, budgetary matters, and union leadership. A third two-month course was aimed at delegates in leadership positions and covered more abstract questions. Each course was run for around sixty students, and the EFS held three of them per year. The EFS also organized regular workshops on historical and philosophical topics, such as the Malvinas conflict, human rights, sexual diversity, and ethics. Finally, the EFS hosted meetings to bring people up to date on issues to do with the health insurance plans and training for delegates from outside Buenos Aires, both at the main city building and through workshops around the country.

In 2009 I attended much of the course for new delegates and a course on oratory (later renamed "oral communication"), in 2012 I attended the final session of the new delegates' course and a session on leadership that contrasted Augusto Vandor and Jose Rucci, and in 2013 I attended the first half of a workshop on negotiation (Figures 2 and 3). In 2014, I presented the results of my research project

FIGURE 3. EFS session, 2013 (teachers)

in a workshop at the school. I also attended the ATE training for new delegates in 2009. I base this discussion mostly on the experience of the two courses for new delegates, beginning from a discussion of the content of the courses and their pedagogical style. I draw out differences and similarities between the two unions in how they conceptualize the delegate as individual and the union as collective and the relationship between the two. I then relate this to ethnographic material gleaned outside the training courses themselves to draw out the two organizational theories that are dominant in each union.

In 2009, the UPCN training sessions for new delegates were organized over the course of two months and held on Tuesday and Thursday mornings. I went to the EFS buildings, then located on Viamonte, where the entrance walls were lined with pictures of Eva Perón and posters for the UPCN cultural festival. Other delegates and I went to the large hall in the basement that served as the lecture theater for the opening plenary sessions. Plastic chairs were lined up on either side of a central aisle, facing the front, where there was a white screen for PowerPoint presentations and a whiteboard. I would usually take a seat in one of the front rows. Gradually, the hall filled up, until around one hundred delegates had arrived. The speakers were either UPCN leaders or experts from outside. Those run by outside experts had a very different feel from those run by leaders of the UPCN Capital Section. The experts were mostly concerned to transmit particular kinds of content—philosophical-historical in the case of the lecturer who gave sessions on the organization of the state and in the case of another, specific legislation related to public administration and public employment in Argentina. They presented PowerPoint demonstrations and even handouts once or twice; and we had to take notes in our exercise books to keep up. The two Capital Section leaders whose sessions I was able to attend gave talks more specifically about belonging to UPCN. Their talks were very popular with the audience: they were on the whole charismatic speakers and held in very high esteem by the newly elected delegates.

Plenary sessions lasted around an hour, after which we all trooped out and went up to the floor where the smaller classrooms were located. Outside those classrooms, tables were set up with coffee, plastic cups, sugar sachets, and biscuits. We helped ourselves and stood around chatting; some people smoked cigarettes illicitly in the corridors or licitly outside on the street before coming to the classrooms. People found out which delegation others came from, whether they knew people in common, what I was doing there, what unionism was like in England. They discussed football, the daily news, the latest ATE antics in their institution, their feelings about UPCN (usually very positive), and so on. After the coffee break we moved into the smaller classrooms in our groups to work in *talleres* (workshops) of around twenty participants, each with two facilitators. These were based around group work. We sat on plastic chairs with small side tables in groups of five or six to discuss texts in detail; we participated in role play, discussion, presentation, and observation exercises and also listened to mini lectures from our facilitators. The topics included leadership, *conocimiento gremial* (union knowledge), forms of mobilization, affiliation, communication, how to produce posters and leaflets, the collective bargaining negotiation commissions, elections of delegates, the role of the delegate, and two of Perón's speeches. The course also included a speech from Andrés Rodríguez to the plenary session and a visit to the CGT offices.[1]

One of the most important aspects of the training session was the opportunity it gave for UPCN delegates from different administrative entities to meet each other and to chat over coffee and cigarettes in the break times. This was containment in action, as they were brought together to build their organization as a whole, as UPCN rather than as their specific delegation, and this dynamic was probably one of the most effective outcomes of the training and the aspect most appreciated by individual delegates. Any criticism of UPCN was only very rarely articulated during the "compound talk" (Tate 2007: 13) of coffee breaks, and then only indirectly, as participants had generally signed up to attend because they were enthusiastic members of the union and were happy to play that role at the time of the course. Attendance did drop off over time, as many people came only to the very minimum number of sessions necessary to pass the course or stopped the course halfway through. Attendees were mostly newly elected delegates, but because the school was a relatively new enterprise in 2009, some more experienced delegates also participated.

The majority of UPCN leaders at the higher levels of the organization have not undertaken this training program, and learning to be a UPCN delegate is something that primarily takes place informally in delegations or even in families. One very high-level leader of the UPCN Capital Section told me that he thought that the purpose of EFS was mostly to "socialize" the delegates, by which he meant educate them in UPCN expectations, forms of thinking, and approaches. However, the school is becoming increasingly important in UPCN's identity and in practices of containment for new and experienced delegates. Undoubtedly it produces a particular official narrative about UPCN, one that was remarkably consistent also across my interviews with multiple leaders of the union. Some key aspects of this included a considerable emphasis on vocation and on the stigma of being a unionist; on UPCN's nature as a union that negotiates but does not confront; on the importance of the *convenio colectivo* (collective bargaining agreement) as the way that negotiations with functionaries should occur; and on the nature of UPCN as a verticalist union.

As one would expect, the official narrative was also at times undermined in discussions during group work and coffee breaks, when delegates brought in other issues. One example is an exercise during a workshop when we were asked to think about how we would encourage workers in our institution to affiliate with UPCN. There was a very clear steer that we should be arguing for the political project of UPCN as a well-organized and coherent union that negotiates on behalf of the workers and needs affiliates to be strong. But several of the delegates joked in the group exercise that they should say that UPCN has the prettiest women and men or gives specific benefits to potential affiliates to incentivize them. The former was less serious than the latter, as UPCN is often accused of buying affiliation, for example, by promising a more long-term contract to those who sign up. People also made jokes in this and other sessions about the role the union plays in getting state employment for relatives and friends. In class, these were mentioned only very briefly and, if so, quickly dismissed by the facilitators as not relevant to the topic under discussion. While these might very well in practice be ways that UPCN delegations gain affiliates (and their existence in joking form shows that they are), they are not acceptable within the official line that is being inculcated in the space of the training school. Despite the hints of an alternative narrative, the delegates present were prepared to be schooled in the official one and on the whole had come to the course predisposed to believe in it as at least an admirable aim if not actual truth. For that reason, this chapter is not an exercise in revealing the ways that individuals resisted hegemonic conceptions of UPCN as political community but rather an exploration of how that hegemony is constructed and a particular kind of collective subject elicited.

UPCN's official self-perception as a union is built in part on a specific notion of the individual delegate as political person with an orientation toward the collective and a desire to change things and stand up for workers' rights. Antonio Montagna, director of the EFS in 2009, began the introductory session by stating that his audience of newly elected delegates had chosen to become union activists. They had made the decision to "renounce a certain individualism" and join "something collective," because they were all "nonconformists" and had the desire to change society. He asked them why they had decided to be delegates, suggesting that if they felt they had been obliged to stand for election, he would like to know. Sure enough, the people who put up their hands to answer his question gave answers that stressed their nonconformist nature, their "solidarity toward the Other," and their desire to stand up for workers' rights.

Contributors also quickly located themselves in a collective context, expressing their irritation with the other unions in their workplace and giving reasons for their choice of UPCN specifically. They located UPCN very clearly as a union that is nonconfrontational but also not "yellow": although it negotiates rather than confronts, UPCN does represent the workers. Since UPCN's identity as a negotiator was also one of the most important themes to come out across the course, it is notable that the new delegates had begun the training with that in mind. They were also very good at producing a familiar story when asked in that first session what they know of UPCN: they pointed to the collective bargaining agreement and to the fact that UPCN is organized and organic, represents the workers, and solves problems. Some of the delegates in that class were experienced members of UPCN, but even for new ones, the training itself did not implant a new narrative in the participants but instead reinforced one with which they were very familiar.

Montagna's two sessions also covered elements that were picked up throughout the workshops and in the plenary sessions run by Capital Section leaders. First, he argued that the delegates should take pride in their being unionists, even though they would be met by "much criticism and little applause." He was referring here to the stigma discussed previously, and in one session when he brought this up, he was met with skepticism from his audience, who thought that in general, unionism was "a bad word." He made a considerable effort to persuade them, pointing out that there are good and bad accountants but nobody says that all accountants are bad, and ultimately arguing that they need to focus on the fact that being a unionist is a vocation, "an interior call," something personal. However, it was a vocation that was necessarily enacted within a collective, even requiring the renouncing of a kind of individualism.

One of the main criticisms of UPCN coming from outside that Montagna pointed to in the introductory plenary, and that was repeated in the workshops and outside the school setting, was the charge "that you [i.e., UPCN] were Menemists and now you are Kirchnerists." By repeating this charge, Montagna and others implicitly reference the ATE critique that UPCN did not defend public-sector workers in the 1990s. Montagna answered by saying that such critics confuse negotiation with betrayal. For him, this position of negotiator was linked to the nature of public-sector employment, since public servants are not opposed to their employer in the way that employees of a private enterprise are; they are part of the state and have the same objectives. "El Estado también soy yo" (I am also the state), he said.

Yet negotiation—especially the decision to negotiate with Menem in the

1990s—was a problematic question for UPCN. In the official narrative, it was a matter of strategy, of what would be the most effective way to defend the largest number of workers (or failing that, affiliates). But for UPCN's critics from outside, it encapsulated all that was wrong with officialist unionism and constituted a betrayal of a whole class by defending only a small subsection and focusing on strengthening the union organization itself, which was as a result essentially bought off by the government in power. Sebastián Etchemendy and Ruth Berins Collier (2007) have argued that the trade unions were compensated for the reforms to individual labor rights by the preservation and even enhancement of their associational power, through the protection of collective bargaining structures and the maintenance of union control over the workers' health insurance companies. UPCN was particularly fortunate in this regard, receiving control over public-sector health insurance provision in 1995.[2] The political tensions around negotiation continued into the 2000s, as critics charged UPCN with being on the side of the employer rather than the workers.

This critique was well known to all of the new delegates and EFS teachers. I had expected that they would ignore or deny it or respond simply by attacking the media and rival unionists as ill informed or otherwise motivated. They did so, but in addition to those strategies, they confronted the critique head-on by presenting an alternative narrative of being an organization that knows how to adapt to circumstances while also knowing "where they are from and where they are going" in the longer term, as one workshop facilitator put it. This mattered because "la organización vence al tiempo" (organization defeats time) and because it also meant effective union action. What was important was to negotiate from a position of power and one of legitimacy with respect to their work colleagues. This philosophy was particularly attractive to the UPCN unionists that I knew and frequently recurred in general discussions across all kinds of spaces, from delegation offices to interviews to public assemblies. It required that delegates be trustworthy, confident, and not promise benefits they cannot deliver. For example, teachers in the EFS argued that although work colleagues might be more seduced by a demand for a 50 percent pay raise, if it is not possible, then UPCN delegates should not promise it. Rather, they should determine what it is possible to offer and what can be done to resolve workplace problems in conjunction with the functionaries who are their employers. I saw this philosophy in action in day-to-day work in a delegation when leaders discussed problems they were attempting to resolve in favor of the workers in their institution, and as they expressed their frustration when they felt that ATE was promising something they knew to be unrealistic.

VERTICALISM

The strategy of determining and offering only what is possible and realistic was linked to one of the most important themes that came out throughout the training course, and indeed throughout all my research with UPCN, that is, the nature of UPCN as a verticalist and organic organization, both of which were very much self-ascribed terms.[3] Indeed, its verticalism was one of the aspects that attracted many of my informants to UPCN: for most, if not all, it was the source of UPCN's strength and power and its ability to negotiate but also to confront where necessary.

Verticalism describes both an organizational philosophy and a means of self-identification and in the context of the Argentine labor movement is understood as inherently Peronist. In sum, it is the notion that those at the lower ranks of an organization must follow the decisions made by those higher up, which provides an organization with the strength that comes from discipline. The facilitator of one of our training workshops explained that the organization is structured in the form of a pyramid, in an image that she drew on our whiteboard (Figure 4), with different levels and qualitative types of authority and participation depending on the level of the pyramid.

Fewer people are at the top, and they are the ones with the power of decision making and the ability to design strategies; those in the middle transmit the decisions down to those at the base of the pyramid and also give their opinions to those above them. At the base, delegates receive information and implement tactics. The facilitator stressed that these delegates have full autonomy with respect to how they execute the tactics decided by those higher up in the organization, and therefore it is incorrect to think that they need to ask permission to do everything. Further, those above must listen to those below them and, if appropriate, transmit those opinions upward. Individuals rise up the pyramid as they demonstrate the ability to use information appropriately. If a delegate does not agree with the strategy decided by the leadership, he or she needs to know how to express that disagreement within the structure but must act in accordance with instructions.

This means that, for example, when organizing and running a labor conflict, the local delegations must keep in constant touch with leaders of the Capital Section; and in theory the strategy for that conflict must be approved by the Executive Committee of the Capital Section. In one workshop toward the middle of the course, our group exercise consisted of working through how to manage a workplace conflict. The delegates came up with what seemed to me at the

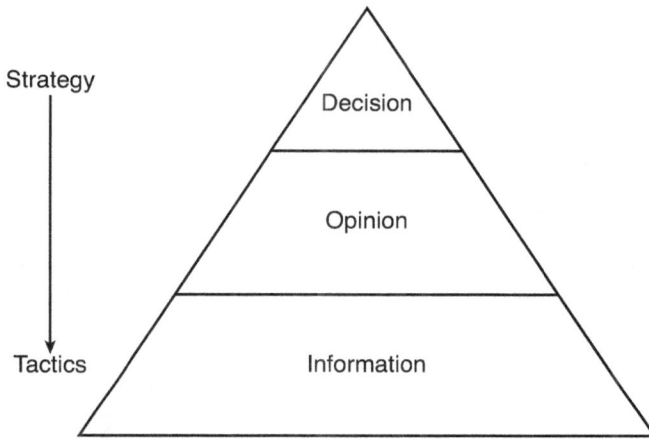

FIGURE 4.   Verticalism pyramid

time highly complex situations, for example, a situation in which, because of the freezing of contracts for ten years, someone was managing a group of people on the same wage as herself. I later discovered that this was a very common problem. Another hypothetical conflict we discussed was the splitting of an organism into two "firms," leading to changing conditions of work for those on temporary contracts and the resulting formation of a (implicitly competing) unionlike structure by the workers concerned. In the group, we suggested that the situation could be resolved through the local negotiation commissions (*paritarias*) and, if unsuccessful, a *paro y movilización* (strike and mobilization). The workshop facilitator came to our group and listened to our suggestion, correcting us on a few matters related to details of what can and cannot be discussed in the commissions and training us in the operations of the collective bargaining agreement. In this session and throughout the course it was made clear to us that decisions about whether and how to mobilize and what to do needed to be discussed with experienced UPCN leaders, either within the local delegation or at the Capital Section or both.

For many UPCN delegates, verticalism is a very positive philosophy, something that makes their organization particularly effective. Verticalism is felt to give UPCN delegates a role, clarity of purpose, and discipline and is explicitly associated with Juan Perón. Carlos Capurro, who is gremial secretary of the Capital Section and therefore something like third in command there, explained verticalism with direct reference to Perón's conceptualization:

There's a verticalism of functioning . . . in the organization that says that first
we have unity of conception, as a first factor, in order to be able to function. . . .
It's not that we all think the same but that we all have the same idea on this
particular point, after having debated it, in order then to have unity of action.
In the unity of action, the execution of that action. . . . [A]nd the most important is the oversight over that execution, which the leadership must have.
That is to say, in this vertical functioning, the unity of conception [in order to
achieve] a unity of action, the execution of that action, and the oversight over
that execution are where you see real verticalism and where each one of us has
a role.

He went on to explain that confusion or a lack of unity of conception would lead
to confusion in the subsequent categories (of action, execution of the action, and
oversight over the execution). His explanation is a very clear description of some
of Perón's most important ideas in *Conducción política* (1971, esp. 155, 215–31)
and uses Perón's own terms.[4]

Perón was very influenced by his own nationalist Catholic upbringing and
military career, but the story of quasi-militaristic organizational structures and
top-down discipline does require some softening. On the one hand, the power
of decision making is concentrated in a small group of people; on the other, a
great premium is placed on the active involvement of all delegates in the activities of the union. Another key aspect of the workshops was in training delegates to take on a full role in activities beyond those specifically connected to
the business of managing conflicts and negotiating with the employer. We discussed things such as how to gain affiliates and run campaigns about workplace
harassment and equal opportunities. All delegates are supposed to know their
role and the official line, especially if they have been through the training sessions. Members of each delegation are encouraged to take on particular responsibilities, such as equal opportunities, cultural activities, and youth activities.
The delegation should in theory work as a team, and a great deal of emphasis was
placed in the training on each delegate knowing who was responsible for which
field of activity.

Thus, the relationship between leader and base is conceived as one of mirror-
ing, of mutual participation in an organic whole, rather than one where the base
members simply delegate their power or right to participate to their representative. We could argue that this is a kind of democracy that privileges participation over representation, one that is common to populist movements (Panizza
2005).[5] However, UPCN delegates do not imagine the question in these terms;
whether democratic or not, what is important to them is that they work together

as an organic whole. They value organicity in and of itself, sometimes arguing that it makes for a more effective and powerful union, sometimes stressing it as a specifically Peronist value, but often taking it for granted as just how the union is and should be.

In addition, UPCN's pyramidal structure does not in practice always stifle discussion. While the structure may channel debate, flows of pressure can work from bottom up as well as top down. One example of this in practice was during the outbreak of swine flu in July 2009. At the beginning of July, the government of Buenos Aires closed city schools and nurseries for the two weeks prior to the school vacations. Over the course of about a week, workers in public-sector institutions were subjected to increasing restrictions on activities that involved large groups of people, with a view to restricting the spread of the epidemic. Initially, and acting on advice given by specialists in the media as well as the official pronouncements from the national Health Ministry, the UPCN leadership decided that it was not necessary to close down the EFS. At one session, however, several delegates expressed their discomfort with the fact that there were nearly one hundred people in a basement room with very little ventilation in the midst of a serious flu epidemic when children were being kept away from similar situations to restrict the spread of the virus. They did so by first expressing their conformity with the decision made, since it was made by the leadership of the organization, but then urging those leaders to reconsider. The educators explained the rationale for the decision, both by giving logical reasons for why it was made and by using it as an example of verticalism. For example, one particular day, some delegates complained vociferously in our workshop about the decision not to close the school. The facilitator's response was that the decision had been made by the leadership and that it was our responsibility to comply with that decision, but she would feed the complaints upward through the organizational pyramid. Soon after, and once the volume of complaints had reached a critical mass, the sessions for July were canceled. Some of those at high levels of the organization told me that they did so because of the complaints, not because their view on the actual need for restrictions had changed. The change of opinion among the leadership was an indication that at least some decisions are informed by their assessment of the reaction of the base. This is contrary to their own ideal story of an organization where the base enacts decisions made by the leadership and only those in the middle layer have the right to give their opinion.

Importantly, and by no means only in that one instance of the swine flu controversy, it is not that discussion and debate do not take place within Peronist organizations, including UPCN. The key is to keep that discussion internal and to present a unified front to all those on the outside. This was constantly reiterated in training sessions, especially those run by Fernando de Sa Sousa on communication. In one, he argued that if a leader has to give an order, it is a failure of persuasion, even if at times it may be necessary; although UPCN is organic, it cannot be like an army because in the army, "nobody thinks; they are only trained to obey." In contrast, UPCN is constructing "a collective power," and that can only happen through debate. Criticisms are important, although "of course inside the delegation," and public disagreement should be avoided. Nonetheless, he also considered it essential to follow the line decided on by the leadership once debate has taken place, and his justification for this was that the leadership is best placed to make that decision because they have the most experience and knowledge. Of course the leadership also has the most influence in determining when a proper amount of debate has happened and when the bases should fall in behind the decision that has been made, but as the swine flu incident showed, this power is not absolute.

As mentioned previously, I was often told that Perón said that Peronists are like cats: when it seems from outside that they are fighting, they are actually reproducing themselves. Yet there is a whole organizational structure built to channel debate, to communicate the decisions of the leadership effectively, to persuade adherents that they are correct, and to enjoin them to enact those decisions even if they are not fully persuaded. Decisions do on some occasions need to be forced through, but the structure is more usually an effective way of managing dissenting voices. In return, the most successful leaders need to demonstrate a modicum of flexibility, to ensure that they are not leading the organization down a path that will eventually become unacceptable to the majority. This must be coupled with a great deal of charisma and power to convince. One of the workshop facilitators proposed the following metaphor to our group: UPCN is a body, with Andrés Rodríguez as the head, and other Capital Section leaders the vital organs, but all members have their place and must follow their function for the body to survive. They are expected to subordinate their individual desires for "this system of which I am part." Each delegation is similarly a body, with the general secretary as head of that part. Actually, this was one of the most extreme statements of UPCN's organicity that I came across during my fieldwork, and very few people were quite as Hobbesian as that. However, it was characteristic for my informants to imagine their political community as an organism, both when they were expressing the official narrative and in more day-to-day practices.

WHAT IS A PERONIST OR OFFICIALIST UNION?

The vision of UPCN political community as an organism is a Peronist vision, and the organizational philosophy and interpretation of union taught by the EFS were also Peronist. However, the relationship between the union and Peronism was also a source of tension. Nearly all the teachers self-identified as strong Peronists, and the majority of the delegates attending the EFS were passionate Peronists with all that entails. Yet when a workshop facilitator asked the participants in our workshop to raise their hands if they were Peronist, a significant minority did not, and the teachers on the whole had clearly decided as a matter of policy to maintain the sense that UPCN is a pluralist union, and that as Antonio Montagna said, "Here nobody is going to Peronize anyone." Although the only texts we discussed in workshops that had attributed authorship were written by Juan Perón, Montagna claimed that they had been chosen only because they were the most relevant; and in subsequent years, these texts were dropped from the curriculum precisely so as not to exclude non-Peronists. They were replaced with speeches by Andrés Rodríguez, the UPCN general secretary, who is in fact a highly committed and active Peronist.

In a plenary session that I attended in 2009, a small conflict arose when one member of the audience said that "if you're a unionist, you're a Peronist." Montagna corrected him and said that not everyone in the union was a Peronist. This sparked off a passionate discussion, with several audience members repeatedly and loudly restating the connection for them between Peronism and unionism. Montagna replied that many unionists were Radicals, to which someone shouted out that he could help them with that—meaning that he could stop it somehow, implicitly by force of something more than reasoned argument. The only two dissident voices in the discussion (apart from Montagna's) were a man saying that unionism did not start with Perón and a woman suggesting that being with the PJ itself might be a source of shame at particular moments (she was likely thinking of the Menemist period). But the debate came to a head when these contrasting views were drowned out by a loudly sung chorus from the audience of "the unions belong to Perón." It was clearly a contentious question, with most of the audience left unconvinced by Montagna's proposal that the relationship between the union and the party depended on the historical moment. Debate on the issue was postponed for a later date, and during the rest of the training course, the teachers avoided dealing with it head-on. Instead, they emphasized the role of the union as union, with a responsibility to represent and act for a broad spectrum of workers and to be able to negotiate with whatever government was in power. As in the case of the family debates discussed previously, dissent was managed by setting aside the topic and focusing on what everyone could agree on.

However, in the context of Argentine history, even the notion of a union that will negotiate with governments in power is generally interpreted as a Peronist one, albeit a particular strand of Peronism. It is especially associated with *vandorismo*, named after Augusto Vandor, who attempted to construct a strong labor movement while Perón was in exile. A number of UPCN delegates thought he had betrayed Perón by seeking to do this. Yet, the tradition of a close relationship between union and government has been a feature of Peronist unionism since the mid-twentieth century (Torre 1998). Alongside it, and often in competition, has always been a more radical position, often associated with rank-and-file members or delegates. This is associated with 1960s *clasismo*, which had Trotskyite and socialist elements but is also viewed by many as a leftist version of Peronism. For some ATE activists this more radical tradition represents a truer form of Peronism.

For the UPCN leadership, negotiation was not a betrayal of their Peronism but quite the reverse. Viewing it as the most effective way to achieve their goals, they stressed that negotiation had to take place from a position of power. This was partially for pragmatic reasons but also to head off accusations of co-optation. The EFS teachers repeatedly emphasized the importance of the construction of power. For them, this involved several factors, especially constantly increasing the number of affiliates, which had both a political and financial impact (since union dues would increase with a growing membership); informants also pointed to the health insurance company as a crucial political tool and to the importance of being seen to be active, of conducting regular elections even when there was only one list of candidates to vote for, of resolving work colleagues' problems, and so on. From the outside, UPCN was also criticized for expanding its power as a union by putting affiliates in positions of power within the state, especially in human resources offices.

UPCN is attacked by members of ATE for precisely this vision of unionism—as negotiators and therefore collaborators. Their response is usually not to deny the accusation but to resignify it as positive. Some even make this discursive move with respect to the union's tactics during the 1990s. One of the main objectives of the EFS, then, seems to be to inculcate in UPCN delegates a pride in their organization, a confidence and inner belief that UPCN was right to do what it did in the 1990s and was right to focus on the institutionalization of its power during the Kirchner years. This is a dual process of personal work for individual delegates and the creation of the organization in the image that the current leaders have decided it should have. It is hard work, hence the need for a very well-developed training school to project the narrative, in addition to the other organizational spaces where it comes into being.

Central to this idealized self-perception is the formal collective bargaining system. Informants often attributed this creation to Andrés Rodríguez, arguing that it was his idea of how UPCN should construct itself as an organization. Whether true or not, attributing it to him makes sense in terms of how UPCN describes leadership and verticalism—that these kinds of strategic decisions should come from the very top. In interviews and in the EFS, this was carried through in the repetition of certain key notions of organizational action: delegates should not promise what they cannot deliver; they should resolve problems and contribute to the construction of power as an organization to be able later to resolve questions for work colleagues.

It was explicitly framed as something that differentiates UPCN from "other unions," which usually meant ATE. Throughout the training sessions, teachers and students referred to ATE as overly combative and promising more than could ever be achieved: promising "all sorts of madness" in one student's words. They thought that ATE produced a seductive narrative, but it was not realistic. In contrast, they considered their organization to be the most appropriate for the contemporary moment: responsible, effective, and powerful, the true inheritor of the Peronist union tradition. Here, the existence of the rival union can be seen as the rhetorical counterpoint to the self-image that they would like to build but also an alternative that can absorb dissension; that is, people can simply join ATE if they are not happy with UPCN's approach.

POLITICAL COMMUNITY AS POLITICAL PROJECT:
ATE TRAINING SESSIONS

ATE activists of course had a different opinion and their own political community to construct. The ATE-Capital training session for new delegates operated on a much smaller scale than those of UPCN; ATE-Capital simply does not have the same amount of resources. The program run by ATE-Capital Formación (the training department of ATE-Capital) incorporated, like UPCN, talks and discussions about questions that the union consider to be important, some training of delegates in their role as delegates, and the publication of written materials. However, the content of those talks, training, and publications was completely different. It would be inaccurate to say that ATE's material is more politicized, since UPCN's material is political in the sense of promoting a particular political vision. However, ATE's material does make its political project much more explicit. Indeed, I would argue that the thrust of ATE Formación's work is to pro-mote a specific political analysis of the contemporary situation for workers in Argentina. That project is linked to the project of the CTA described previously, and—as it was for UPCN—the message was remarkably consistent between the training sessions and the interviews I conducted.

The workshop that I attended took place over two days in 2009. It was held in a basement room in the office of ATE-Capital and attended by around thirty new members of ATE *juntas internas*. They were ordinary ATE unionists: men and women mostly in their thirties and forties, casually dressed in jeans and T-shirts. They gathered around the door to the room, smoking cigarettes and chatting, until enough people had arrived to start the session. We sat down on our plastic chairs, arranged in front of a wall acting as a projection screen. The lights were dimmed, and the young university students who acted as facilitators showed us a short DVD program about the recovery of democracy within ATE in 1984. One facilitator introduced me and said that I would be participating in and observ-ing the workshop, and everyone nodded in agreement. Later on, during the first coffee break, a few came to introduce themselves and ask for more information about what I was doing, and I took the opportunity to generate interviews and note down cell phone numbers. Mostly people seemed unperturbed by my ac-companying them and noting down the discussion. When the DVD finished, we were told to form two groups, so we moved our chairs into two circles to talk about the film. After that, we discussed different models of unionism, with vol-unteers nominated to summarize our discussions for the plenary. In the after-noon, we talked through the role of the delegate in our groups, and the first day finished with a talk back into the general group from Marcelo "Nono" Frondizi, at the time gremial secretary of ATE-Capital, who had been an ATE delegate for forty-two years. The following day focused on the question of conflict and began with a talk from one of the workshop facilitators. We then moved into two com-missions (groups) and were given the task of designing a hypothetical conflict for the other commission to discuss. We then discussed our conflict and what kinds of strategies we might choose to deal with it. Then the group was brought together, and the facilitators asked for students' comments on the course. After that, they asked me to comment, and they then finished with a closing speech from one of the facilitators. In fact, a student had asked for my comments before the students expressed their ideas, but the facilitators said that it would be more appropriate for me to speak later so as not to prejudice the discussion with my viewpoint. So I had some warning and time to prepare what I would say.

The DVD was clearly designed to set the tone for the workshop. Produced in 2004 to celebrate twenty years of the recovery of the union, it put forward the closest ATE has to an official narrative. It described the experience of the 1976–83 dictatorship and the internal elections of 1984, as a small group of men in the ANUSATE list took on the union hierarchy who had been close to the military junta and won the elections against considerable odds to recover the union for democracy. The group discussions after the DVD centered on the question of the kind of union model that ATE and the CTA are constructing. Delegates in my group argued that the DVD had shown them the kinds of things that ATE was doing. One man said that there would be very few unions that could show a video like that and mobilize young people in a democratic and participatory way. A woman said that she came from a *familia luchadora* (activist family) and had found that ATE gave her an opening, a containment that enabled her to do something beneficial, but it was important to show work colleagues that as ATE delegates they were not wasting their time. At this point, the facilitator brought the discussion back to the nature of the union model and we moved to a general discussion of what that might be. This consisted of two linked threads: first, a positive discussion of ATE's "model," as a union with a particular *concepción de clase* (class theory), autonomous of political parties, that recovers what was the workers' movement in its earlier socialist and anarchist phases and that is internally democratic. The facilitator summed up our discussions of the two models as "horizontality versus verticalism."

The question of internal democracy was a particularly important theme for the participants and leads to the second thread of those initial discussions, a critique of "other unions," especially UPCN and SUTECBA. In the plenary, one delegate said that in her group's discussion they had decided that one of the best ways to help define ATE's union model was by defining "the other," that is, describing what ATE is not. They had focused on questions of autonomy from political parties and internal participation. In the general discussion, delegates argued that ATE does not have a "hegemonic position" or a line that is "sent down" (*bajado*) from the general secretary to the delegates and the workers but that it "awakens in the *compañero* the intent to participate." That awakening needed to happen because ATE was not about resolving problems but about a political position that was concerned with defending the workers. There was tension during the group work and the plenary as some participants wanted to enter into a broad debate about the role of the state, exploring a critique of its absence and what its new functions might be in a neoliberal era, while the facilitators wanted to keep the focus on the union model, especially because they were due to address the role of the state in a later module. However, they let the talk flow, interjecting when they felt they could draw it back to the topic at hand for that session.

When we moved in the afternoon to debating the role of the delegate, similar themes were repeated, and delegates pointed to questions of honesty and coherence and of the need to be an example of a new kind of unionism in their own personal action. It was important to them not to be like the classic image of unionists as corrupt, as *los gordos*, the fat ones (CGT unionists are known as *gordos* because they are seen as having enriched themselves through their union activity). As in interviews with me, delegates confirmed that ATE unionists had not enriched themselves, often telling the story with reference to key consumer items: for example, "no one has a house in a gated community; if they have cars, they are old." This is in accord with one of the facilitators' opening gambits at the beginning of the day, when she said that Andrés Rodríguez represents the oligarchy because he goes hunting and has a horse. She said, "Our leaders are not like that; they live in a workers' neighborhood—they have a dog maybe, but not a horse!"

The delegates were clearly concerned about the importance of encouraging workers to join them in ATE, and some were worried that work colleagues ask, "What does ATE give me?" Rather than directly address that concern, the workshop promoted the idea that ATE gives a political project, a "horizon" or place from which to struggle. It is not an entity that gives but something that corresponds to the workers by law but is their right; it struggles to recover what the "other union" had sold off. It was important to the participants that ATE "contains me; it listens to me" (*me contiene, me escucha*) and that for some, such as contracted workers, it was the only union that would affiliate them. But not all the delegates present were convinced that this would be enough to generate interest and commitment, especially when ATE asks them to go on so many marches.

ATE's political vision is very seductive, which was brought home to me in the talk given by Frondizi. Speaking without notes, he ranged from a historical perspective of constant class conflict to a personal appeal to the delegates to construct themselves as protagonists in a collective. This was very important to him, because, he said, contemporary society is so individualistic, and that makes a collective construction difficult. He argued that they should be patient and work out how to deal with any obstacles, but "for me, heroes are not individual, but collective."[6] He moved into giving advice, about how to act as a delegate. He suggested that they needed to contain (*contener*) their work colleagues, by which he referred to the therapeutic understanding I described earlier but extended it in a more political direction. For him, containment consisted of listening to work colleagues but also connecting their personal problems to wider structural issues. He warned delegates to take care of themselves as well so that they don't succumb to the difficulties of daily life and the struggle. In their daily work, he said, delegates should take note of silences in assemblies, participate in marches, and defend the CTA as a place of identity, a structure for the struggle. He referred to the collective bargaining agreement but said that legislation was less important than knowing how to interpret an assembly; and he gave advice on how to negotiate with functionaries from a position of strength. He put everything into a context of a long-term historical struggle: "History is the struggle of the people; we the workers are the motor of history. We have nothing to lose [because] the final objective is to break with capitalism." He was an immensely inspiring speaker: committed, with a clear political vision that seduced an audience ready to participate, and with the experience and aura of one who had been a unionist in the 1970s. This connection of militancy to the 1960s and early 1970s holds a powerful appeal for contemporary ATE delegates. There was a palpable buzz in the room as we finished the workshop for the day and went home, ready to return the following day for more sessions.

The second day of the workshop consisted of a module discussing conflict. We had been told that conflict was an everyday condition for ATE activists and workers more generally, and in the introductory session, one of the facilitators told us that specific workplace conflicts were "the moment of living militancy." This moment was a space "between rage and happiness," and, she said, "with this moment we make politics," which encapsulates the shared desire and fantasy in participation in a conflict and contrasts distinctly with UPCN's wish to avoid conflict through negotiation. She then moved into more practical aspects, which she listed in the following order on the whiteboard:

- what the chains of decision making are
- where they should place the drums [i.e., who should be disturbed by them]
- what the problem is
- what the strategy is
- how not to close all doors [including negotiation]
- how to communicate with ATE-Capital's central office, in advance and with suitable planning

The order in which she wrote these elements is revealing in its contrast with how UPCN organizes conflicts. It was quite clear both in the introductory session and in the group work that ATE's approach to conflict was very different from that of UPCN. The group sessions worked mostly as a means to discuss ongoing conflicts that delegates were experiencing, although the facilitators drew out general principles as the discussion progressed. Much of the discussion turned on the problems that delegates had in common with the structures of state employment, reductions in budgets, and so on. We developed a hypothetical conflict for the other commission to discuss and in the afternoon discussed the conflict that they had set us, which was about a municipal government making cuts to overtime payments.

During this session, the shared understanding was that a *junta interna* would manage the conflict on the basis of decisions made at assemblies. We debated various strategies, such as short stoppages, assemblies held at the door of the functionary's office, or an hour of drums per day, a tactic known as a *batucada*. We discussed principles of negotiation, such as not to go to the negotiations alone and to be sure to have the most complete information possible. We were also told to keep up the momentum of the conflict, not to let it "get cold," and to keep assemblies as part of a scale so that the conflict could be ramped up gradually. At each assembly it is important to give a date for the next one and to be able to move up the scale of protests—for example, from one hour's *batucada* to two. We were encouraged to keep a "back and forth" with ATE-Capital throughout the conflict and to provide support with press, posters, possibly also lawyers.

The discussion in the workshop was consistent with how I saw conflicts managed in day-to-day practice, for example, in the Colón Opera House and the Buenos Aires city accounts office (see Lazar 2016b for a discussion of the former). My ATE interviewees also tended to stress the idea that their central office should provide support for conflicts that are directed by local *juntas internas*. That support comes in a number of forms: a PA system for marches, posters, advice, and the convening of representatives of other *juntas internas* for particular demonstrations, of which there are usually many. Delegates are expected to attend both those demonstrations called by ATE-Capital and by the CTA and those called by local *juntas internas* or workplace assemblies, the latter in order to show solidarity and help pressure the employers. Frondizi was particularly concerned to emphasize the importance of this. In interviews, ATE delegates would describe this as the facilitator of the first day of the training did, an example of their horizontality in contrast to UPCN's verticalism. The organization of conflicts was one of the key aspects of horizontality for them, as was the assembly. Underpinning both is the ability for individuals within the union to profess and act on different viewpoints.

Both in the training sessions and in interviews and daily practice, ATE delegates placed a great deal of symbolic weight on the internal democracy of their organization. They contrasted this absolutely to UPCN and SUTECBA, and it was indeed one of the two most significant differences between the organizations that my ATE interlocutors highlighted. The second most significant for them was the way that UPCN and SUTECBA were seen to work with the employers rather than in favor of the workers and was understood as an outcome

of the first. It was crucial to ATE informants that ATE was not a verticalist organization, that there was a space for dissidence, dispute, and alternative perspectives, even though some criticized the heavily ANUSATE-inflected start to
the training workshop, and by extension the union hierarchy. Nonetheless, it
was very important to them that they could critique the dominant electoral list
within ATE (i.e., ANUSATE's candidates) and were not frozen out because they
did not share those political views. And the dissent expressed in the "compound
talk" of the cigarette breaks was ultimately part of the hegemonic vision of ATE
as an organization that could bear critique.

Still, ATE was attempting to build a political community in accord with
a vision of unionism that was in essence the vision closely associated with
ANUSATE, the project founded by Víctor de Gennaro and Germán Abdala to
first recover ATE and then build the CTA as an autonomous workers' central.
It is political community as political project, and many ATE activists were very
powerfully attached to that project. Their vision of militancy was one of an activist self in an activist political community that aimed to build a better society and
a more just state. In practice, the political community of ATE was much more
fractured than that of UPCN, a feature that UPCN unionists saw as a weakness. However, for ATE informants, that fracturing was precisely its strength because it was evidence of democratic debate and action. They were often therefore
highly critical of their leadership and the workshop itself during breaks and in
group work sessions. This was evidence for them of the value of democratic debate itself as a public good. That said, the image of fractious but democratic debate within ATE must sit alongside a recognition that ANUSATE, known now
as the "green list," had tended to win most key leadership positions in ATE very
comfortably since they recovered the union in the 1980s until September 2015,
when they lost ATE-Capital. Such powerful electoral hegemony cannot hurt.

By 2013, ATE was suffering from the effects of the CTA split into the Yasky
and Micheli factions, as some activists had left while others voiced criticism of
Micheli's politics. And the tensions within ATE, between pro-Kirchner groups
and those who wanted to be more autonomous, posed difficulties to me with
respect to gaining research access to ATE unionists. While I was conducting
fieldwork, ATE's strength tended to be concentrated in individual *juntas internas* rather than extended across the whole organization, even in the city of Buenos Aires. So, while once I had permission, I could gain access to UPCN spaces
that crossed the city and that held power over their component parts through
their strong organizational structure, ATE was much more fragmented. As a result I had to negotiate access multiple times with individuals and small groups,
who were often very open to granting me interviews and very willing to have

me accompany them in public campaigning events. In contrast, UPCN leaders assigned me to delegations that they were comfortable with me researching or spaces like the EFS that they considered to be appropriate for me.

PEDAGOGIES OF EXHORTATION

In addition to the promotion of two contrasting narratives of political community, the training processes I have described elicited—and attempted to elicit— particular kinds of subjectivities among the delegates present. The workshops and plenary sessions were spaces where the unions worked on individuals and got individuals to work on themselves to create an orientation toward the collective that put their union's vision of political community into practice. Thus, in this section an analysis of pedagogical style and experience complements my previous discussion of the content of both educational endeavors and explores the implications of the creation of particular individual dispositions for the construction of collective ethical political subjects.

This possibility of a collective subject is in tension with Foucault's work, which tends to imply an individual ethical subject who cultivates his or her self often in dialogue with another, such as a teacher, confessor, or recipient of letters. That other may be potential and not actual, such as God (in prayer) or oneself at a later point in one's life, but it is still primarily a dyadic relationship. Other discussions of ethical formation have kept a focus on the individual, even if it is the individual in relation to others. For example, Cheryl Mattingly (2014) uses the moving example of a woman who forms herself as the kind of mother who is fighting for her disabled son's ability to live a particular kind of life. Yet Mattingly does not explore how the mother might cultivate her son's self or make him into a particular kind of person.

Nonetheless, an ethical subject does not necessarily have to be individual, as Laidlaw acknowledges (2014: 105). Faubion (2011) described his relationships with his two principal informants as constituting an ethical system that makes them into a joint ethical subject that is greater than the sum of its parts. Naisargi Dave (2012) also shows the collective construction of a collective ethical subject in her account of the coming into being of a political community of queer activists in India. Without actually describing the groups of activists as collective ethical subjects, she does describe the activist construction of a community of like-minded women who become collectively able to enact the ethical practices she identifies as key. Maple Rasza (2015) also details the way that anarchist activists in Slovenia constructed themselves as an unruly collective subject greater than themselves through everyday and spectacular acts of political commitment. Webb Keane's discussion of Vietnamese communists' making of ethical subjects under Ho Chi Minh explores what he calls "the expansion of the moral circle and the fostering of an expanded sense of agency" to evoke a collective subject beyond the immediate circle of kin and village (2016: 228).

There remains a tension between the individual and collective, and a number of anthropologists working on matters of morality and ethics have critiqued approaches to ethics that rely conceptually on an individual subject (Fassin 2014; Englund 2008; Keane 2016). Fassin calls it "the autonomization of morality" and argues that it has contributed to "a form of depoliticisation" of anthropological studies of ethics (2014: 433). Because both ATE and UPCN were focused so strongly on the creation of collective subjects and their practices sought, often explicitly, to cultivate particular collectivities, it would make little sense ethnographically in this case to focus only on individual technologies of the self, even in relation to others. We need to shift our perspective and examine both the individual and the collective and the tension between them. This may help to "repoliticize" ethics.

This shift in methodological emphasis brings to the fore some important aspects of the role of education in ethical-political subjectivation in the two unions. Crucially, the mode of education was at least as important as the content transmitted, an insight about education more generally that comes from theories of critical pedagogy (Giroux 2005; see also Lazar 2010). Both courses were grounded in a practice of learning as exhortation: They sought to elicit particular orientations of self—of the individual in the political community—through exhorting people to recognize themselves as that person. In the EFS, this was especially evident with the repetition of the emphasis on the sense of vocation held by the attendant delegates, as plenary lecturers and facilitators repeatedly told the delegates that they had chosen this path because, for example, they wanted to change things or renounce individualism. Delegates were repeatedly enjoined to persist despite the negative perceptions of unionists and public employees and despite the outside perception of UPCN as a Menemist union and therefore traitor. One facilitator in a workshop said that the delegates have chosen to join UPCN, which meant that they carried a heavy "backpack" (*mochila*) of the union's history but could carry it with enormous pride.[7] She used the metaphor of the backpack a few times in the workshops and added at another point that they had chosen a place where they are very exposed, and they represent UPCN all the time. For example, she told us that a *compañera* had happened to change her car two weeks after she had been voted UPCN delegate, and immediately people had begun to talk, suspecting her of corruption linked to her union activity.

The ATE workshop similarly encouraged students to feel pride in what they were doing, to see themselves as honest participants in a historical struggle for the benefit of their class and their society. Frondizi in particular appealed directly to the members of the group, telling them, for example, that it was normal to be nervous but that being a delegate is a process of collective construction. He discussed the personal consequences of being a delegate: "You hear everything [*escuchas todo*], and you can take on a lot [*cargar*]," with all the stress of the struggle and personal problems of affiliates, so it is important to be able to set limits. He said, "I tell you this so that we can be introspective and think [*introjectimos* [sic] *y pensemos*], as the psychologists say." His use of the singular second-person verb form was a direct appeal to each person listening, but then he switched to the first-person plural and fell into psychological language. This way of understanding union action was quite common among my informants, from both UPCN and ATE, and draws on understandings of psychotherapy and psychoanalysis that are popular among *porteños*. He was implicitly speaking of the problem of containment as a therapeutic relationship between union delegate and affiliate (Lazar 2013). His reference to psychology points to an important aspect of how the unions envision their political community as a collection of individuals who are embedded in a collective self. That embedding is an active process of construction, as he said, rather than something that can be taken for granted. The process of construction and containment must take place within individuals, through reflection and conscious work.

Yet it can also be prompted, often by the rhetorical means of proclaiming what is already the case: we are committed to the struggle; "ATE contains me, listens to me"; we are better than the other unions. In both ATE and UPCN spaces, the teachers were seeking to elicit particular orientations, values, and beliefs mostly through repeating them, albeit in a way that assumed that they were preaching to the converted. This is an interesting move both pedagogically and in terms of the theory of the self that it implies. Pedagogically, the important point is that the teachers do not assume a "banking" model of empty students needing to be filled with knowledge—rather, they are adults who have particular predispositions and can be molded to a certain extent, but mostly enjoined to take pride in their decisions and to keep strong in their beliefs. They are being "socialized," as Felipe Carillo said. That socialization happens through repetition of what should be (the individual with a particular orientation) as if it already were (you have a vocation; you have made this decision).

With respect to a theory of the self that we might identify, it is notable that the union training uses the basis that the particular orientations of self discussed previously can be elicited through exhortation. Delegates are not understood to have a core, true self that needs revealing or that cannot change. Rather, their sense of self as political actor can be constructed through the formal processes of teaching in lectures and workshops by repeating to them how they already are. They both are and can be created through repeated enunciation; essence is both there and mutable, cultivatable. In a further layer of representation-as-creation, these selves were then enunciated to me in the form of an interview. A cynical perspective might see the whole process as merely a charade, interviewees simply providing me with the narrative they thought I should hear. However, failing to take their pronouncements seriously does my informants a disservice. Instead, we should recognize that unionists do not necessarily live up to the representation of self they produce in formal training venues or research encounters but that the representation itself is an important aspect of an elicitation or cultivation of the kinds of selves they aspire to and achieve much of the time. That means that "compound talk" against the grain was actually mostly eliminated from the educational space, but took place more often, if at all, in discussions about the training on the way back to the delegation office, or once back there. Where they talked about the training, usually I heard people say that they thought it was very helpful, and if they criticized, they would criticize specific participants or matters of fact, but very rarely the facilitators. Dissent would rarely be made explicit and instead would show up in simply not following the exhortation to be that particular kind of self. There just was general agreement on some goods—specifically, for UPCN negotiation, for ATE contestation. But I came to realize that the reason for this is that those goods are so determining of the organization; it is those qualities that attract their activists. So those who disagree do not join, much less sign up for a training course. Those who do decide to be elected as a union delegate and then attend training were predisposed to go along with its content, at least while the course was under way.

This practice of cultivating the self through repeated verbal representation is in part influenced by the dominance of psychotherapeutic language and practices in Buenos Aires. For example, in the EFS, some of this elicitation took the form of specific exercises seeking to draw out orientations understood to be internal; delegates were expected to work on their selves as part of the workshops. In an early workshop delegates were given an exercise to work out their own personal strengths, opportunities, weaknesses, and threats—an exercise known as the FODA (Fortalezas, Oportunidades, Debilidades, Amenazas; Strengths, Opportunities, Weaknesses, Threats) matrix. They were then supposed to measure those characteristics against their view of what an ideal delegate would be. In a further version of that exercise, they were asked to think through the following five points:

1. What are my virtues?
2. What are my defects?
3. As a union delegate, name two or three opportunities that you consider as such.
4. As a union delegate, name two or three questions that could be considered as threats.
5. Keeping in mind the self-examination (*auto-examen*) that took place in your answers to questions 1 and 2, what should be the profile of a delegate?

This is a formal version of the process of *askesis* identified by Foucault as crucial to self-cultivation in the ancient world and discussed at length by Faubion (2011).

They were also given a set of questions to answer, which measured their knowledge of their local delegation and UPCN more broadly and included questions on matters such as the numbers of affiliates in a given delegation, the name of the equal opportunities secretary there, and details about UPCN's structure. The point was for the delegates to find out the information by the end of the course if they did not already know it. Delegates also needed to absorb knowledge of the key legislation that UPCN considered to be crucial for their action as a unionist. The most important of these according to the workshop facilitators were the law of collective bargaining in the public sector (Ley 24.185, 1992) and in the private sector (Ley 14.250, 1988), the law of educational leave for workers (Ley 25.165, 1999), the law that regulates trade unions (Ley 23.551, 1988), and the decree establishing the *convenio colectivo* for SINEP (Decreto 214/2006).

Some knowledge was therefore important as content that could be transmitted to students, but in addition the presentation of knowledge was part of the process of eliciting particular kinds of selves because knowledge is something that not only can be known but can be *asumido*. *Asumir* does not mean "assume," in the English sense of knowledge that is assumed to be the case without needing to be questioned. In part because it is a transitive verb, it has a more active meaning, such as "to take on" or "take responsibility for." It is an important descriptor of how the union and the delegates create political selves: the delegates assume in an active sense a particular kind of selfhood as they continue to be activists and go through the educational experience. That is, that they take on or internalize this version of their self, changing themselves in the process; to speak metaphorically, it is a kind of clothing that can become the person. This assumption of self is not a one-off event but ongoing, and it can be generated or sped up through exhortation. We might call it a process of "exhortative creation," one that was directed to creating distinctive forms of both self and political community. UPCN delegates were exhorted to create themselves as committed, loyal unionists who understood their place in the organic whole and submitted to the verticalist discipline, while ATE delegates were encouraged to be political activists with class consciousness and a commitment to combative action and their vision of a better society.

CONCLUSION

UPCN and ATE have, therefore, two different projects of collective subjectivation or political community: for UPCN, one that is organic and verticalist; for ATE, activist and horizontal. Both are collective projects that require distinct orientations of self to the collectivity. The differences between the two are revealed both in the values they profess and cultivate among their members (the hexis they seek to construct) and in their contrasting organizational praxis, where praxis refers to explicitly theorized action with a view to transforming the world. The latter is articulated in contrasting terms of verticality and horizontality, which thus become metonyms for the political, a particular matrix of relations between values, philosophy (both organizational and political), practice, and self. This is ethical-political subjectivation in one of its more formal enactments: education or training as containment in the sense of group encompassment of the individual. The training consists of ongoing attempts to elicit particular dispositions, which are subject to questioning or lack of engagement on the part of their subjects but which are also remarkable in their coherence as a hegemonic project in both organizations.

The cultivation of specific values among individual delegates links back to the previous discussions, as educators seek to bring out the same set of values that people explained to me in interviews as part of their character and the reasons for their militancy and that they reproduced as ideals to aim toward in day-to-day conversations. Thus, my interlocutors told me of their sense of vocation, passion, commitment, rage against injustice, and so on, and educators sought in their pedagogical practice to draw out those values in the delegates attending the sessions. In part they did so by stating that it is already there, as in phrases such as "you are here because you have a vocation for service." This is a particular mode of hexis, an exhortatory mode, where values and dispositions are elicited from the delegates through a pedagogical relationship with tutors and union leaders, most prominently by asserting that these dispositions already exist internally among the delegates. In these spaces (and times), essence and hexis form a dialectical relationship with each other, and they both take place in and through the collective.

5   CONTAINMENT AS CARE

My emphasis on the collective continues, but the focus shifts to the union as collective subject in everyday life through containment. Containment is both a therapeutic practice of containment through counseling, derived from Kleinian psychoanalytical practice, and a kind of encompassment of the individual by the group, often described through the verb form (*me contiene*—[the union] contains me, *me siento contenido*—I feel contained). Thus, it names a complex of union activity that is also an idiom of political community and a means of collective ethical-political subjectivation. Here I examine practices of containment particularly characteristic of UPCN and later explore two practices of containment that are especially (but not exclusively) associated with ATE, the assembly and the street protest.

Previously I described quite formal processes of building political communities. Here I show that the union also comes into being as collective ethical subject through practices of kinning, which include commensality, sociability, ritual action, care, and problem solving. The union delegation works in the interplay between personal interactions and the actualization of the fluid structures that organize state employment. These are both formal and informal, to be found in the collective bargaining agreement and in kinship and friendship networks of recruitment and union activism, as I illustrate through the case of one UPCN delegation. Encompassment in these networks or frameworks is not automatic but entails work on several levels, from informal and formal negotiations over specific problems to the affirmation of union presence and strength through visual and ritual means. Importantly, this is underpinned by forming relations within the delegation and the workplace through the sociality of both special events and the everyday.

THE MINISTRY DELEGATIONS

Much of the ethnographic description in this chapter draws on a period of field-work with the UPCN delegation of a central ministry in late 2012. I was sent there by leaders of the Capital Section because they considered it to be a large and well-functioning delegation. For obvious reasons, they did not want me to spend time with a conflictual or ineffectual delegation, and Felipe Carrillo in particular wanted me to go to a delegation of substantial size, mostly because he thought it would be more interesting and varied for me. Of those he suggested, I chose that particular ministry because I thought that I would find it easier to understand its institutional structure than those of the two social services agencies he recommended, which do not have a direct equivalent in the United Kingdom.

Two delegations operate in the central ministry building: the delegation that serves the workers in the building itself, who are the administrative workers for the ministry; and the delegation for the whole ministerial structure. I spent most of my time with that delegation, whose office is on the tenth floor of the build-ing and is a complex of three rooms: an entrance corridor with a couple of desks where people sit and answer the phone or deal with initial queries, the office of the general secretary, and a back room with a large table and two desks with computers. Once the Capital Section had sent me to the ministry and the gen-eral secretary of that delegation had met me, he and another two leaders took me around the building, introducing me to some of the office workers. They then al-lowed me to come to the delegation offices in the afternoons, which was when they tended to arrive themselves. I mostly sat at the large table in the back room and drank coffee, soda, or mate with them while listening to their discussions, following the often impassioned and always multivocal and overlapping debates, and responding to their questions about me, my research, British politics, the Malvinas, and the weather. Sometimes I asked for clarification when I lost the thread of the discussion because they had used names of people I did not know or used slang with which I was unfamiliar. We often watched TV and joked to-gether, and from time to time the leaders took me to other ministry buildings to meet people there and find out what they did or to events like ceremonies and lunches. When people wanted to discuss something out of general hearing, they went into private offices; and by the end of my stay, the two or three times that there was something they thought that I should not write about, they told me to hold it "in reserve" (*en reserva*). They were on the whole very willing to explain their work to me and very keen that I understand as well as possible even some of the more arcane parts of their employment structure in the ministry and the is-sues they dealt with on a daily basis.

Not everyone is in the tenth-floor office for the whole day, as many have their own institutional delegations to manage as well. While I was there, three peo-ple worked there regularly, answering queries and dealing with different aspects of administration. One young woman acted mostly as a receptionist. She was transferred to the union office after having had problems at her previous job in the ministry. She was often accompanied in the office by Diego, who was once a goalkeeper for the Argentine national team.[1] Diego told me he was known as the "demon of Berisso" in his day. He spent the day gathering forms that peo-ple brought him and that needed to be filled out properly and taken to the office of the health insurance company. His knees and hips were no longer in a great state, so walking was difficult for him, but nonetheless, once a day, he would usu-ally go over to the health insurance or Capital Section office to hand in the forms on behalf of the affiliates. Tufo was also there, usually in the mornings. He took care of administrative matters, such as filling out forms to claim expenses for travel on union business.

The members of the delegation who dealt with more political business would come in as the day progressed, arriving around lunchtime. The active leaders of the delegation are flamboyant characters, although they probably would not ap-prove of that particular adjective. Lionel is the general secretary, and he is a very jovial, expansive person, passionate and very knowledgeable about Argentine politics and history. He teases everyone, argues and jokes nearly all the time. Martín and Carlos are his deputies. Martín was the general secretary of one of the main institutes of the ministry, and Carlos is his adjunct secretary. They are both large, twinkly men. Martín is a Radical—early on, he told me with a wink that I should include him in my writing to show that UPCN is not solely made up of Peronists. Carlos appears at first to be quiet and unassuming but has a steely character. Fernando and Sergio are in their early to mid-forties. Fernando comes from a different institution within the ministry. He enjoys photography and of-ten travels around to ministry institutions in the interior of the country. Sergio is a committed and thoughtful man who puts in a lot of legwork at the ministry building itself. He gets teased for coming from a poor background, but the rib-bing does not bother him, not least because he knows that he has done remark-ably well for himself. The teasing is also recognition that the others know this, too. Juanito is a former general secretary who also works very hard at the day-to-day business of negotiation, problem resolution, and so on and combines that with a keen sense of irony. He is immensely knowledgeable and experienced, has a great understanding of realpolitik, and smiles nearly all the time. Once, when Lionel chided the young receptionist for wearing a skirt that was too short for someone who attends people, Juanito deliberately came in the next day wearing shorts, undoubtedly to provoke Lionel. Pablo, an older man and very committed Peronist, is often to be found quietly surveying the conversation and accepting the jokes thrown his way with a smile. He was pretty much the only regular occupant of the office who still smoked, the others having given up a few months before I arrived.

Fabiana was responsible for Acción Social (Social Activities), in particular for signing people up for the kids' summer camp. She tended to come to the tenth floor toward the end of the afternoon when she had finished at the fifth floor. She laughs easily and happily participates in the risqué jokes and discussions— once Lionel explained to me (and to much hilarity) that she was a "man-woman," and that's why it was okay to tell sexist jokes in her presence. Florencia has a degree in psychology and was the representative for training, responsible for organizing attendance at the EFS. She has strong opinions and is happy to express them. Mercedes has a background in social work and a son who is a delegate at another institution within the ministry. She is petite and kind. Vanesa works mostly at a local delegation but often comes over to the tenth floor once she has finished there for the day. She has a very close friendship with Lionel and from time to time runs errands for him, such as standing in line at the bank to pay his monthly taxes and utility bills.

Delegates come and go from the tenth-floor office: for example, to recount some problem in their workplace, relay concerns of or gossip about their colleagues, or ask for a signature on a form that gives them leave of absence for union duties. The composition of the group around the big table at the back changes constantly. Cell phones ring all the time. Small groups go off to Lionel's room or to other less public parts of the office to have private conversations. People grab each other to go meet with colleagues or their bosses; and when they return, they tell the room how the meeting went. As the day goes on and work gradually stops, the table becomes a companionable social space: cards may come out, or the TV gets switched on; the mate gourd is filled and passed round, and people enjoy refreshments. The joking, debates, and gossiping get louder and more intense as passions rise and subside as people gradually peel away as the time comes for them to go home. A small group stays until around 8:00 p.m. most days.

The fifth floor has a different feel and is more a space where members of the delegation attend to their affiliates rather than discuss matters with other delegates. In something of a contrast to the tenth floor, it was more often a place of administration than a hotbed of political activity and debate—although neither was exclusively one or the other. The fifth-floor office is one large room with a picture of Evita on the wall over a whiteboard that announces news and keeps a tally of numbers of affiliates. There are two desks, each with a computer, and at least one person is at one of the desks from quite early in the morning until about 5:00 p.m. They attend to affiliates who bring forms for the health insurance plan or to register their children for the summer camp. From time to time, people gather to talk politics and prepare posters and events. Each time I went to either floor, someone offered me a coffee, until I got used to helping myself. People were often a little bemused at my desire to spend some time there but were unfailingly friendly and welcoming. They would ask me about British politics, or we would talk about the weather, the air conditioning, current events, or our families. The union delegation was a space both of political activism and of quotidian administration.

CONTAINMENT

In addition to being a space of administrative and political work, the delegation was also a space of containment.[2] The concept "containment" appeared in multiple contexts in my fieldwork, from informal conversations to interviews, when we were discussing the role of the union delegate, but also with respect to the relationship between individual affiliates and their union. The word is used to describe both political membership of the community of the trade union and an important activity of political leadership. That is, individuals can be contained by the group, which provides a "place of containment" (*lugar de contención*), a context for self-realization and political action. But containment also names an active form of leadership, most particularly in the way that unionist leaders contain others through therapeutic relationships. With respect to the former, a UPCN delegate who wanted to remain anonymous told me in 2009 about the sense of protection, family, and personal support provided by being an active member of the trade union:

> UPCN gave me identity, I feel part of UPCN, I don't feel alone; whatever happens, I'm from UPCN. And UPCN is everywhere, it's going to protect me, it helps me with my children in school, it gives me a summer camp [for the children], it gives me social coverage. . . . UPCN gave me identity—wherever I am, or if there is a demonstration and although people come from other ministries, we're all from UPCN, and that's fantastic. UPCN embraced me [*me abrazó*], and it's a paternalistic figure.

To me, UPCN gave me an identity that I needed and an embrace that I lost when I moved to Buenos Aires city, when I left the party, and UPCN gave me this Peronist identity that encompasses me [*que me abraza*]. I feel contained [*contenido*]; it gave me identity. I am from UPCN. . . .

I'm part of UPCN; I'm part of an organization in an individualistic society. . . . UPCN gave me a place where we're all equal, where it gives me everything that I need, or they give me everything they can give, and they protect me. That's what UPCN gives me.

UPCN is like my family. I have my wife, but UPCN is also my family. . . . Perhaps it's difficult to explain with words, but UPCN is like a feeling [*un sentimiento*];[3] we're part of something. I'm not alone in the street or at work; UPCN is always there with me.

Note his phrase "I feel contained." Quite often I was told that part of the job of a delegate was to "contain" (*contener*) the affiliate or that "there's a lot of containment" (*hay mucha contención*). Containment was not the only mode of relationship between delegate and affiliate, but the *claim* by some activists that it was such an important aspect of their job and experience makes it deserve some scrutiny.

There are several dimensions to containment in everyday talk of union activists, two of which I discuss.[4] First, containment refers to the therapeutic practice of containment conceptualized by Wilfred Bion (Douglas 2007; Hinshelwood 1989; Bion 1959). Freudian psychoanalysis has been popular in Argentina since the 1950s,[5] and British Kleinian theories were the most influential in Argentina until Lacanians began to dominate in the 1970s (Plotkin 2001). So it is plausible that the notion of containment traveled from Britain to Argentina and entered into everyday speech through the influence of Kleinian psychoanalysts in Argentine society, which is quite a good indication of the general popularization of psychoanalysis in Argentina, as described in detail by Mariano Ben Plotkin (2003). The therapeutic ability to contain the person with a problem, meaning to be able to process the person's "emotional communication" (Douglas 2007: 33) without being overwhelmed by it, was part of an understanding of containment among middle-class residents of Buenos Aires, and some of my interlocutors spoke of containment in very similar terms. For example, Ariel Negrete, general secretary of the ANSES delegation, told me,

About containment, well the worker seeks out the union delegate not just for union problems. He or she has a problem and goes to talk to the union delegate, and the first thing the delegate does is listen to all the comrades. And . . . what we do is contain from that place [*contener desde ese lugar*], listen. . . . People have to go to someone who helps them rethink, recapacitate themselves; and well, we do that task, and we do it a lot.

Informants also used the term just in passing, when referring for example to delegates' abilities to deal with affiliates' problems, using phrases such as *capacidad de contención* (capacity for containment).

My informants also often simply called the union a *lugar de contención* (place of containment) and used containment to talk about a kind of group encompassment of an individual. Thus, the term has gained extra layers of meaning, specifically being extended from an understanding of a kind of therapeutic practice to a politicized notion of group belonging, the second meaning of containment I discuss here. This refers to the way that the union offers delegates a kind of context, both in the sense of a political context and as a space of protection and for self-actualization. ATE is particularly associated with the former and UPCN with the latter, but both unions do both kinds of containment. Containment thus involves not only a therapeutic effort but also one of political encompassment: giving people something to belong to as a means of creating a better society. Within the unions, that aspect of containment is practiced in a variety of ways: for ATE in particular, delegates enact their belonging through political activity such as meetings, demonstrations, and political discussions in the union office over mate and cigarettes.

UPCN delegates also participate in such explicitly political activities as street demonstrations and other mobilizations, although at nothing like the frequency of ATE. But they complement their political activities with a wide range of organizational activities revolving around encompassment as the provision of a space of protection and for self-actualization. They have a significant program of professional training in public administration; they hold regular meetings of the delegates responsible for equality of opportunities, youth, culture, and so on; and they promote cultural activities, such as photography or creative writing competitions. They have a stand at the annual Buenos Aires book fair, where they hold debates and presentations. My interlocutors were very proud of these last two activities. Particularly active UPCN delegations also hold events at their place of work, for example, to celebrate International Women's Day or the Day of the Activist. Some produce material and give advice for the workers on their office on a wide range of topics outside the progress of political actions or collective bargaining, such as workplace bullying (*violencia laboral*), preventive health, or swine flu.

A major practice of encompassment was enacted through care, in particular, care for the health of individual affiliates. As Lionel pointed out in a workshop

I organized at UPCN to discuss my research findings, this is consonant with unions' very early roots in the mutual organizations for immigrant workers established in the mid-nineteenth century. These mutual assistance societies were set up to pool resources by means of a monthly quota to assist members who were suffering difficulties such as illness, unemployment, or the death of a family member. They were organized by groups of immigrants or workers, unions, firms, political groups such as the socialists, and the Catholic Church (Senén González and Bosoer 2012: 35, 36). Today, UPCN is especially proud of the fact that it controls the health insurance system for civil service workers, Union Personal. UP is widely considered to be a very effective health insurance—unlike some of those controlled by other unions—and it is open to all civil servants, whether affiliated with UPCN or not. One delegate told me that the health insurance was "an important source of containment." It is also a key means by which the union makes social citizenship substantive for its affiliates and for the workers in its sector, since it is the mechanism by which the union delivers the social right to health care. Delegates often saw one of their most important services to their affiliates as providing support and advice in managing the health-care system: they would help affiliates through bureaucratic procedures such as the authorization of a particular operation and maintenance of telephone clinics to make appointments or check whether test results were back. One of the most common reasons for people to come to the delegation offices is to process their *chequeras*. The *chequera* is a piece of paper that confers an extra 20 percent discount on the cost of medication when presented to the pharmacy with the prescription. It is available only to UPCN affiliates and grants a discount in addition to the discount they get from being a member of UP.[6] Affiliates buy *chequeras* in groups of six, and the application to purchase a group of *chequeras* must be accompanied with copies of other identification documents proving their eligibility. They can go to the Capital Section office themselves, but the ministry delegation will also collect up a pile of applications each day, which Diego then takes to the office. He returns with the *chequeras*, and people come to the delegation office to pick them up.

Sometimes the union delegation takes on wider responsibilities associated with the health of workers; for example, one delegate told me that he joined UPCN because when his baby daughter fell very seriously ill, it was only the UPCN activists who took care of him, even though he was not an affiliate at the time. They arranged for hospital treatment and ensured that he was granted paid leave from work to be with his daughter in the hospital. The concern was not merely logistical though: on a quotidian basis, the delegation members I knew often concerned themselves with each other's health. For example, one day the office was buzzing with the news that a friend had had a heart attack the day before, and another person's baby was affected by hydroencephaly, but they had been able to arrange for treatment through UP.

UPCN also has a well-developed range of subsidies (*subsidios*) for affiliates, which are gifts, mostly of a stay in a hotel, that mark particular life events, from the birth of a child to weddings, wedding anniversaries, and death of an affiliate. UPCN also negotiates discounts with travel agents, kindergartens, and other medical services; it provides school materials for preschool and primary school children each year; it also has three recreational facilities for its affiliates.[7] One of the day-to-day activities of the delegate in charge of Acción Social is to assist affiliates in applying for these gifts and benefits, although in that particular ministry they are not able to help with vacations and death gifts and must send affiliates to the Capital Section office.

But what Fabiana spent a lot of her time doing in the final weeks of 2012 was organizing registration for the children's *colonia de vacaciones* (summer camp) for the following January and February. Located at Ezeiza, the camp is available to all UPCN affiliates and is much cheaper than commercial summer camps. Included in the cost is a bus from near the affiliate's house at 8:00 a.m. on the days the child is registered, which returns the child at around 6:00 p.m.; clothing and the relevant equipment; and teachers to supervise the activities. To administer the registration process in the ministry building, Fabiana had first to collect the names of people who wanted to preregister their children for the upcoming camp and take them to the Capital Section office. Then her responsibility shifted to collating all the necessary documents for registration from each of those who had signed up. In the past, individuals had had to go to the Capital Section office to sign up their children for the camp, and I was told that they would have to queue from 3:30 a.m. until the office opened at 5:00 a.m. Nowadays, the delegation official (Fabiana) makes an appointment to take the group of registration forms and payment, and they are returned to the parents with the receipt and their documents.

Registration of affiliates for these benefits is one of the most important administrative jobs of the delegation and one of their most tangible activities. ATE also has a program of Acción Social, including discounts, other benefits, and a children's summer camp, but not health care. It is administered from the central office of ATE-Capital, not by local delegations. In the ministry, the local UPCN delegation office acts as broker for the union, meaning that individuals do not need to take time off work to go to the union or the health insurance office to gain access to their social benefits, nor do they have to queue from early in the day. The delegation is an intermediary between affiliate and union, and through these practices, UPCN makes real the social rights encapsulated in union-controlled systems of health insurance and other welfare provision, especially child care. It thus makes its affiliates' social citizenship substantive, or at least it does so for those affiliates prepared to come to the union to request assistance. Union provision of social citizenship was more extensive in the past, when unions not only controlled health insurance, child care, and discount schemes as UPCN does today but also provided vacations and even sometimes housing. Nonetheless, today a big part of the delegates' job is to help affiliates access care and benefits by assisting them administratively. This is a kind of containment or group encompassment through care, enacted through the position of broker between affiliate and the union.

BROKERAGE BETWEEN EMPLOYEE AND EMPLOYER

For many formal-sector workers the union can have a great deal of influence over the lives of its members beyond the benefits that it administers, most obviously through control over the conditions of working life. The unions, UPCN especially, have historically played a central role in how state employment is structured, and how workers are contained within that structure. During the 1990s, UPCN even co-designed the Argentine state's structural adjustment.

Today, it continues to shape the state but in more localized ways. It does so from the position of intermediary between workers (or affiliates) and their bosses, known as the "functionary." The functionary is the occupant of a position of leadership of the civil servants within a ministry, just below the level of the minister and his or her deputy. Many of the delegation's brokerage activities are institutionalized in the form of the processes of collective bargaining, which was extended to the public sector only relatively recently, after legislation passed in 1992. In the private sector, collective bargaining has taken place at least since the labor code was incorporated into the 1949 constitution and continued despite successive military constitutional suspensions. The constitutionalization of labor law is important for preserving worker power with respect to employers and union strength in negotiations, as it sets some lower limits (e.g., on hours, holidays, right to representation). It has some downsides in potentially putting limits on negotiation, but in any case the application of the parts of the code has varied according to the regime in power (Cardoso and Gindlin 2009). Collective bargaining takes place usually at industry level, and there is a monopoly on union representation by economic sector or industry in the private sector; that is, only one union can officially represent workers of a given sector—such as metalworkers, truck drivers, bank workers, or transport workers. Agreements negotiated with the truck drivers' union apply to all truck drivers, and workers who are not members of the union are all subject to the collective agreements, or covenants as the industrywide ones are known. The strict monopoly of representation does not apply to public-sector workers, as both ATE and UPCN have *personeria gremial*, the official status that allows them to participate in collective bargaining. In both the public and private sectors, norms that are established by high-level industry negotiations cannot be derogated by local agreements, and collective agreements remain in force until they are renegotiated, even if they have nominally expired (Cardoso and Gindin 2009).[8] ATE withdrew from the negotiations for the first national administration (civil service) collective agreement in 1998 but joined in for the second covenant of 2006, which is the one in force today. For UPCN, collective bargaining is a central achievement of the last two decades. Many UPCN delegates told me proudly that in 2005 they had held a mass demonstration (thirty thousand people) to demand the return of collective bargaining, and Néstor Kirchner was forced to respond.

The collective bargaining agreement was enacted through discussions between the employer and representatives of UPCN and ATE in commissions known as *paritarias*. They cover four broad sets of issues: environmental conditions (CYMAT), equality of opportunity and treatment (CIOT), professional training and capacity building (FOPECAP), and COPIC, which interprets the collective bargaining structure and negotiates salaries.[9] The first two operate at both central and local levels, while the second two operate only at a central level. Not all ministries have well-developed local *paritaria* commissions, but where they do, they discuss local questions and can take issues higher to the central commission if necessary. The commissions discuss questions of sexual harassment, violence at work, bullying, and so on (CIOT); the condition of the work environment, such as matters of refurbishment to offices, repairs to elevators, and air conditioning (CYMAT); the allocation of scholarships for further study and professional training (FOPECAP); and salaries (COPIC). The COPIC *paritaria* applies across the system covered by the SINEP agreement. This *paritaria* was the one that was most opaque to me, unsurprisingly. Although there are official meetings, much discussion is informal, and it is a sensitive matter that outsiders are not welcome to scrutinize. Most people think that agreements to increase salaries were actually negotiated personally between Andrés Rodríguez and President Fernández de Kirchner, by cell phone. I have no way of verifying this, but Rodríguez did appear to have a good personal relationship with Cristina.

Some of the *paritarias* cover areas of employment law that in other legal systems might be covered by the judiciary. For example, CIOT hears cases that might in the United Kingdom be heard by equal opportunities commissions or employment tribunals; some of the CYMAT discussions might cover questions that would come under health and safety legislation. But both commissions also conduct educational and awareness-raising activities, with CIOT being particularly active in this regard. The presence of the union representatives as well as the representatives of the *estado empleador* (the state as employer) means that the unions have considerable say in the development of employment conditions—even, to an extent, the development of employment law, such as case law on harassment and bullying at work. The number of representatives is carefully protected: the state has three representatives, UPCN sends two, and ATE sends one. This particular proportion relates to a count conducted in the 1990s that determined that UPCN had around 75 percent of the union affiliation among those in the national administration subject to the covenant, with ATE holding nearly all the rest. Needless to say, ATE frequently questions that count nowadays and argues that it should have greater representation on *paritarias*. UPCN delegates on the whole are very proud of their majoritarian status and assert it repeatedly, with a common phrase pointing to their sense of having "the responsibility of being the majority union." One of the points of contestation that arises from this is that the unions, UPCN in particular, not only represent employees but also administer them, often on behalf of the employer. This is what ATE argues about UPCN—that the employers in fact have five representatives at the *paritaria*, while they as the truly representative union have only one delegate.

The role of the union in administering the workers is not confined to the *paritaria* and happens in multiple interactional spaces, but even some of the less institutionalized spaces for negotiation are shaped by the broader collective bargaining agreement. One example that illustrates informal brokerage actions is a case of employment contracts that arose while I was accompanying the ministry UPCN delegation. It could have become a point of conflict between labor and management (and ATE sought to make it so), but the UPCN delegation successfully negotiated that possibility away, by—in their eyes—resolving the situation.

Problems with employment contracts are particularly acute toward the end of the calendar year, as budgets need to be spent before the slate is wiped clean at the beginning of January, and most temporary contracts come up for renewal at that time. This matters because in a number of institutions people are not paid from when their contract terminates in December to the signing off of the renewal, which can be as late as March the following year. This saves money but leaves people feeling very insecure. Practice in the different parts of the ministry varied: at some of the well-organized and smaller institutions, I was told that the union ensured sign-off of contract renewals in early January each year.

One afternoon, a UPCN delegate came to the main delegation office and explained that a group of ministry drivers had raised some concerns with him. They were employed on temporary contracts, in a form known as *pasantía universitaria*, designed to enable people to be employed temporarily through subcontracting with universities for a specific project. Everyone at the delegation agreed that this was a highly precarious form of employment—*totalmente en negro* (completely in the black, meaning informal),[10] as one leader said to me. (He thought that probably 20 percent were contracts with university students and the rest were contracts that had gone to *conocidos*, friends and relatives of the bosses or the union, in his ministry and across the state administration.) The drivers in question were most concerned that their contract might not be renewed for the following year, but they also had complaints about work conditions, including the payment of their daily allowances for long trips and uncertainty about paying for fuel. They did not have insurance for workplace injuries and thought that one driver in particular would not have his contract renewed. ATE had picked up on their discontent and was preparing to organize an assembly and other protest measures to demand better working conditions and to protest against the precarity of their contracts. This galvanized the UPCN delegation to find out more about the complaints and to convene a meeting with the drivers for the day before ATE's assembly. They did so even though they were not, strictly speaking, supposed to represent workers on these kinds of temporary contracts, since they did not fall under the collective bargaining agreement so did not pay union dues and therefore could not even really be members of UPCN.

A week later, ATE scheduled a *batucada* to protest the situation of the university-contracted workers. The day before at the UPCN office I found Lionel discussing the drivers' complaints with their (UPCN) delegate, asking whether the one who was in danger of being fired had done anything to deserve it and clarifying what the problems were. Sergio was also present and rang the functionary in charge. When she answered, he passed the phone to Lionel, who said he would like to talk, so she invited him to come to the office straightaway. He told her he would be there in five minutes and then waited considerably longer for Sergio to finish what he was doing and for another leader (Juanito) to arrive at the building so they could go together. Meanwhile, he read through the list of complaints. After the meeting they returned and filled us in on what had happened. The functionary was, it turned out, "one of us," a UPCN affiliate. She had told them that the drivers did in fact have workplace insurance, all the contracted workers did, and that the question of daily allowances was up to the university that was officially their contractor, so there was little anyone could do about it either in the ministry or the delegation. Here, Lionel said, "What am I going to do, go to the rector of the university? Why are we defending these guys? If they aren't our affiliates and she [the functionary] is?" She had teased Lionel that she was an affiliate and he had not defended her in a previous case, yet now he was coming to her to defend others. Regarding the individual at risk of firing, she would check the situation by speaking to his boss. However, and most important, she had assured them that the contracts would be renewed; there was not a problem with anyone on that front. For Lionel, this was an acceptable resolution.

This example illustrates two points. First, the apparent simplicity and neatness of the system as contained in the collective bargaining agreement obscure the messiness of how state employment has actually evolved over the years. One of the leaders of the ministry delegation spent two afternoons taking me through the structure designed in 2000 and 2006. In theory, the SINEP system has six job categories (A–F), each of which has eleven wage points within it, numbered 0–10. A person may be hired, say, at D3, and over time would move up every two or three years through D4, D5, and so on until reaching D10, with a gradual pay increase. It also is possible to get 25 percent extra pay by finishing a university degree or some other form of tertiary education. Each year, the boss evaluates the individual's work and gives a mark of "Regular," "Bueno," "Destacado," or "Muy Destacado." To move up through the pay scales, the employee needs at least "Bueno" in the evaluations and is rewarded an extra month's pay with an evaluation of "Muy Destacado."

In practice, this has never reflected the reality of state employment, even in an institution like this ministry that has a very effective union delegation overseeing the implementation of the collective bargaining agreement. One issue is that a flattening out of people's official pay grade has gradually emerged, because promotion from the top of one grade to the bottom of another (e.g., from D10 to C0) is not possible without a *vacante* becoming officially available. A *vacante* is the name for a new position that has become available in the ministerial structure and that should be filled by competition on the basis of merit. However, the filling of *vacantes* had been frozen since 1997 as part of the restructuring of the Argentine state under Menem, a process that meant that whenever somebody retired from an administrative position or left to go to another job, the vacant position was not officially filled. The freezing of the *vacantes* had begun to thaw across the national administration from around 2009 but was proceeding at too slow a pace to significantly regularize the structure of employment. According to UPCN, by 2012 there were officially 411 *vacantes* in the ministry. For the UPCN delegates and for many of the employees themselves, the people most deserving of taking up *vacantes* in the *planta permanente* (under terms of permanent employment with full labor rights) should be those working either as contractors or in the *planta transitoria* (transitional employment regime under which regime workers have all the rights of permanent employees but on a fixed-term contract). The competition was really, as Juanito said, only to filter out the "donkeys." As far as the delegates were concerned, the number of *vacantes* should then correspond to the number of workers in the ministry on temporary contracts. That was around 1,500, they thought, so 411 was a woeful underestimate.

If you want promotion, you must enter the general competition to fill that *vacante* once it becomes available, even if you have been doing the work of the higher grade for years. This is a particular problem for categories D and C, because C is a supervisory grade, while D is an administrative one. Fernando explained to me that it would not be sensible to have too many people at the C grade; otherwise, who would do the actual work? But many people at D grades are in practice doing supervisory or C-grade jobs. Since there were no competitions from 1997 until very recently, a lot of people have reached the top of their salary scale but have nowhere to go from there. Additional salary increases at the top of a particular category (e.g., D10) have taken the form of "extraordinary" allocations, on what appears to have been largely an ad hoc basis. Further problems are that the evaluations conducted by bosses can often be delayed, or good evaluations may be given out on the basis of personal connections rather than good performance.

Moreover, over the years different forms of temporary contracts have been designed to get around restrictions on hiring or to move wage bills off the books and hide them from the eyes of international financial institutions. These have taken various forms, the latest being the "university contracts," the contract regime for the drivers mentioned previously. These are contracts initially designed so that university students can do what amount to internships as part of government projects, particularly those cofunded by agencies like the World Bank or the United Nations Development Programme (UNDP). However, their use has been extended beyond these specific criteria. It helps, perhaps, that they circumvent the more rigorous, visible, regulated, and costly form of temporary employment represented by the *planta transitoria*, which was negotiated in 2002.

One of the problems with the temporary contracts of all kinds is that they are often associated with a particular boss, so when that person moves to a different department, sometimes the new functionary is not so bothered about renewing specific people's contract or wants to make space for some of his or her own people. He or she may try to fire people by not renewing their contract—

which the union suspected was the case for the individual mentioned previously. Sometimes he or she just creates new sets of contracts, leading to overlap, as new groups come into state employment with each new functionary. This is thought to be a particular problem in the city government of Buenos Aires, rather than so much in the national federal administration, although it is not something that delegates were likely to admit to happening in their own institution.

Different institutions have different local arrangements, which have developed over decades. The result is a situation where the union stakes its legitimacy on the basis of a structure that it advocated for and helped design but that cannot possibly happen in practice as intended. UPCN activists are very proud of their role in first getting and then enacting the collective bargaining agreement, and its symbolic force is very strong. It is a form of law, both a commitment to regulate a particular systemic arrangement as if it actually existed and a statement about how things should be. It thus has a dual nature as both aspiration and description. And in practice delegates continually need to work around that system to find people a place in it. As one said to me, "We mostly sort out problems created by the state."

This leads to the second point illustrated by my example. In the face of anomalies that have built up over the years, as well as budgetary constraints that mean there will never be a match between the real numbers of employees and the numbers contemplated in the formal structure, strong personal relationships are essential to sort out the problems that inevitably arise. These were mediated through a friendly sociability between union and employer, one that often had a pragmatic edge: despite the joking and teasing that Lionel reported about his meeting with the functionary, it was clear that he was unwilling to defend someone who actually deserved to be fired nor was he very keen to defend a cause that might be unwinnable. This was a particular risk for the question of those on university contracts because of the complex nature of how their employment was organized.

This pragmatism is all very much part of UPCN's style, something that often infuriates ATE activists because they think it shows that UPCN is on the side of the employers. Yet from my position as observer it seemed that the resolution of the problem of the contracted drivers had two threads: ATE threatening to take protest action, by means of an assembly and associated *batucada*, which prompted both UPCN to find out what was going on; and the functionary to talk with the union with whom she had the best connection. UPCN "resolved" the situation and ensured that the contracts would be renewed, but it is likely that this would not have happened as it did if ATE had not been at the same time loudly denouncing the precarity of the drivers' employment conditions. UPCN members generally do not like to consider that they exist in this kind of relation-ship with ATE (and vice versa), even though at times that is how it appeared to me. Each union considers that the other causes it—and consequently the work-ers—more harm than good: ATE activists think that UPCN is too close to the employers and simply enacts what the employers want, explaining that to the workers and keeping them from protesting. The workers do not then get all from the employer that they might. UPCN in turn considers that ATE is overly com-bative, that it does not stick to agreements that have been negotiated and makes utterly unrealistic demands, thus raising workers' expectations to a point where they are always going to be disappointed.

On a local level, it is often necessary to use personal relationships to resolve problems and gain benefits for the workers in the everyday. Indeed, it is proba-bly essential if the intricacies of state employment are going to be managed and the system made to work in real life. UPCN and ATE both had to deal with the capricious nature of their employer and the complexity of the system, and both sought to benefit their constituency: where possible, all the workers, and where not possible, their direct affiliates.

NETWORKS: "WE'RE LIKE A FAMILY"

However, the union is not merely a body that represents workers' interests to the boss. UPCN has played a central role in the negotiation of the formal structure of employment over the years and continues to negotiate the day-to-day actual-ization of that structure through both formal and informal lines of communica-tion. Its brokerage role extends further, as it also plays an important part in the structuring of state employment along the lines of kin and friendship networks. This less formal logic of shaping the state is longer-standing than the *paritarias* of the collective bargaining agreements of the 2000s and is visible especially—al-though not exclusively—in the allocation of jobs. Here, two systems overlie each other: on the one hand, the Weberian allocation of office on the basis of merit as assessed through open competition (Weber 1968) and, on the other, the op-eration of personal networks to allocate jobs to friends and kin. The union's ac-tualization of friendship and kinship networks operates both before and after employment by drawing in friends and family members to the circle of those employed and then active within the union and by fomenting friendships be-tween delegation members and a strong group sentiment as part of the local union. This is achieved through processes of kinning (cf. Howell 2006), consist-ing of particular forms of sociability and commensality.

When people working for the state told me that their institution was "like a family," they often meant it both in a figurative and literal sense; and they were frequently very open about the fact that most people had obtained their job through some kind of family connection. One ATE delegate said in an interview:

> Well, nobody goes to work for the state by presenting their CV at the reception window; people get work for the state because they are someone's family member, through the unions or through the functionary. . . . An eighteen-year-old kid doesn't get in on his own merits; he gets in because he is someone's family. In the Radical party epoch, I got in in 2002. At that moment because of the [union's] relationship with the minister we could fill up [job] contracts. But, well, that's how you get a job working for the state. . . .
>
> One of the businesses that [the unions] have always done is getting people jobs—always, always. Every local office of any union in the state has a file of CVs from friends, family members, from affiliates, who ask you. That's how it works.

Although few of my interviewees were as frank with me on record as this particular person, the role of union networks in getting state employment for family is not especially hidden in day-to-day interactions. In informal conversations, friends discussed where they might find a state job for their children when they come of age, for instance, and when I asked members of the ministry delegation about their family histories, many of the stories they told me included how they had got a place for a family member. The phrase is *hacer entrar* (to make [someone] enter), and it is used in an active sense—so, *hice entrar mi madre, sobrino, hijo, etc.*, means "I got a job for my mother, nephew, son, etc." One delegation leader told me that his mother had been widowed when he was very young and worked as a domestic worker paid by the hour to support him through school. Once he was in the union delegation, he got her a job as a cook in a nursery, which he said was "the most dignified job she had had in her life."

The prevalence of family networks varies according to institutions, with a few more concentrated than others. For example, a delegation leader described one institution as "like a religious fraternity" (*como una cofradía*); he said that "we pile up all the relatives there" (*amontamos todos los familiares ahi*). Family networks do not always correspond directly to union networks but are a more broadly used means of recruitment to state employment in Argentina. This has a long history, especially in state-run industries, as Elana Shever (2012) has shown for oil workers and Sandra Wolanski (2015) for telecom workers. In the past, jobs used to pass from father to son; and, indeed, Wolanski argues that the telecom workers saw this as a right that had been lost on privatization and partially recovered after 2005. Of course, the allocation of jobs according to particular social networks is a feature of public-sector employment across the world, including in the supposedly more Weberian bureaucracies of the North Atlantic region.[11] Probably in no part of the world does a civil service fully conform to what was after all an ideal type even for Weber (1968).

However, the overlap between kin and job recruitment networks was a delicate question, and some members of the delegation were more comfortable discussing it than others. Where they were uncomfortable with the practice, it was mostly because of how they thought it might look to those on the outside. Wolanski (2015) suggests that the reason is that this is a matter from the private realm and that talking about it would be to wash dirty linen in public. For me, part of the issue was that people thought I would disapprove, so it fell into the realm of the slightly embarrassed sideways glance. Recruitment based on family connection is an open secret that sits alongside a genuine commitment to Weberian ideals of bureaucratic action, which include recruitment based on merit. Internally, it could even be seen as unethical not to incorporate a family member who would be appropriate for the job.

The fact that a given ministry is often staffed by people connected to each other through kinship or friendship helps maintain an easy sociability, which is in turn generally considered to be an indicator of a well-functioning workplace. When I first arrived at the delegation office, Lionel and Sergio took me around a few of the offices, greeting the workers with a kiss, introducing me, explaining to me who everyone was and how they were connected to each other (cousins, nieces, etc.), joking with them, and asking them how things were going. Not all of the workers participated in the exchanges, and some kept their heads down at their computers; but Lionel was at pains to show me how well the delegation leaders know the affiliates personally. Some members of the delegation go to specific offices more frequently than others, but all value personal connections with the workers, and in general the union places a great premium on "getting close to people" (*acercarse a la gente*), as Juanitos urged delegates at one meeting. It is not enough for these networks simply to exist; they must mean something in the day to day.

The friendly sociability was one of the most distinctive aspects of my experience at the delegation and indeed was one of the most appealing aspects of conducting research with unionists. Sociability is important both in everyday and on special occasions, as when delegations organize social events, such as lunches to celebrate birthdays, or excursions, such as a guided visit that Juanito, a small group of UPCN women, and I took to the Evita Museum. In addition to locally organized events, delegations convene people to attend cultural events organized by the Capital Section or the EFS, such as guitar festivals, trips to the theater, and art exhibitions. The social gatherings are core to how the union keeps people together, contains them. By getting its delegates together regularly, the group continually reaffirms its collective purpose and sense of collective identity. In moments of commensality and shared enjoyment, the group cultivates itself as a group.

Increasingly, this collective sociality happens also on digital platforms, especially Facebook, as people post pictures and videos, share their thoughts on the issues of the day, and discuss politics and personal matters. Facebook enacts sociality at multiple scales: individual, as people post about birthdays or achievements, their children, parents, holidays, and daily life; within networks of friends as people post photos taken at different union events; and with respect to the delegation as a whole. This is quite a recent phenomenon: the delegation has run its own Facebook group only since late 2013.

Further, I spent much time sitting in the delegation office with the delegates: chatting, smoking, debating, having refreshments; playing cards; watching football or the news on TV; watching YouTube videos that someone received by e-mail or on Facebook; discussing stories in the newspapers; gossiping about functionaries or tensions elsewhere in the building; and poring over leaflets produced by groups within the building or by ATE.

Mate in particular is associated with unionists and public-sector employees. It is an herbal infusion prepared in a round cup: One person packs the cup with the yerba mate leaves and pours boiling water over them from a thermos. The person sips from a metal straw until all the liquid is consumed and passes the cup and straw back to the person with the thermos, who pours more water on and then passes the drink to the next person. Although people do also drink mate on their own, the conventions of sharing make drinking mate into a very social endeavor. It is so associated with a particular attitude that from the outside it has come to represent a lack of commitment to the job, for example, when people make comments about public servants just drinking mate all day instead of working. But it is also considered to be the national drink, a rite that affirms Argentinianness as much as the barbecue does. Ministry delegates usually prepared mate in the mid- to late afternoon, when we came together to discuss the issues of the day, such as topics internal to the ministry—a report of a meeting with workers or with a functionary—or matters of current affairs or debates about interpretations of Argentine history. The latter may have been often prompted by my presence, and the topics of conversation did become less intellectual as my stay went on. However, it was clearly not uncommon for them to talk about weighty matters, and delegation members evidently enjoyed debating nearly as much as they enjoyed joking and teasing each other.

The union actualizes existing social networks and brings new people in all the time. All this is a kind of containment and kinning (Howell 2006). In using this term, I also draw on Marshall Sahlins's definition of kinship as "mutuality of being," by which he means "people who are intrinsic to one another's existence" (2013: 2). Beyond explicitly defined relationships of family, his notion makes good sense as a description of how the Argentine union comes into being as a political community, especially at the level of those who work together on a more or less daily basis. He says, "Generally considered, kinsmen are persons who belong to one another, who are parts of one another, who are co-present in each other, whose lives are joined and interdependent" (ibid.: 21), and this would also describe rather well the relationships between union activists.

As Janet Carsten has pointed out, Sahlins's focus on mutuality of being emphasizes the benign aspects of kinship as relatedness and does not quite account for practices of "dekinning" (Carsten 2014) and separating. This is a fair point, and here I also focus on practices of kinning in a positive sense, as they construct rather than destroy collective political subjects. Unionists tended to downplay the elements of tension and difficulty within those projects of collective self-cultivation. It was evident nonetheless that they all demanded a considerable amount of work, work that was never finished. Along with the internal focus on building community, collectivity, and kin, these processes of collective construction also from time to time required the delineation of the group self as opposed to a rival Other, which depending on the context might be their employers or the wider society that was suspicious of their activism and thought it corrupt. Alternatively, ATE delegates defined themselves and their political project against the officialist unions; for the very pro-government UPCN activists, the rival Other was often the anti-*kirchneristas*, especially from about 2012. Each union differentiated itself from the other on the basis of its organizational philosophy. These could all perhaps be seen as processes of dekinning in the separating out of different groups of working people from each other, the breaking down of working-class identity as a whole. Certainly, the factionalism that is part of any set of organized social forces is an example of both kinning in the internal cohesion of the faction and dekinning in the distinguishing of different groups from each other.

Practices of kinning were crucial to UPCN's daily work in the ministry, and in this sense they are no different from many other (unionized) workplaces in the country. Elana Shever's (2012) research on the oilfields of Southern Argentina illustrates the overlap between kinship, economic practice, and politics. Her analysis brings together the daily practices of collective politics and economic organization with the symbolic registers of nation building, exploration, adventurous masculinity, and good parenting in the development of the oil town of

Cutral Có, originally built by YPF to explore for oil and build the Argentine nation. In the 1990s, YPF was privatized and organized in part through a series
of kin-based subcontracted collective enterprises. That was an economic process bound up in the symbolism of the building of the nation but also intimately
related to how the local union of oil workers organized itself, not least as they
brought in workers and union members through family relations. New arrivals
were brought into the family of oil workers by the creation of avuncular relations
through the barbecue and mate (Shever 2012). Although it is mostly implicit in
Shever's work, the union structure in fact overlaid this family and oil-worker
structure, as all workers had to be members of the union; and state employment
in the more administrative institutions is little different.

Those networks need considerable work to be maintained, even if they operate on the basis of preexisting relations such as those of family. The work of
maintenance, creation, and re-creation happens through repeated social interaction. In the case of the ministry delegation, that interaction is facilitated by particular kinds of personalities, especially that of the general secretary, Lionel, who
was held in great affection by many of his delegation. His expansive, jovial sociability is a crucial aspect of his charisma and leadership. He is not alone in this, as
other leading unionists I know have similarly charismatic personalities, consisting of an avuncular sociability that draws people to the individual while maintaining hierarchies of office, knowledge, or experience. It is particularly associated with but not confined to men: for example, Marcela Manuel, director of the
EFS, is similarly jovial almost all of the time, exuding confidence and friendli-
ness, and giving the impression that she knows everyone without losing authority. We may consider it a form of politicized sociability, characteristic of many
successful politicians, especially in personalist systems (see DaMatta 1991; Gay
1998; Albro 2000). This is not to suggest that it is necessarily artificial or inter-
ested but rather to propose that the social dynamics of political power favor particular personalities.

PRESENCE

The concept of politicized sociability is a feature of individual personalities but
also something that operates on a collective plane, for the union continually creates itself as a collective in multiple ways. I move now from the more intimate
forms of negotiation and kinning to public ritual events and visual practices.
The union power to do all the work of making the state requires strength—and
importantly, the display of that strength. The union delegation is in large part
an instrument for the resolution of problems, the administration of state em-

ployment, the actualization of social networks, and the containment of its members. Yet one of the most important kinds of political work that the delegation does is to make itself present, to the employer, the employees, and to itself. From UPCN's perspective, it is crucial not only to build an organization that is coherent, is organic, and can negotiate from a position of strength but also to be *seen* to be so. Social events are a part of maintaining that perception, along with other elements, especially poster displays and public events.

As the case of the contracted workers shows, much of UPCN's most effective activity is actually constituted by behind-the-scenes negotiation, in contrast to ATE's techniques of presence through mobilization. As a result, it is very important to the delegation and to the Capital Section office that UPCN be active and be seen to be active. Delegates constantly read visual clues about how active their union is—and they thought other people read the clues in the same way. For instance, at a meeting of the ministry delegation, one woman complained vigorously that at the entrance to her institution you could see only ATE posters. She had been unwell so unable to redress the balance, but it was important to her that UPCN attempt to change the situation, even if in practice it was a matter of a single individual putting up the posters. That ministry was not particularly conflictual, but in other institutions there were frequent battles where one union delegation would rip down the posters displayed by the other, who would then retaliate, and so on. Most state institutions bear the imprint of both unions, and for both, posters are crucial to their activities. The location of the ATE or UPCN notice board made a statement about the relative weight that employers gave to each union, and delegates would sometimes grumble about employers who granted one union a less prominent space for its board.

Usually, especially where relations between union and employer were good, posters would be located at entrance halls or outside elevators and doors to corridors. The ministry had a regularly rotating series of posters, with the ATE delegation there making itself appear rather more prominent than the relative numbers of affiliates would suggest, by virtue of the regular appearance of ATE-branded posters. Posters emphasize the unions' activities through imparting information about benefits available to affiliates and through their presence in the hallways and beside elevator entrances. They also advertise union-organized events: assemblies and protests in the case of ATE and cultural events and other ceremonial acts in the case of UPCN.

Those acts in themselves were a key part of the delegation's work. Their role in making the union visible in a certain way was also a topic of explicit discussion, with Juanito very emphatic that delegates should tell people about public acts so that they know the union is doing something. While I was there, two ceremonies were held in late 2012, one on the second anniversary of Néstor Kirchner's death in late October and one on the Day of the Activist in mid-November. Notably, UPCN did not celebrate the traditional Peronist Day of Loyalty, 17 October, with official public acts in 2012, as I had expected. I had been asking whether something would take place and had in part organized that field trip so I could be present on a 17 October because of its prominence in the annual Peronist commemorative cycle (Robben 2007). That year, some said that they thought the union had decided to take a low profile or that it was not the correct "conjuncture" for a large demonstration of loyalty. In the ministry building, 17 October was a normal day, in fact, one where much of the activity on the fifth floor concerned planning the ceremony to pay homage to Néstor. Although local Peronist basic units had held celebrations on the seventeenth and there were official ceremonies, the multiple gatherings to mark the anniversary of Néstor's death a couple of weeks later seemed to have a higher profile that year. Those gatherings were especially notable for the number of young people present. Perhaps the key pro-Kirchner groups so close to government in late 2012 were making a statement about the (literal) rejuvenation of Peronism: no longer based so much in trade unionism but in youth activism.

Similarly, the homage to Néstor Kirchner was the initiative of a group of young people in the UPCN delegation, including the youth secretary, Roberto. One day about a week before the ceremony, I came across Roberto choosing an image for the poster and banner they would display on the day itself. He was discussing the choice with a young woman from the youth group La Cámpora. They were particularly concerned to pick an image of Néstor that was inspiring but not "too La Cámpora." On the day itself, groups of UPCN delegates from the different ministries came to the main building, some wearing T-shirts and others carrying signs, flags, or umbrellas indicating their allegiance to UPCN and to their group in the ministry. One such band played the drums as they crossed over the road and continued in the foyer of the ministry building and the corridor outside the salon where the ceremony was to be held. The drums were astonishingly loud, amplified by the marble hall in the ministry foyer. After only a few minutes of being in close proximity to them to take photos and recordings, my hearing was so dulled that I found it difficult to hear the speeches that followed. Delegates squeezed past them fairly quickly, invigorated by the sound but also unable to bear it for a very long time, particularly in the small marble-lined corridor outside the salon.

I entered the room and found a seat in one of the front rows. The room was high-ceilinged and starkly decorated, with marble walls and wood paneling (Figure 5). A large UPCN banner was attached to the wall at the back. At the front

FIGURE 5.   Unionists awaiting the ceremony in homage to Néstor Kirchner

was set up a large free-standing screen, a lectern, and public address system. Lionel, Martín, Carlos, Fernando, and Sergio stood at the front of the room greeting all those who entered, until someone decided that enough people had arrived to start, and they sat down. The ceremony began with a minute of applause for *el compañero Néstor*, and then a young UPCN delegate I did not know introduced a video he had produced, saying that when Néstor died, "you lost a political leader, the opposition lost a rival, and some lost an enemy, but many of us, we've lost a father." He was speaking of himself as part of a generation of young people who felt the loss of Néstor deeply. The video depicted Kirchner among crowds of Argentinians and with the Madres de la Plaza de Mayo. It showed footage of the crisis of 2001 and subsequent economic recovery, the repayment in full of the debt to the IMF in 2005, and the defeat of the Free Trade Area of the Americas. It also emphasized Néstor's regional politics, as pictures of UNASUR (Unión de Naciones Suramericanos; Union of South American Nations) gatherings and excerpts from the homages to him by Lula, Correa, and Chávez accompanied pictures of him with Luis Inácio Lula da Silva, Hugo Chávez, Evo Morales, and Fidel Castro. Throughout, the video returned to the connection with the Madres, ending with a quote by Estela de Carlotto, one of the leaders of the Abuelas de la Plaza de Mayo. She said, "Néstor, es un hijo" (Néstor is a son), thus evoking his connection to the children of the Madres, the disappeared. In later discussions at the ministry delegation office, people agreed that it had been very poignant, and indeed many people were crying by the time the video ended.

Lionel then rose to speak. He said that the Kirchners had stopped thirty years of decline (*decadencia*), and for him the last eight years had been the best years of Argentine democracy for a long time. He said, "I come from a Peronist family, and I thought we would never recover our dignity as a country," and he attributed this to Néstor but also implicitly to Cristina. He told the story of how he heard from his daughter that Néstor had died, his voice breaking as he spoke. He referred to a conversation I had had with him previously, when I had asked him what all the fuss was about Néstor. At the time, he had said he wasn't too sure, maybe just that Peronists like to worship the dead, but maybe it was because in recent years there had been a significant move toward social justice. During his speech, he said that although he had told me that there is a Peronist "pantheon," in reality there were not so many figures that had arisen from the workers themselves, and he named Hipólito Yrigoyen, Perón (and Evita), and Néstor. And, he said, the desire for homage had not come from an order from above, or even from his delegation, but from the young people themselves. He continued—to applause—that these figures are part of the pantheon because they deserve to be. At the end, everyone rose to sing the *marcha peronista*, gesturing with their right arms,[12] increasing the volume as the song went on, and feeling the sense of togetherness and shared commitment that the song evokes. Then people gradually dispersed, and the band played them out.

It is quite something to place Néstor Kirchner as the latest in that line of figures: Perón and Evita are iconic figures for almost all Argentines, whether Peronist or not, and Yrigoyen, the cofounder of the Radical party, is one of the most celebrated progressive presidents of the twentieth century. But there is no doubt that the figure of Néstor Kirchner has appealed very strongly to a newly invigorated Peronist youth. The UPCN delegates later analyzed the appeal in generational terms: for example, Lionel said that he would not have emphasized so much the question of human rights in the video; for him it would be more important to emphasize the issues of social justice. But, he said, for *los pibes* (the kids), the pursuit of the dictators is very significant. And although his voice broke during his speech,[13] and Néstor's death had clearly touched him, some of the young people at the ceremony were in floods of tears by the end.

The ceremony was well attended, the *marcha* sung with high passion, and it seemed that those present had enjoyed the experience. The sound of the band had taken over the building. The union had asserted its presence, to itself and to others, and had collectively reiterated its passionate connection to Peronism. The members had demonstrated their support of the government by participating in Cristina Fernández de Kirchner's reverent attitude toward "Él" (her way of referring to Néstor), and they affirmed the importance of the *kirchnerista* political and economic project of a strong state, the attack on commercial monopolies in the media, a determination to pursue the violators of human rights in the courts, and a strong position in the face of international financial institutions.

Three weeks later, a delegation from one of the ministry institutions organized a public event to mark the Day of the Activist. This is explicitly a Peronist celebration, commemorating Juan Perón's first return to Argentina from exile on 17 November 1972. At the time, he stayed for a month, returning definitively the following year, but the second return was marred forever by the massacre at Ezeiza airport. The ministry delegation celebrated this day for the first time in 2012. On the morning of 17 November, I went to the building to find groups of people milling outside, listening to the band and drummers, and twirling their UPCN umbrellas. I went into the office, found the delegation rooms, and chatted with the UPCN delegates there. They asked me also to record a message for a video for their end-of-the-year ceremony, so I took the opportunity to thank them on camera for their help and welcome. At some point, the signal was given to begin the ceremony, and we went to unveil a plaque that named their room in honor of Leonardo Favio, a Peronist filmmaker who had recently died. Then we all entered the Leonardo Favio Auditorium and sat in front of a large screen, ready to watch the video and listen to the speakers. The event started with a short speech by Roberto, the youth secretary who had played a big part in the organization of the homage to Néstor. He introduced a video and said that although some people think that militancy is a duty, it is in fact a choice made every day, a way of life that you can choose. It is a feeling of solidarity, of meeting, of *convivencia* (living together)—of working "with friendship and *compañerismo*." He said to audience applause that he was "profoundly Peronist," even if some laugh at that, but "we are all activists [*militantes*]"; and his hope was that after this event, the group would be more united and perhaps a little more Peronist as well. The video developed these themes, opening with some footage of Perón responding to a question about the "combative" wing of his party, in which he stressed that "there are orthodox [Peronists], there are heterodox, there are combatives, there are contemplatives, but everyone works." This segued into images of Perón and of notable activists such as Evita and José Ignacio Rucci—who is thought to have died for his loyalty to Perón—and of the Juventud Peronista, accompanied by a 2010 song, "Militante," by Ignacio Copani about 1970s student activism.[14] These were followed by an interview with Oraldo Britos, billed as a "historic Peronist," someone with a long trajectory of militancy, and the speaker quoted in the Introduction. The video then moved to images and video clips of members of the UPCN delegation, at demonstrations and social events such as a football tournament, in their offices, and playing the drums, all to the accompaniment of the *marcha peronista*. At this point, the mood in the room lifted and became more animated, as people spotted themselves and their friends, laughed at the poses and costumes in some of the photos, and remembered the activities they commemorated.

Then Carlos paid homage to Perón, for giving his life to return democracy, and to other key figures, including Alicia Moreau de Justo and Hipólito Yrigoyen, all of whom tried to build a better country and "forge a future of love over one of hate." He said, "These are genuine activists who believe in something," who believe in this "great Argentina" that San Martín dreamed of and the reality that Perón achieved. Martín followed him and spoke about activism for the union; as the Radical in the leadership, he spoke, he said, to include the non-Peronists present, to demonstrate that it was possible to have a militancy that was not necessarily Peronist: what was essential for him was the defense of the union and of the rights of the workers. He also emphasized the way that militancy is "un estilo de vida," an expression of "this love for others" that they have inside. Both the Peronist and Radical speaker used rhetorical tropes of a piece with the construction of activist selfhood described previously.

At these kinds of official ritual events, the sentiments expressed in public speeches are of course carefully staged, the discourses unlikely to undermine official narratives. As is the event itself, they are a way of making the union and its ideology present to its members and to itself. They can also be read as exhortatory forms, like the training at the EFS: by emphasizing that the audience has chosen militancy out of their feelings of passion, commitment, solidarity, and love, the speakers draw forth those dispositions anew. They create activists by telling people that they are already this kind of activist, just as the trainers in the EFS do. Much emphasis was also placed on feeling, especially feelings of solidarity and love toward the group and Argentina. This is a way of enacting containment, which involves both the encompassment of the individual by the group and the desire of the individual to be contained, "embraced" in the words of the anonymous UPCN delegate quoted at the beginning of this chapter. That desire does not necessarily exist a priori but can be elicited through exhortation; indeed, it may need to be continually elicited for containment to be successful.

Rather like the collective bargaining agreement, which collapses together the *as if* of the agreement as description and the aspiration for the future, these ritual events also collapsed different temporalities together. Within one morning, they embody what is, what can be elicited, what may (or may not) be necessary for the future, and what is created in the moment itself. Through their commemoration of past events, the two events described here temporarily locked contemporary participants into a chain that consisted of key moments: Hipólito Yrigoyen's regime, Perón's first return from exile, Néstor Kirchner's death, and Cristina Kirchner's national popular government in 2012. The chain is created anew with each new event and could take on a completely different cast if desired and according to each participant. The choice in 2012 to celebrate the day of the Peronist activist rather than the 17 October Day of Loyalty meant that the chain as instantiated in the ministry that year included Perón's return but not the mass demonstrations of the Plaza de Mayo calling for his release from prison in 1945. Of course, many had participated in local events called by their Peronist neighborhood group, so each person's chain was different. The kind of militancy that came into being in late 2012 through these events had a specific character: it was intensely contemporary, youthful. The acts drew on the technological expertise of the younger delegates in producing videos that projected their vision of militancy. But it was also a reconfiguration of a militancy with a longer history, incorporating long-standing modes of belonging expressed in Peronist rallies, of passion and collective orientation, and stressing elements such as loyalty to Perón and the focus on his return from exile.

The collective experience of effervescence, of confirmed and reinforced group identity in social and public events, is a way to demonstrate, reinforce, and enact the group's encompassment of the individual and to create and re-create the individual himself or herself. Containment comes into being in the act, but the act also recognizes containment as already existing: the temporality of causation collapses in on itself so that the staged event is at least three things at the same time: a recognition of a priori containment as enacted through all the day-to-day practices described, an act of containment in itself, and a promise of future containment.

CONCLUSION

Importantly, neither of the celebrations just described was restricted to the most active delegates or even solely to UPCN affiliates. They were open to all who wanted to come, including some of the functionaries who identified as Peronists and supported UPCN. This is clearly an important contributor to UPCN's ability to maintain its social networks within the institution. The ritual events help make networks that may need to be mobilized in the future to defend the interests of their affiliates.

The union therefore goes well beyond being merely a representative institution or a mediator between the different interests of worker and boss, or citizen and state. Instead, it is part of the complex of institutions and practices that bring the state into being as a collective entity composed of its workers. Through informal brokerage and formal negotiation, the union actualizes social networks and the formal structures found in entities such as collective bargaining agreements. The social networks and formal structures overlie each other and relate in complex ways, and often the expertise of the union leadership lies in their ability to make the two compatible. That ability relies on the personal connections and social skills embodied in different leaders, the "expansive sociability" I have identified as a characteristic of union leaders. It is also crucially connected to the strength of the union as a collective, something that is continually reaffirmed in a wide spectrum of social activities as well as practices of encompassment in day-to-day activities, through care. A union is strong when it is both well connected to the functionaries and very present—to the bosses, the workers, and itself. So containment is a multivalent process, consisting of many threads, from individual relations of counseling and trust to collective identification and effective brokerage.

The threads are mediated by practices of kinning, through care, sociability, and ritual. Those practices come together to constitute containment as cultivation of the collective ethical subject. It is what grants the union its strength, enabling effective negotiation with the employer in the resolution of problems and the gaining of benefits for its affiliates. This chapter has described this collective subjectivation for the level of the delegation (one that is well functioning). The previous chapter described these processes of subjectivation at a broader scale, where both ATE-Capital and UPCN Capital Section build a sense of collective subjecthood at the level of the citywide union through explicitly pedagogical activities. Those were formal and carefully theorized processes of the building of collective subjects, but as in the ritual acts and day-to-day sociability described here, even in the training exercises, the explicit learning was combined with more implicit experiences of kinning, in the cigarette, coffee, and pizza breaks; informal conversations; excursions; and so on. In the training plenaries and workshops; around the office delegation table; in the ceremonial acts; and in excursions to restaurants, museums, cultural activities, and other union offices, activists build concord and friendly feeling among themselves, to use Aristotelian language of ethics; in the language of anthropology of kinship they build "mutuality of being" (Sahlins 2013: 2) and cultures of relatedness (Carsten 2000) by means of commensality, learning together, and ritual action. Collectively they cultivate and circulate ethical values of loyalty, passion, solidarity, love, and vocation. Thus, the group encompasses the individual, bringing to the fore charac-teristics that already exist deep within and cultivating the group hexis of collec-tive militancy. That group hexis then enables the praxis of increased collective power as an organization and successful brokerage between workers and the state.

6   CONTAINMENT AS

POLITICAL ENCOMPASSMENT

Containment is a form of encompassment that gives activists a context, a space for being and acting and for constructing themselves as collective ethical subjects and political actors. This dimension of containment operates in conjunction with containment as therapeutic relationship and care but is more collective and public in the case of ATE in particular. One ATE activist described it as follows:

> Well, the fact of belonging to a group, to a collective, at least it contains you [*te contiene*]; it makes you feel good, because you might be with people, some more your friends, others less so, but you feel contained [*te sentís contenido*]. In four or five small things you feel contained; you know that we're here for something in common. . . . There's something that unifies us, and it's something that isn't material; rather, it has something to do with living together, with conceptions of life.

This quote comes from a group interview with the ATE *junta interna* at the Malbrán institute and is a response to my question about why they continued as delegates, which I asked just after they had described to me their most celebrated and successful mobilization of 1996 against state reform.[1] The speaker was referring to how containment involves an effort of political encompassment: giving people a context, something to belong to as a means of creating a better society or dealing with the problems of contemporary society. For him, that need not require the sharing of political ideas but was about belonging to an organization.

That belonging was enacted for both ATE and UPCN activists in collective activities of political participation. Especially for ATE activists, the most important of these are the assemblies, while UPCN activists tend to engage more frequently in commemorative or celebratory performances or social gatherings. In this chapter I explore how ATE activists create political community and act politically through assemblies and street protests. I argue that these kinds of collective action consist both of subjectivation and of "reflection and action upon the world in order to transform it" (Freire 1996: 51). They thus combine the cultivation of hexis with praxis. In *Pedagogy of the Oppressed*, Paulo Freire said: "Human activity consists of action and reflection: it is *praxis*; it is transformation of the world. And as *praxis*, it requires theory to illuminate it. Human activity is theory and practice; it is reflection and action" (ibid.: 125). Freire was arguing in the context of the debate between vanguardist Marxism and his popular education project aiming to promote revolutionary change. Praxis, understood as an explicitly political project that combines action with critical reflection, describes well many aspects of unionist action, including the pedagogical activities discussed previously. ATE activists in particular held a very well-theorized political project of transformation of their worlds. I have described earlier how they outlined that project in personal ideological terms, but here I explore how they enacted it in practical action in assemblies and on the streets.

I begin with a discussion of assemblies and then analyze street protests as collective subjectification and critical action. Protests are embodied experiences with a particular relationship to time and space and open to diverse readings. In addition to being forms of praxis, both kinds of collective action are practices of containment as kinning. That is, they create deep relations between the activists as values of solidarity, passion, commitment, and friendship circulate in the experience of common purpose and "mutuality of being" (Sahlins 2013: 2) on the streets and in assembly halls. This combination of hexis with practice enables the unionists to constitute themselves as collective ethical-political subjects.

THE ASSEMBLY

ATE's principal mode of containment was probably the assembly, and the assembly also played a crucial symbolic role as the crystallization of ATE's ethical self-construction as a political project of autonomous and democratic unionism.[2] It was very important to most of my ATE informants that ATE convenes many assemblies, both at the level of the administrative entity where people worked and at the union's central offices. As Ruben Mosquera, a leader of ATE-Nacional, summarized, "If we stick to one principle within ATE, it's that the assembly is in command," and this was constantly drawn out in the training session I attended.

Assemblies are public meetings, held either in the office of ATE-Nacional or ATE-Capital or at the place of work. I first attended an ATE-Capital assembly in February 2009. Because ATE-Capital was refurbishing its own auditorium, the meeting was held in the auditorium belonging to ATE-Nacional, which has glass windows the full length of the walls to the back of the audience that look onto a sculpture of steel pipes representing members of ATE disappeared during the military junta. The room has the shape of an amphitheater, with the audience on three sides, facing a stage. The hall was almost full to its capacity of around 150 for every assembly I attended in 2009. At the front of the lecture theater, seven leaders of the union sat at a table on the small stage and spoke into microphones set on the table. They began by calling for a minute's applause for the recently deceased general secretary of ATE-Capital, Leopoldo González. The adjunct secretary of ATE-Nacional gave a speech in homage to him, as did González's successor at the head of ATE-Capital. They said that his legacy would best be served by continuing to follow his example in struggle. They then announced newly elected *juntas internas*, each of which was applauded, and an audience member from the *junta interna* of the National Institute of Statistics announced the upcoming march there for the following Wednesday. Audience members indicated their willingness to talk and, when given the cordless microphone, stood up to give their speech, usually lasting about five minutes each. The second person from the audience to speak at that assembly was Jose Piazza, general secretary of the junta of the Teatro Colón, who linked his fight against firings to the struggle for the National Institute of Statistics (see Lazar 2016b). Everyone clapped at the end of the speech, and a succession of speakers rose to share their local concerns and struggles or announce more protests for the upcoming weeks, to which the adjunct secretary of ATE-Capital responded each time. After two hours, he declared that they would close the list of speakers so the assembly could be brought to a close, to shouts of "yes! yes!" from the audience. Throughout, the presence of the microphones gave a mediated quality to the discussion. It is not that undesirable people are not given the microphone, although I assume that this happens from time to time; rather, the need to pass the microphone through the assembled people gives a sense of formality and performance and requires that the debate proceed in a linear fashion. It also enables discussion to be easily cut once enough people have given their views. Smaller-scale assemblies operate on a similar model, albeit not necessarily with amplification equipment. The speeches are constructed as beads on a chain of discourse, with the leaders of the assembly as interlocutors for each speaker. This happens whether in an assembly hall, an office, or a corner of the street, as sometimes occurs for assemblies held by the Teatro Colón workers.

Especially at the larger scale, this is a style of meeting well suited to the delivery of information, with contributors from the floor seeking to clarify, comment, or ask questions to move the leaders in a certain direction. UPCN tends to use assemblies in this way: primarily as information delivery mechanisms, but with the audience not merely consuming the information but responding to it and encouraging or gently criticizing the leaders. UPCN assemblies that I attended took place in large auditoriums at workplaces, once with the union band at the door, which played us out after the assembly had heeded the call of the delegation leaders to mobilize on behalf of a recategorization process.[3] ATE seeks to promote discussion in its assemblies, but in practice what happens is not so much a full deliberation about policy, or even tactics, as a presentation from the leadership of what their suggestion is (marches, other mobilizations), followed by comments from the floor on that position. This was very clear in the assembly just described, when some speakers were pushing for the leadership to demand permanent contracts for all workers. The dynamic that I usually saw in the meetings of ATE-Capital was that the audience comments tended toward a greater radicalism than the leadership position, creating pressure on the leaders to take more radical action than they had initially proposed. One particularly clear example happened during an assembly at the audit office of the city government of Buenos Aires. Delegates of the *junta interna* were fighting restructuring plans that they thought would disperse their workers across the city and lead to job cuts, and also greater corruption, because they were more isolated from each other. They organized an assembly because they wanted to call for a twenty-four-hour strike to begin the following day. I joined that assembly, held in the open plan part of the city office. Office workers gathered at the appointed time, standing or perching on desks, and listened to the leaders explain their plan for a stoppage. Once they had done so, people put up their hands to speak in turn. Some expressed doubts, but most supported the measure, until one young worker stood up and said that not only should the stoppage start immediately but that it should last seventy-two hours. The applause from the rest of the assembly participants indicated that this was a popular idea.

Whether leaders choose to heed the more radical dynamic from the floor or not depended on several variables, but undoubtedly it is helpful for the leaders negotiating positions to be able to say that the assembly wanted them to do more. In ATE-Capital, the fact that more conservative voices are not often heard in the fairly high-tension situation of an assembly does not mean that they do not exist but more likely that they either are not prepared to speak up or they do not come to an assembly. Assemblies for ATE-Capital happen during working hours, at the central office, and sometimes at a frequency of once a fortnight or even more often. Attendance is the responsibility of delegates from the *junta interna*, who get an allowance of time away from their jobs to conduct union business. As a result, assemblies are populated by the more politically committed workers, and there is considerable incentive not to voice criticism of the leadership from a conservative position. In more local assemblies, of workers rather than simply union delegates or affiliates, some more tentative or conservative people were more prepared to make interventions, as in the case in the audit office, when one person hesitantly suggested that a strike might not be the best idea for them. Usually though, the general mood of the assembly often favored either the position of the leadership or a more radical position.

Assemblies are often held to be a simple and frank exchange of views, theorized by ATE activists as the enactment of horizontality in a practice that prefigures the kind of democracy that activists desire and thus creates them as a specific kind of collective ethical subject. Individual assemblies do not always live up to this ideal. Nor are they spaces where leaders simply manipulate the assembled masses because so much happens outside the explicitly verbalized part: in the discussions in the run-up to the meeting, the comments made to union delegates when they are encouraging workers to come to the assembly, or in the decision of ordinary workers or union affiliates not to attend or not to follow the resolutions of the assembly. The audit office *junta interna* spent time just before the assembly going around the office and encouraging people to attend, discussing the issues, and answering questions about the proposed course of action. Assemblies are also highly varied, and levels of participation and range of views expressed change according to factors such as who is in charge and how frequently they are held. What was common to all of the assemblies that I have attended is that whenever a decision came to a vote, it was rare to find dissent from the position argued for most vociferously by the leaders. By the time something comes to a vote, the will of the assembly is usually pretty clear, and it is usually consonant with the leadership position, as is the case for most collective meetings.

Despite the variability in actual assembly practice, my ATE interlocutors often made a rhetorical slippage between the fact of holding an assembly and the assumption of internal horizontality or democracy. ATE activists are not alone in this; plenty of other activists, as well as academics, use the holding of an assembly as evidence of democracy: for example, in discussions of internal democracy within the famous worker-controlled factories of the early 2000s (Atzeni and Ghighliani 2009). In practice, assemblies are a technology, which may be used to promote, sidestep, or even stifle internal democracy, depending on circumstances. Indeed, a number of European and US social movement groups, especially those influenced by anarchism, have developed a forceful critique of discussion and vote-based assemblies, along with alternative technologies to foster discussion in small groups as part of consensus-based decision making (Maeckelbergh 2009; Graeber 2013). Of course, internal democracy is very much more than what occurs in meetings. Assemblies can only appear to create a common analysis of a situation because the leaders of those assemblies put in much effort beforehand in assessing feelings among their bases so that they come to a decision acceptable to the majority and afterward in persuading the bases to agree with a particular position (see also Polletta 2002). Assemblies therefore may not always quite live up to the promise of exposing political differences and resolving them through discussion during the course of the assembly itself. The time around the edges of any assembly is probably much more important. Nonetheless, rhetorical emphasis is placed on the assembly itself as evidence of internal democracy.

Much effort is also expended in the organizing and holding of assemblies as a form of political action in themselves. When a problem occurs in a workplace, ATE activists will almost always propose to hold an assembly as their first course of action. The assembly should decide on the next step, and repeated assemblies will be necessary during a particular conflict to inform the workers of the actions of the union delegates and put proposals for future activity to the group. ATE activists also place great emphasis on assemblies as the correct space of decision making in regard to ending a particular conflict. When negotiating with the employers, leaders know that they must not agree to anything as representatives of the workers but instead take the precise proposals to the workers directly for their agreement. Assemblies are crucial enactments of ATE praxis in the construction of their political project of autonomous and democratic unionism, described previously for individual activists. In some instances, assemblies also become a form of street demonstration, as, for example, in the case of the workers of the Teatro Colón, who gathered regularly on the Avenida 9 de Julio in the early months of 2009 to discuss their conflict with the management (see Lazar 2016b).

THE PROTEST: TEMPORALITY

Probably ATE's second most important technology of containment is the street protest.[4] Demonstrations are a central political technology for most social movements, and unions and other political organizations frequently call for public mobilization—usually marches—to press their demands. I discuss two dimensions of demonstrations, the temporal and the spatial. The temporal dimension of protest is important because for activists, being part of a social movement is as much about inhabiting different lived social experiences of time as it is about participating in networks or fighting for inclusion, rights to public space, or even the very notion of the public, some of the very spatial metaphors that inform the academic literature on social movements.[5] Here I describe two such social experiences of time, which I call "historical time" and "attritional time," and argue that this temporal dimension is a crucial aspect of ATE activists' ethical-political projects, which are confronted (repeatedly) with their limitations and forced to adapt but also persist in the face of limited possibilities for change. Yet this question of success (or its lack) is still undertheorized in much of the anthropology of ethics, which tends to assume a more teleological temporality of self-cultivation toward a given set of goals. I discuss this particular question at greater length in the book's Conclusion.[6]

When I was working with the UPCN delegation described previously, it was rare to turn up at the ministry building in the center of the city and not to see some kind of street march there or nearby. ATE also rarely stops demonstrating, apart from during holiday months. Even when not in direct conflict with their employer, delegates attend local and citywide assemblies, marches, blockades, days of action, protest festivals, CTA demonstrations, and so on. They are on constant alert to react to government and employer initiatives both real and potential, such as policy changes like the proposed lowering of the age of criminal liability in the city of Buenos Aires; employer initiatives such as not renewing some people's contracts, firing others, or reorganizing offices; squatter clearance; and increases in fuel bills, and they also instigate recurrent demands for wage increases. Finally, each month ATE and associated groups hold a demonstration outside the national statistics office when inflation figures are released. This is part of a pattern of protests that have taken place since 2007 when, ATE and others argue, the National Institute of Statistics became subject to government interference aimed at disguising the true rate of inflation.

Common modes of demonstrating include a street march; creative events, such as a carnival or music festival; a dance event; or a mock funeral. The Teatro Colón workers were particularly creative in their protest repertoire, drawing on their artistic resources. In early 2009, they held a regular protest outside the city government building on the Avenida de Mayo, which combined a dance performance (modern, ballet, and tango) and the singing of the national anthem with the more usual speeches and placards. On another occasion they paraded around the Teatro Colón with a coffin on which the word "Culture" was inscribed, as a declaration of the death of culture that would result from the attack on them as they saw it. The protest repertoire on which contemporary actors draw is extremely broad, incorporating multiple events and understandings, as well as what people can design using their own creativity, and there is a strong tradition of eye-catching creative protest events in post-dictatorship Argentina, known as *escraches* (Benegas 2013; Kaiser 2002; Lessa and Levey 2015). Past protests inform current ones, providing models on which those planning protests can draw. For example, on one occasion, Teatro Colón workers briefly installed a temporary white tent outside the city government building, referencing the famous white tent installed in front of the Congressional Palace by teachers protesting Menem's reforms in the 1990s (Guano 2003).

The Teatro Colón conflict of 2009 contested the "modernization" of Argentina's preeminent opera house (see Lazar 2016b for more details). As an example of neoliberal economic policies in miniature, in recent years there has been a sustained attempt to change this state-owned opera house from what the workers call a "factory theater"—one that puts on its own productions using its own technical and artistic workforce—to a venue for productions mounted by other (subcontracted) theater and opera companies. This involved both the reduction of the workforce and a highly contentious refurbishment of the building. Some of the workers, led by key figures in the ATE local delegation, tried to resist this process in a series of almost constant mobilizations, which have ebbed and flowed over the years. Indeed, it is possible to declare "a state of permanent mobilization," like a state of emergency, which happened in early 2009. Mobilizations included assemblies, demonstrations of different kinds, press conferences, and support festivals, and they occurred at different frequencies, but up to once or twice a week for months at a time. They were punctuated by particular scandals and events, such as parliamentary hearings, court cases, and a building inspection. Between early February and late August 2009, there were twenty-three separate mobilizations that I knew about, just for the Teatro Colón. Members of other ATE juntas internas accompanied the Teatro Colón workers at many of these mobilizations, while they joined broader ATE or CTA mobilizations as well. Over the same period, I logged an additional twenty-two ATE-sponsored assemblies and mobilizations. These included five in conjunction with the CTA and four on behalf of the Buenos Aires city audit office. This totals forty-five, constituting a rate of over 1.5 per week, and I did not learn of all of the demonstrations and assemblies held in that time.

As the discussions have shown so far, both ATE and UPCN activists conceptualized their work in historical time, the context of a distinctive historical narrative of political action (Lazar 2014). This narrative involves a linear sense of time, albeit one that does not flow smoothly but is punctuated by iconic events, epochs, and people. In the case of many of my interlocutors, this required the splitting of historical time into specific periods, specifically 1946–55, the first Peronist regime; 1955–69 and 1969–73, resistance and radicalization; 1976–83, the military dictatorship; 1989–99, the neoliberal period; to some extent the banking crisis of 2001–2; and 2003–15, the Kirchner regimes.

The narrative flow of epochal time (Harris 2004) was not only divided into identifiable periods but also punctuated by key events, as Robben (2007) ar-

gued. He suggested that mass, often violent, street demonstrations have punctuated Argentine political history and changed its course at several significant moments. The archetypal example of this is the 17 October demonstration that has
come to be understood as led by Eva Perón and that secured Juan Perón's release
from prison in 1945; also crucial were the Cordobazo of May 1969,[7] the demonstrations at Ezeiza airport greeting Perón's return from exile on 20 June 1973
(which became a massacre), the protests against the Falklands war in 1983 that
toppled the dictatorship, and the riots of 19–20 December 2001 in response to the
financial crisis. The importance of these events, all of which began as street demonstrations, shapes how Argentines interpret day-to-day mobilization on the
streets. In April 2016, one friend posted on Facebook about an upcoming demonstration to support Cristina Fernández de Kirchner as she attended court to
answer charges connected to the sale of dollar futures:[8]

> I'm convinced that historical events don't warn you in advance; you just have to
> be there. Wednesday 13 [April] could be just one more date, but it could also be
> as important as 17 October (which I would have loved to live) and 20 December
> (which I did live). Let's not lose the opportunity to write history. And never for-
> get that the happiest days have always been Peronist. [V-sign emoji].
> Everyone with Cristina!!

Street mobilization is not confined only to these momentous events; of course,
the vast majority of street demonstrations do not become revolutionary. Some
might be associated with exceptional events but not lead to an abrupt change in
the course of history—for example, the large-scale street mobilizations associated with the deaths of leading political figures. Recent iterations of this include
the wakes held for Raul Alfonsín in 2009 and Néstor Kirchner in 2010, both of
which evoked the mass mourning for Evita in 1953 and Perón in 1974.[9] On a
smaller scale, the key moment can also be a specific event in people's workplaces,
such as a particular campaign against the firing of a group of people or individuals, changing an employment contract, or making a collective bargaining agreement. Demonstrations may also be called in response to political events, such as
a particular presidential election, or a demonstration in favor of, say, collective
bargaining rights.

As some events and dates come to be symbolic in the flow of narrative time,
so do particular people. We can point to Juan and Eva Perón and to their iconic
presence within street mobilizations of all types today. Their faces appear in
huge awnings at the side of the stage in CGT demonstrations; on posters, banners, and placards carried by different groups; and in the naming of the groups
themselves (e.g., the Movimiento Evita). I previously discussed the incorpora-

FIGURE 6.   ATE banner featuring images of Germán Abdala and Leopoldo González

tion of Néstor Kirchner into that pantheon through ritual events. Such practices of making the past present are not confined to traditional Peronists, and
other figures have a similar iconic afterlife, such as Germán Abdala for ATE.
He is a crucial figure (*referente social*), a powerful symbol of the resistance to
Menem's reforms of the state. Abdala died from cancer in 1993, and his death
continues to be commemorated by ATE activists, in homages on its anniversary and in naming new ATE delegations or offices (see Martuccelli and Svampa
1997). His image features in the large banners displayed by ATE at demonstrations (Figure 6).

Thus, historical time and memory are of crucial importance for the shaping
of political activism in these unions and for containment as politicized encompassment. The chains of connection to past events are created and re-created,
personalized and shared, in different acts, including street demonstrations but
also in the videos and speeches delivered at public events like those described
previously. It is a regime of time that shapes the past, especially the immediate past, but leaves the "near-future temporal frame" (Guyer 2007: 417) actually quite indeterminate: the future is open, not quite stated, to be constructed

through praxis. But ATE activists do not on the whole seek to construct a knowable utopia, either in the near or distant future; in fact, in their daily political life, much of what they do is reactive, to events and to rumors of events.

This reactive mode is a kind of "attritional" time, one of constant protest or negotiation. It is the continuance of the day to day of political life when there is no resolution to a particular conflict or problem in sight, coupled with a dramatization of what can become quite banal over time. The different varieties of demonstrations called by ATE give a sense of what I personally experienced as a somewhat grinding and dispiriting repetitiveness. Individual demonstrations were an opportunity for the repetition of particular political arguments and the constant rehearsal and refinement of political narratives and understandings, in formal speeches and audience/participant commentary. This is the mundane, repetitive, constant struggle that makes up political activism and containment in the everyday. It can be extremely draining, as UPCN delegates often pointed out when discussing ATE's particularly combative approach to their employers:

> Because ATE—ATE is confrontation, ATE is struggle, ATE is conflict, and life just can't be like that. ATE in itself is—well, everything is struggle-conflict, struggle-conflict, struggle-conflict, and that is not a reality that a worker wants. A worker wants to work; she or he wants to work. After that, better conditions, better benefits, all the rest. ATE begins with the struggle, ATE is stoppage, ATE is strike, ATE is conflict. That's what an anarchist wants, a political activist. For this reason, I have never felt represented by ATE. (anonymous UPCN delegate)

> FERNANDO DE SA SOUSA, UPCN LEADER: What I mean is, I can do a strike or a mobilization tomorrow, but the day after, every day, no. If I have to live from stoppage to stoppage, it's unsustainable; there isn't a worker in the world who can support it.
> MARCELA MANUEL, UPCN LEADER: It creates a lot of anguish; it's impossible.

My experience of that temporality and the UPCN critique was not shared by my ATE interlocutors. For many the participation in attritional time is also coupled with an underlying sense of fun and drama. Demonstrations are often entertaining and inspiring. They reaffirm collective faith in the overall struggle for class liberation, against neoliberalism, and so on; they are chances for people to meet and maintain friendships with like-minded fellows and reaffirm their commitment to the cause and to each other and to feel that they are doing something worthwhile.

Further, there is the possibility that each demonstration could be, potentially, a key moment in the struggle. It could tip from participation in attritional time to participation in momentous historical time. Although, having said that, I am unclear whether this feeling of potential for more was one shared by my informants. While there, I assumed that they continued to demonstrate and mobilize because each demonstration could prove definitive in some way, but the more I reflect on my material, the more I wonder if that analysis has more to do with my own personal desire for these events to have some significance. Certainly, I kept searching for the Event (Badiou 2005) that would or could resolve all the structural contradictions against which the unions were struggling—the revolution— and of course it never happened and (probably) never will. The Teatro Colón workforce was successfully reduced and the refurbishment conducted in what the workers maintain is an extremely damaging way. Legal struggles continued to defend those workers particularly targeted by the management, and until late 2014 I received regular e-mails notifying me of press conferences, court cases, and other events and campaigns. In October 2015, I ran into one of the protagonists in the ATE *junta interna* at a meeting in the Parque Centenario called to protest the possible election of Mauricio Macri. My friend told me that ATE had been so weakened by the fight that disaffiliation was at the point where they did not have enough members to legally form a *junta interna* anymore. Workers had become exhausted, and SUTECBA, the more officialist union, had poached them from ATE. However, the monthly demonstrations at the National Institute of Statistics continued; struggles over intended reorganizations at the city government audit office neither abated nor were resolved. These projects for the transformation of worlds are continuous, and praxis is a process of constant construction with no identifiable end point.

The ultimately unfulfillable desire for certainty or for demonstrations to have a real effect is, I suspect, one of the elements that lead people to drop out of activism. Yet the churn of activists at all levels of leadership was lower than I had expected. A surprising number of people stayed the course, and those middle-aged and older activists I knew seemed on the whole comfortable with the ongoing and attritional nature of their struggle. This was partly because they saw themselves as a small part of a much larger narrative, a longer tradition of struggle, and thus they folded this attritional experience into their experience of their place in historical time. Others simply enjoyed the repetition, the day-to-dayness of activism. For both groups, the future is one of continued struggle, not one of utopia achieved; their ethical project is not only a process of self-cultivation toward a particular end or goal; it is also about quotidian conceptions of life and living together.

The rarity of revolutionary moments may actually not be something to la-ment, since often the element that tips a mass mobilization into history-changing event is fatal violence, either because demonstrations become riots or because the state violently represses them. The December 2001 demonstrations quickly became riots, with people sacking shops and attacking banks and the state responding with tear gas and rubber bullets (Auyero 2007); earlier, the Cordobazo and the Ezeiza massacre were characterized by confrontation between the state and protesters, and the Peronist resistance was galvanized by the massacre of around five hundred people in the Plaza de Mayo after the 1955 coup. Mercifully, policing of routine protest in Argentina is usually fairly light on the day, despite an increasing criminalization of protest (Svampa and Pandolfi 2004), which refers to how successive governments have sought to control street demonstrations by pursuing demonstrators in the courts. However, relative to conditions in the United Kingdom and United States, Argentines are actually very free to demonstrate. In contrast to the lines of fluorescent-jacketed police officers along the routes of British demonstrations or the pepper spray–wielding US agents, Argentine police tend to take a low profile at street marches. Generally speaking, they do not try to control the demonstrations that take place regularly. Their role is mostly to direct traffic around the route of the march: they park their motorcycles across the roads that they want to block off, removing them once the tail end of the march has passed (Figure 7). In order to hold a demonstration, in theory the unions have to register the route of the march with the city police seven days beforehand. However, they are not asking permission to march and often do not meet this deadline.

This may mean that street demonstrations are somewhat routinized and therefore toothless (cf. Juris 2008). Certainly, this is the critique that UPCN members make of ATE's tendency to take to the streets regularly. They argue that it should be only a last resort to conserve the power of the act. So, for them, the fact that UPCN called out thirty thousand members to the streets in 2005 to demonstrate for collective bargaining indicates that they can convene large numbers if they want to but that it is a mechanism they choose to use selectively. ATE activists argue differently, saying that their combative nature makes them into a significant *factor de presión* (pressure factor), potentially making employers wary of future action, if not changing their minds on present decisions. For example, in the case of the restructuring of the state in the 1990s, they argue that it would have been considerably worse if they had not been prepared to take to the streets and protest loudly when state employees were fired and institutions privatized.

Nonetheless, the experience of attritional time has, as I have suggested, a significant relationship to historical time in that each demonstration *could* be the

FIGURE 7.   Police directing traffic away from the route of a demonstration

one that changes the course of history. Furthermore, the powerful do have a sense that they need at least to be seen to be responding to the demands of the protesters. So, it may be that ATE activists are right and that employers bear in mind previous demonstrations when they are considering changes that could negatively affect the workers. They do also seek to resolve issues in the face of a threat to demonstrate, as I discussed in regard to the ministry functionary negotiating with UPCN in the face of ATE's bellicose statements and upcoming *batucada*. The Argentine state is no different from other large and bureaucratized entities in that change is very slow, including change to the detriment of the workers as well as to their benefit. The balance of power between employer and unions may be one explanation for that. In the meantime, often a demonstration will provoke a favorable response from the employer: for example, someone will not be fired or will be instead moved to a different job, proposals from the employer to adversely change working conditions will founder and be forgotten, or actions will move to the legal sphere and become mired in endless court cases. Or an agreement will be reached, for the employer to renege on when it seems feasible to do so. So it continues.

SPATIALITY: EMBODIED EXPERIENCE

If street demonstrations are boring, draining of energy, routinized, and largely ineffectual, on the one hand, or outright dangerous when the state does send in the security forces, on the other, protesters seem to be caught between a rock and a hard place. Why participate? Of course, there is not a single answer to this question: A Durkheimian approach would point to the functions of the ritual act in promoting solidarity as a means of enacting containment. One could also suggest that street demonstrations have merely become a kind of habitus for activists today or alternatively highlight the thrill of demonstrating, associated in part with the sensorial experience of being in a street march. I combine the latter two approaches and argue that the protest is a way of experiencing, inhabiting, and acting on the urban environment. It creates the city as political space and exposes the embodied nature of citizenship action. It is at the same time a mode of political being-in-the-(urban-)world and a source of excitement and experiential power informing processes of collective subjectivation as particular kinds of political actors. Here, spatiality returns to my analysis, as I explore the relationship between bodies and urban space during marches.

The street march was the most common form of street mobilization in which ATE and CTA activists participated. Marches usually take place around the political center of the city of Buenos Aires, which is constituted by the principal avenues, the Avenida 9 de Julio and the Avenida de Mayo, which cross each other. The Avenida de Mayo runs from the Casa Rosada at one end to the Congressional Palace at the other. Protesters convene in a number of places: if it is a big march, at the obelisk at one end of Avenida 9 de Julio or perhaps at the Congress but also at the corners of streets that feed into the avenue, including the "Diagonales." They then march to a specific end point. If it is a big march, the traditional end point is the Plaza de Mayo at the front of the Casa Rosada, where almost all of the very important mobilizations mentioned by Robben ended. However, protests may also end at the seat of the city government of Buenos Aires, the city legislature, or outside a ministry building, such as that of the Labor Ministry. Pensioners have been protesting at the Congressional Palace every Wednesday for over twenty years. Figure 8 maps out this spatial organization, with the caution that, as Michel de Certeau points out, the "act itself of passing by" or, in this case, marching by (1984: 97), cannot be grasped through visual depiction on a map, which can only show trajectories.[10]

Technologies for protest and the assertion of presence are intimately linked to the affordances of the local urban environment. The massing of people along

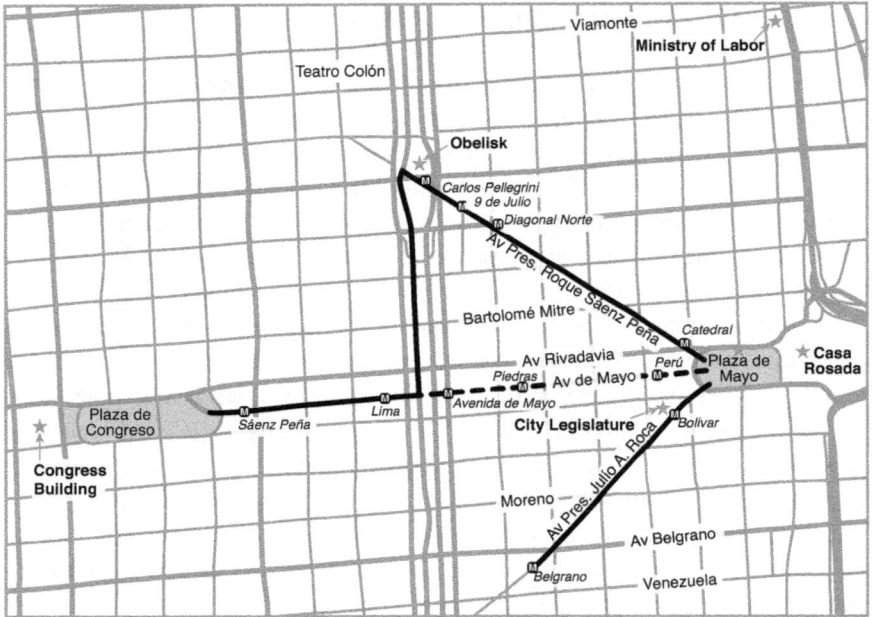

FIGURE 8. Protest routes in center of Buenos Aires (bold black lines) and the main route along Avenida de Mayo (dashed black lines)

a main central avenue is more easily achieved in densely populated areas, where only a small proportion of the residents need to take to the streets to create a mass gathering. I have been to multiple ATE and CTA protests in Buenos Aires and always find them exhilarating, as protesters march down the long straight streets in groups, shouting and holding up their flags and banners, then mass in the square at the end to listen to fervent speeches from leaders stationed at the "stage" (*palco*), usually a truck hooked up to a high-capacity public amplification system. The sounds of the protest, especially the drums of union marches, echo off the buildings at the sides of the streets and enter the bodies of the participants as vibrations of the sternum. People can lean out of high windows of government buildings and shower the protest with small leaflets detailing the demands—a practice called a *papelazo*; they can hang banners out of the windows or watch and encourage. The streets channel the flow of people forward; crowds mass and bodies bump into each other or, when numbers are not too high, spread out to fill as much space as possible. Those watching TV at home or following on Twitter can easily reach the demonstration, and protesters can call, text, or tweet their friends and each other to decide where to go and how to avoid the police. Media outlets can take advantage of tall buildings to photograph images of large numbers of people; they can easily find the leaders of a demonstration at the head of a column of marchers or speaking on a stage at its end point. Building windows can be targets for graffiti or attack, trash cans can be overturned or set on fire, parts of the street and buildings can be picked up to use as missiles or barricades, and demonstrators can disappear down side streets quickly if they need to.

Urban protests are intensely physical and embodied, in different ways than more rural ones, where protest technologies may take on a more topographical character, as in land invasions or the blockade of an arterial road. In other ways, too, protest marches are well adapted to different urban environments, most particularly in how they focus on specific government buildings and take over key nodal points for transit through the city. This is especially evident in smaller cities. In Buenos Aires, it is not so easy to bring city transport to a halt by taking over a defined set of spaces or to provoke much more than the usual gridlock. However, there are some popular places for blockades, such as the Puente Pueyrredon, which was especially important for *piquetero* blockades in 2001–2.

When there is a protest that cuts off part of Avenida 9 de Julio, traffic can be directed around, but it slows down considerably. The avenue has nine lanes of traffic running in each direction—the central avenue has seven in each direction, and there are side streets running alongside, each with two lanes (Figure 9). Although it is not essential for cars to travel down Avenida 9 de Julio to get from one side of the city to the other, it should be evident that blocking such a large number of lanes quickly creates a considerable buildup of traffic in the surrounding streets. *Porteños* have developed strategies for working around marches: for example, on the day of an evening demonstration that was expected to be very large and planned to concentrate at the obelisk, workers in the center of town left early, and by the time that demonstrators began to arrive, traffic on the avenue was minimal. Taxi drivers keep up to date on news of traffic cuts because of demonstrations—as much as they pay attention to news of roadworks or accidents—and if there is a march, they take customers to the point where they consider that they can still escape the traffic and continue their business outside the affected area. Although often people grumble about the ways that demonstrations prevent others from working and moving around the city, on the whole people accept it as part of life in the city.

Thus, the relationship between urban environment and protest is not unidirectional: protest shapes the urban environment as much as the other way around. In her study of the 1871 Paris Commune, Kristin Ross (2008) investigated its creation of social space through various mechanisms. She argued,

FIGURE 9.   View of Avenida 9 de Julio (with the obelisk in the distance)

for example, that the commune horizontalized and made space less hierarchical, particularly exemplified in the destruction of the Vendôme column. Christos Lynteris suggested that this opposition shares an elective affinity with the
distinction Deleuze and Guattari make in *A Thousand Plateaus* (2004) between
smooth and striated space, the latter referring to the organized, often grid form
of space of the state.[11] For Deleuze and Guattari, there is an important distinction between nomadic smooth ground and agricultural striated land. The city
is striated space par excellence, although no space is entirely striated or entirely
smooth. One might speak, then, of the communards as "smoothing" space.[12]
It seems self-evident that state repression striates urban space during and after a protest and that riot horizontalizes and smooths, but what does routinized
(union) protest do? Perhaps the hierarchical forms of organization, the defined
route, the appeal to government authorities, and the careful observance of principles of nonviolence and respect for property all help preserve hierarchies and
maintain striated space. Yet the protest, however well disciplined, also always
contains the potential for excess, as I have suggested for its temporal dimension.
Further, it trains bodies in demonstrating, educating people in a common language of protest but also meaning that political gatherings can happen outside

more conventionally organized marches. These forces ensure that the potential for smoothing space is present within the demonstrational form at all times.

Whether smoothing or striating, protest is a means of acting on the urban environment. As in de Certeau's analysis of walking as a way of reading the city, protests "constitute a 'wandering of the semantic' produced by masses that make some parts of the city disappear and exaggerate others, distorting it, fragmenting it, and diverting it from its immobile order" (1984: 102). They collapse the distances between the obelisk, the Plaza de Mayo, and the virtual spaces of social and mainstream media, for protesters and audience alike. A single protester can participate in all of the spaces of protest, even if physically present only at the start of the demonstration but then make his or her way home to watch it on TV. In this way the protest becomes greater than the sum of its parts. It is an operation on space, a practice that produces space (De Certeau 1984). Somewhere between the unconscious tactics of the walker and the ordered strategies of the planner (ibid.), the protest is a special event that is nonetheless not so unique that it cannot be routine.

De Certeau argued that the "act itself of passing by" is a "space of enunciation," a way of reading the text (or "immense texturology") of the city, and thus producing it (1984: 97). This is important because, he argues, the totalizing processes of apprehending the city as Concept-city—that is, the kind of city that is depicted in maps, plans, statistical surveys, and so on—forgets space and overprivileges time. Beyond that, I would suggest that a focus on walking or protest as productive operation requires a consideration of both space and experience in relation to each other. De Certeau suggests that Merleau Ponty made a similar distinction, between "geometrical" space and what he called an "anthropological space" (ibid.: 117). That "anthropological space" is constituted through experience, and for the demonstrators, the experience of protest is a kind of urban and political being-in-the-world, an ethical phenomenology that is part of what creates them as activists.

That experience begins when ATE and the CTA advertise a protest by means of their e-mail lists, website, group Facebook pages and the personal pages of affiliates, and importantly, posters, cell phones, and assemblies. At the appointed time, groups meet at the convening point, bringing their banners and flags. One of the earliest groups to convene is often the drummers. They start the rhythmic drumming that is the main sound track to the march and welcome all the protesters. When enough have convened, the leaders of the protest set off at the head, arranged in a line across the street, and holding a long thin banner in front of them (Figure 10). Photographers and, if they are lucky, TV cameras can get a good image in this way, of masses of people behind the leading figures. Only the

FIGURE 10.   CTA demonstration, October 2012

drummers usually precede the leaders, and if not, they are located near the beginning of the march. When marches are large, there will be several groups of drummers. The march proceeds along its route, to the stage at the end point. Here the drumming stops, and the leaders of the protest give speeches to the assembled crowd.

I have been present at and participated in street protests in Bolivia, Argentina, and the United Kingdom. All are intensely sensual and have distinctive characteristics and different ways of relating to space, sound, and sight. In Argentina, the dominant sensual experience for me has always been sonorous and associated with the drums. The drumming is an immensely powerful way of asserting presence, especially in this architectural setting. The sound is amplified to the point where those close by cannot help feeling it in their bodies. It is channeled down the Avenida de Mayo or one of the other arterial streets and echoes off the high walls of the six- to eight-story stone buildings. It provides a rhythm for the slow walk and occupies space through sound. Accompanied by a sea of flags and larger banners, of stewards in tabards that indicate their membership in ATE (green) or the CTA (blue), and occasionally a *papelazo* where thousands of leaflets are thrown into the air or thrown down from high windows along the route, the experience is often exhilarating.

The use of drums is now associated with organized demonstrations, especially those organized by unions. The *bombo* is a large drum that has been used in Argentine folkloric music (especially that of the northeast) since the arrival of the Spaniards. Folkloric websites concur that the *bombo leguero* was traditionally made out of a hollowed-out tree, with animal skins drawn over it, and was influenced by European military drums.[13] It has been a feature of protest demonstrations since at least 1945 (Amato and Boyanovsky Bazán 2012; D. James 1988a). Drumming bands do not come out only for large street demonstrations: they may be present, for example, at small quasi-spontaneous gatherings such as the one associated with a short strike called by ATE at the city audit office. As the discussion at the training workshop suggested, an hour of drumming—a *batucada*—is considered by ATE delegates to be a legitimate strategy within a workplace conflict, one that can be escalated if necessary, starting at one hour, moving up to two or three, or longer. Often in informal conversation, UPCN delegates used ATE's willingness to get out the *bombos* as illustration of their conflictive nature; that is, the *bombos* were symbolic for them of combative union activity. ATE activists thought the same; for example, Pablo Sanseverino said, when asked about the negotiation based on the collective bargaining agreement, "Now we consider that we have to be there and that we have to prepare ourselves for that—because we're geniuses with the drum [*para el bombo*], but we also have to be experts so that we don't get crapped on [*para que no nos caguen*] in the negotiations."

UPCN was also not averse to the use of drums, despite the way that its activists characterized ATE as too ready to create a fuss, to engage in "these things that seem to be just for ignorant people, for brutes, the drumming thing, the thing of going out from one side to the other, screaming, noise, rockets, fireworks, that type of thing," which—for this interviewee as other UPCN activists—should really be more of a last resort. In fact, drumming was quite common for UPCN. For example, the National Lottery delegation held an assembly asserting their right to contribute to a process of recategorization of employees and underlined this claim with a loud and strong drumming group that played at the beginning and end of the meeting. The ministry delegation took out their drums on two occasions in one month while I was accompanying them. First, the act commemorating the death of Néstor Kirchner began with the arrival of delegates from other parts of the ministry, one group of which is particularly known for having a number of young men who like to play drums. They arrived in full voice, not stopping until we had all entered the room where the ceremony was being staged. What this meant was that they played the drums in the marble-walled foyer of the ministry building. The amplification was astonishing: the sound of the drums occupied my whole body and dulled my ears for hours afterward. On a second occasion, on the Day of the Activist, the drummers gathered outside the building and played for twenty minutes or so on the street, accompanied by an audience of those who were coming to attend the ceremony, many carrying UPCN flags and umbrellas. The band also featured prominently in the video shown at that ceremony.

Drumming can therefore symbolize combativity, it can constitute a *factor de presión* in and of itself as a strategy for use during a conflict, and it can bring people together in a joyful and exhilarating collective moment. The flags, umbrellas, tabards, and banners are a visual means of occupying space and asserting presence, while the drums do so aurally. They also bring together the people participating in the demonstration—the sound enters individual bodies, takes them over, encompasses them, and pulls them in, making each individual part of the group.

For UPCN, the assertion of presence and collectivity in this way is preemptive, while for ATE it is reactive: UPCN members use their assertion of presence to bring attention to their potential power and warn their employer to keep the UPCN delegation on their side; in addition, they advertise their weight to potential affiliates within the ministry. ATE's drumming usually responds to specific concerns and says to the employer that the members will continue to embarrass and make the employer feel uncomfortable unless demands are addressed. This is not at all accidental and indeed quite self-conscious. It is praxis as theorized action on the world in order to change the world; leaders need to decide whether and why to hold a protest, for how long, and what kind of demonstration to engage in at any moment—a strike for twenty-four, thirty-six, forty-eight hours; a one- or three-hour *batucada*; or a street demonstration, a funeral for culture, a dance, a press conference, a music festival, a carnival, an occupation. They make these decisions based on experience and their assessment of the risks, and they consider very carefully what might be the effects, on their employers and on the workers. These decisions are subject to debate within the leadership, in the assemblies, and during the events themselves, and leaders must constantly assess the mood of the participants and their willingness to commit to further action.

PROTEST AND THE STRUGGLE OVER MEANING

The self-conscious and strategic aspect of any protest makes it different from the act of walking in the city as described by de Certeau. Even though many of the

ways and forms of protesting might not be overtly conscious and might have become something akin to Maussian techniques of the body (Mauss 1973), the act
of mobility itself is designed to act on the city and its inhabitants in a specific
way. Unlike walking, a demonstration is not about getting from A to B. So, as
well as being a particular way of reading the text of the city, the protest itself is
also a cultural product, a kind of text. That text is a form of praxis produced in a
self-consciously strategized way: it requires organizers who ask what exactly are
the demands of the demonstration, who will play the drums, what route will we
take, which building shall we congregate outside, do we need a PA system, and
will we have dancers? As a text it is also open to contested readings, as the politics of protest shapes citizen action, legitimizing some forms of political participation and claims making and delegitimizing others. Politics becomes distilled
into the struggle over meaning and display (see Lazar 2015).

The political agency of street demonstrations as a collective subject in themselves, or as the praxis engaged in by the collective subject of the union or other
political group, is as much about the readers of any particular demonstration as
it is about the demonstrators themselves, and the two groups are not mutually
exclusive. In everyday Buenos Aires demonstrations, audiences are important:
in physical proximity, tourists and citizens alike watch big demonstrations that
happen to be passing by and are given pamphlets by protesters; taxi drivers and
their passengers discuss routes to take to avoid the congestion caused by protests.
Indeed, the possibility that citizens are inured to street protests, that they have
become a kind of "anti-audience," is always present, and more creative tactics are
constantly being evolved to capture audiences. For other mass demonstrations,
the principal audience is on TV, as news channels transmit rolling images of the
large numbers of protesters massed in the streets and interview individual participants. For political demonstrations of all kinds, there is little point if there is
no audience, even if the audience is not physically present at the time of the presentation but is constituted by politicians, national or international media, other
protesters in different places, or public opinion defined more nebulously. The audience and participants make the event together, it is not something being produced by authors and consumed by readers. Communication between protesters
and audiences is, of course, always contested, because readings vary.

The very multiplicity of readings and their mediated nature have become increasingly important for Argentine politics since the presidential election of
2011, as the political environment as filtered through mainstream and nonmain-
stream media became significantly more polarized. This resulted from multiple
factors, from the increasing vehemence of opposition in media outlets associated
especially with Grupo Clarín to the emergence of youth groups like La Cámpora,

whose support for Cristina is equally passionate. By the presidential election of late 2015, political debate had become a war of signs and interpretations: Are the Kirchners (Néstor and Cristina) the phenomenally corrupt politicians painted by the journalist Jorge Lanata in his Sunday TV show and Facebook posts, or are they the fearless defenders of human rights and youth painted by the various Movimientos K? Were Cristina's plans for the elections of judges a means to pack the courts with party-political lackeys who would pursue her enemies or a democratization of the judiciary that removes it from the hands of the oligarchy? Did she order the murder of the prosecutor Alberto Nisman in January 2015, or did rogue intelligence agents murder him to discredit her government?

Unions like UPCN are in the middle of the two opposing forces, seeking to gain benefit through institutional mechanisms of support and relation with the president, which work through formal and personalized channels. Meanwhile, many of their activists moved to a much more hard-line position of support for Cristina in the face of what they perceived to be personal attacks, and this became even stronger after she lost the election and during the subsequent cases brought against her for corruption. ATE fractured between its *kirchnerista* and non-*kirchnerista* wings as politics polarized. In such a situation, those who live politics are continually watching and debating who takes to the streets, for what motives, and how spontaneously. They enact their day-to-day activism in this context.

CONCLUSION

Union activists experience the temporality of protest as a mixture between routinized responses to specific threats at their place of work or to working conditions more generally (such as when protesting a particular proposed piece of legislation) and occasional moments of tension that cut across specific union demands and reach out to expose societal stresses. Protests are multivalent practices, experiences that take place within contrasting but often overlapping temporalities and spatialities and that shape the time and space within which activists operate. As embodied experiences, they are often powerful, inspiring, creative, and entertaining. Like the assembly, they draw the group together, affirm collective identity, and enact collective political agency. Much of the power of a street protest lies in its potential: most will not become history-changing events, but they all might—if not on their own, then in concert with others. Each protest has the capacity for excess but is also vulnerable to contested understandings and at times state repression.

Protests are also multisensorial experiences. I have focused mostly on visual and auditory experiences, but in principle there is no reason why one could not extend the analysis to the senses of smell, taste, and touch. Thus, when we analyze these—and probably other political rituals—it will be worth heeding de Certeau's warning against the "cancerous growth of vision, measuring everything by its ability to show or be shown and transmuting communication into a visual journey" (1984: xxi). We can "read" street demonstrations as cultural products but should not restrict ourselves only to that which is visually evident or captured by statements in the media or by informants.

Protests are part of the texture of everyday political life. Thus, and returning to the main theme of this book, they are both hexis and praxis, especially when part of conscious union action. That is, protests are techniques of ethical self-cultivation as collective subjects through containment, as well as critically theorized action on the world in order to transform the world. Through the experience of collective action in assemblies and on the streets, ATE activists construct themselves as subjects with clearly defined political projects for transformation and betterment. They experience and debate effervescence and mutuality of being within several different collectivities, for example, as Teatro Colón workers, members of ATE-Capital supporting the city audit office workers, or as CTA members. Values such as autonomy, democracy, political commitment, and rage against neoliberal injustices circulate with the sounds of the *bombos* and the physical experience of collective action to act on the city and create the group as kin and friends.

The assembly and the protests are spaces of kinning, through practices similar to those described in the previous chapter, as people join together in effervescence and circulate values as well as material objects (banners, musical instruments, leaflets, cigarettes, sandwiches, empanadas, and pizza). In this case, the kinning works in a more explicitly politicized sense or toward a more explicitly politicized aim, which is to transform the world (and the city). Thus, the link between containment as collective self-cultivation through kinning and praxis as explicitly theorized action to change the world becomes clearer. The street protests and assemblies are excellent examples of the combination of hexis and praxis: both are actions of kinning that make the collective and collective actions that make the world.

CONCLUSION

I have focused on two groups of especially committed activists in what might be considered one of the more powerful labor movements in the world. Historically, the Argentine labor movement has had significant and continuing ability to be an effective interlocutor with the state and to protect the position of the movement and its members. Today that strength is derived in part from the movement's history and in part from its place in a particular national political context. Crucially, it is also self-constructed through political organization. I reiterate my point that political organization should be seen as a collection of processes of more or less consciously constructed collective subjectivation, understanding the term "subjectivation" as *assujettisssement* in Foucault's usage but with a less solipsistic and more political edge. In turn, understanding union activism as a necessary combination of different kinds of ethical-political action requires us to acknowledge the importance of organization to social movement success. What that does is open the possibility of moving beyond a dichotomy of rational choice versus ideological manipulation as the dominant means available to us to explain political and social mobilization. This affects how we understand the dynamics and practices of collective citizenship in Argentina today.

Organization is essential to political struggle and political identity formation, an observation often applied to class formation. I have focused not on a class in (for) itself but on a subsection of a class, unionized public-sector workers. I have explored how their political subjectivation comes into being, what social practices and values inform and constitute it, and how activists understand their participation. I here consider how these ethical and political dimensions relate to each other and argue that, for the unionists studied here, activism is an ethical mode of existence that is a combination of whole-life experience and action to transform society.

ETHICAL AND POLITICAL SUBJECTIVATION

There is a complex relationship between will, cultivation, and essence in the political subjectivation of activists. As this book shows, for many activists, from both UPCN and ATE, militancy is a life experience, mapped out along different pathways of union, neighborhood, and party activism. As unionists, both groups produced narratives of commitment, passion, and love, which they frequently explained through quasi-biological metaphors, describing their activism as a virus or an addiction, for example. However, mostly it was seen as a natural outcome of their personality, so the way that they made themselves was often articulated in terms of their (preexisting) essential being. Only rarely did they narrate their activism as a choice made after rational calculation of interest, nor was it something that they felt needed particularly active or conscious work on their part.

Yet this narrative of inevitability does not tell the whole story. For activists were also acutely aware of the difficulties of activism, in their personal lives or with respect to the stigma attached to unionists in the eyes of the general public, but they continued nonetheless. Furthermore, the daily life of activism is actually something that in practice demands considerable commitment, effort, and time. At different points in history it has also been physically very dangerous. Yet they continued, often taking considerable pride in the fact that they did so. By describing their activism as *militancia*, they were also knowingly evoking a whole series of historical resonances, of 1970s militancy or Peronist heritage and resistance and even exemplary figures such as Eva Perón, Juan Perón, or for ATE unionists, Víctor de Gennaro or Germán Abdala. Finally, the values and personality traits held to be part of their essential being could also be elicited from activists through schooling. So an activist disposition was in fact not an automatic outcome of being born with a particular character but could be and was generated through particular pedagogical and practical mechanisms.

Yet essential being was still central to the practices of self-making in the unions. For example, the elicitation of particular personality traits or deeply held values and beliefs in pedagogical spaces such as the union school of UPCN was achieved mostly through exhortation, by saying, "You have this commitment, vocation for unionism or social justice; you are this kind of person." Delegates were also encouraged to examine their own strengths and weaknesses in workshop exercises such as the FODA matrix exercise. This "self-examination" is an example of a technology of the self in the pure Foucauldian sense, as delegates were encouraged to measure—and work on—their own virtues and defects with a view to achieving a particular profile as a delegate.

Complex notions of essence also came through in understandings of how activist disposition is transmitted across generations and through kinship. Peronism is understood to be something in the blood, or "from the cradle." This phrase takes the biological metaphor of activism to the point where it becomes almost genetic: the predisposition to activism can, it seems, be inherited from one's mother or father and is therefore clearly part of one's inner essence. Yet Peronism can also be transmitted from early infancy and in the mother's breast milk, pointing to the crucial fact that it is also transmitted through experience. So people told me about parents, uncles and aunts, or grandparents telling stories of Evita, teaching them particular political values, or taking their children along to demonstrations and other political events from an early age. People's children "grow up in the midst of the chaos" as one UPCN delegate said. Family members—especially uncles and aunts—can be exemplary figures as well, teaching an activist disposition to members of the next generation through their own behavior in addition to the stories they tell and the political discussions in which they engage. Yet activism is *also* about will, since not all children or nieces and nephews will have the same response to an older generation's activism, with many choosing a nonpolitical pathway. So the disposition to activism is something that both "just is" and is mutable, described as part of someone's inner essence even when it was a choice.

Thus, much of my interlocutors' talk about their subjectivation was articulated in terms that downplayed the role of reflection in their action and focused more on essential aspects of their being or character. Their cultivation of self was only partially amenable to reflection, in specific contexts such as a research interview or discussion or formal workshop exercise. In my experience it was not in itself a daily topic of conversation outside those contexts, not even when people were considered to be not measuring up. If someone was not prepared to be a good activist, the person would simply withdraw from activity. No one would attempt to bring the individual back into the fold; there were no sermons directly describing correct behavior and bearing as can be found in some religious contexts (Lazar 2008). Nonetheless, activists did develop a certain style, bearing, and commitment. Out of what they understood as essential, even biological characteristics, they created a particular cultivated disposition, or hexis.

A crucial aspect of those activities that constituted activist hexis was their collective nature: activists understood themselves as individuals located in specific collective contexts, and they were convinced of the need for collective solutions to political problems. These convictions, which had the status of unquestioned and often unarticulated truths, were achieved in part through the highly social mechanisms that I described as containment. They consisted of social gatherings, commensality, day-to-day care, and quasi-therapeutic relationships, combined with the more self-conscious elements of schooling, speeches at ritual events and political rallies, and so on. I have suggested that all were practices of kinning, achieved through the circulation of substances such as food, drink, and importantly, values. Both ATE and UPCN shared the value of collectivity itself, but other circulated values that differed according to the union concerned commitment to governmental figures or to autonomy, verticalism or horizontalism, discipline or democracy for UPCN or ATE activists, respectively.

PRAXIS

In contrast to the selves of late Foucauldian thought (Foucault 1988, 1990) and a number of subjects of the contemporary anthropology of ethics, unionists' practices of self-cultivation are not aimed primarily at improving themselves as persons or even especially living in accordance with conceptions of the good, although both do apply. Their principal aim is to transform society, so for them, self-making combines with "praxis," a term that points—especially through its Marxian use—to action for social transformation.

Foucault used the term "autopoiesis" to describe self-cultivation, drawing— via the Stoics—on Aristotle's notion of poiesis, usually defined as "making or fabrication" (Faubion 2011; Foucault 1988). But Aristotle also provided an understanding of self-cultivation that extended beyond poiesis and autopoiesis into praxis, usually defined as "doing." Aristotle's discussion of making and doing in Book VI of the *Nicomachean Ethics* forms part of a description of a series of intellectual virtues, all related to different kinds of activity. For example, *sophia* (wisdom) maps to *theoria* (theory), while *techne* (skill or art) maps to poeisis. Finally, *phronesis*, translated by J. A. K. Thomson in the *Ethics* as "prudence," maps to praxis. For Aristotle, wisdom, skill, and prudence are all virtues that should be developed within the person to result in the different modes of action (theory, making, and doing). They culminate in the desired hexis, or cultivated moral state of the person.

Prudence is eminently political, since the prudent man is able to deliberate on what is good not only for himself but also for the good life generally; the quality of prudence "belongs to those who understand the management of households or states"(Aristotle 1988: 209). Thus, prudence was especially associated with the realm of citizenship, which excluded legislation but included deliberation and judgment (ibid.: 214, 1992; Arendt 1998). Hannah Arendt (1998) was particularly inspired by this and developed a notion of action that was very much about how to live with others, how to participate in the web of human relations, particularly through speech. The latter characterizes political life in Argentina as much as it did for Arendt and can be seen in this book in practices as varied as workplace assemblies, ceremonial events to pay homage to Néstor Kirchner or to the Day of the Activist, speeches at street demonstrations and political rallies, negotiations with functionaries, and discussions of national politics. To understand Argentine unionists' action and activism, it is important then to reinstate the explicitly political aspects of Aristotelian and Arendtian thought on ethics and intellectual virtues: to recover prudence/*phronesis* and, especially, praxis.[1]

In doing so, we must also consider Marxism, the main philosophical field associated with the term "praxis." Antonio Gramsci, following Antonio Labriola, called Marxism the "philosophy of praxis" in his *Prison Notebooks* (1998: 321–472). From its beginning, this philosophy of praxis has held extraordinary political and social power in addition to its philosophical charge,[2] encapsulated in the famous Eleventh Thesis on Feuerbach: "The philosophers have only interpreted the world, in various ways; the point is to change it" (Marx 1845). Although ATE and UPCN disagree about the mechanisms to promote desirable change, and perhaps the extent of change necessary, they both seek to transform their worlds for the better; or, as in some historical moments such as in the 1990s, they sought to ameliorate change for the worse. And in fact there is a range of opinion across both unions about what change might be desirable and possible. Nonetheless, both unions see themselves as acting for the betterment of their members and for workers more broadly; and in doing so they put considerable effort into self-making, both individual and collective.

The recognition of the importance of social and political action for philosophy as encapsulated in the Eleventh Thesis has clearly had many implications, one of which was the entry into Marxist political thought of what we might understand as processes of subjectivation. Marxists as different as Ernesto "Che" Guevara (1965) and Herbert Marcuse (1969) acknowledged at least to some extent the role of self-making in the construction of desired political subjects. Marcuse was especially excited about the prospect of the New Left of the 1960s for creating a "new sensibility" based on art, imagination, and the Great Refusal (of dominant systems of thought, including capitalism). Paulo Freire, more directly embedded than Marcuse in practical political and social action, linked praxis to subjectivity via pedagogy. He defined praxis as "reflection and action upon the world in order to transform it" (Freire 1996: 51) and thought that it could be brought into being through radical education that enabled people to perceive their own position in a given—oppressive—social structure. Both unions' training programs are conceived at least partially in this way, although ATE's more so.

However, a focus on revolutionary transformations might blind us to more mundane forms of praxis that are nonetheless transformational, although on a small scale. There are multiple examples of nonrevolutionary praxis described in this book, actions that are often moments of interaction and common construction and circulation of values. For example, the street protests described in Chapter 6 are a series of creative moments of common construction of meaning, located in the political history of the labor movement itself and in the city as space. The rituals paying homage to Néstor Kirchner or celebrating the Day of the Activist are moments of collective affirmation and circulation of common values and interpretations of politics as well as social experiences of effervescence, commensality, emotion, and communitas (Durkheim [1915] 1965; Turner 1969). They state and restate a political agenda and contribute to building it in the present moment, through bringing protagonists together and making collective strength evident by means of sonorous and physical presence (drums, shouting, banners, and bands). Unionists also engage in more quotidian moments of praxis, such as negotiations over individual employment contracts; making and displaying posters claiming particular political goals; engaging in acts of care through the provision of welfare and social rights such as child care or health care; holding cultural competitions for poetry, essay writing, art; campaigning against workplace harassment and for equal opportunities. Finally, the two unions engage in particular kinds of pedagogical praxis, as they train their delegates in particular understandings of organization, political action (negotiation and contestation), history, professional bearing, and personal values.

ORGANIZATION, KINSHIP, AND ETHICS

Together, all these amount to a whole-life experience of politics and ethics, shaping citizenship through the interaction between self-making and collective political action—two processes that appear in day-to-day language in Argentina as militancy and containment, respectively. Collective politics is thus an ethical project (in fact, many ethical projects); it is the praxis that consists in and becomes possible from multiple individual and collective self-making projects and that in turn shapes those projects.

I want to take this one step further and argue that much of the power of this collective politics derives from the fact that it is also a kind of kinship. Specifically, I suggest that containment is both ethical practice and kinship mode. It is a term used by Argentine unionists to describe processes of kinning, which include ritual, political, and educational practices as well as caregiving and the distribution of welfare. They might include discussions over mate in the afternoons and evenings around the table, workshop sessions on the collective bargaining agreement, assemblies at the workplace and the central union office, campaigns for equality of opportunities, and the other multifarious activities of unionism. In all these spaces, common values circulate and are reinforced, new recruits are drawn into the group, and the group is strengthened in the face of its opponent—whether the managers, the rival union, or the city mayor. People make each other as kin, as they become friends and experience "mutuality of being" in Sahlins's sense (2013: 2), perhaps a kind of mutuality of political being. They also draw kin in in very practical ways, as they find jobs for sons, daughters, nieces, nephews, cousins, and family friends and then bring them into the union delegation as well.

Thus, kinning underlies both ethical projects and collective politics more generally. It happens differently in UPCN and ATE: while both engage in social processes of kinning through conversation and commensality, UPCN emphasizes more the elements of care, service, and negotiation, and ATE emphasizes explicitly politicized action such as assemblies and protest events. UPCN also has a very highly structured educational program that makes delegates as both kin and persons. These distinctions are consonant with the contrasting historical trajectories of development for the two unions. The Peronist labor movement has long been associated with a kind of service unionism (what some of my informants called *gremialismo*), which can be described as business unionism (Mollona 2009), bureaucratic unionism, officialism, even yellow unionism. UPCN leaders of course resist this more negative evaluation of their union praxis and argue that it is the most effective choice for their affiliates and for the workers in general. ATE activists envisage themselves as part of a contrasting union tradition, more influenced by social movements in the present moment, with a history of anarcho-syndicalism from the early twentieth century, and radical rank-and-file unionism from the 1960s. Their opponents argue that this position is ineffective, exhausting, and unappealing to most workers, while ATE contends that this is the only truly autonomous stance to take in opposition to management.

So the ethical modes of existence I have described have a structural context: they are activist but also exist within an organizational ecology. An implication of this is that they come up against limitations, one of which is the question of "attritional time," the constant grind of political activity where ultimate success is impossible. I argued that this was made possible for unionists because they saw themselves as part of a longer project of "historical time," a narrative of ups and downs in a much longer-term political project. Their praxis is not revolutionary (or not always), but it is a struggle against oppression. Yet it does not always come from a clear subject position, and the tension between pragmatism and ideological purity is another limiting factor in the political-ethical projects of the unionists. This can be seen especially in ATE's critique of UPCN for being overly ready to negotiate, so much so that UPCN is actually really on the side of the management, while UPCN activists consider ATE to be unnecessarily dogmatic and therefore harmful to those it is supposed to represent.

That in turn relates to the particular question of the kind of political subject represented by these organized public-sector workers. In contrast to the archetypal industrial proletariat, public-sector workers, especially civil servants, find themselves in a complex structural position in two ways. First, both unions have trouble encouraging their affiliates to identify as workers in contradistinction to the state employer: some UPCN delegates even said to me that as public servants they were actually their own employer, in their capacity as Argentine citizens. The range of jobs covered by both unions promotes an extremely broad range of identifications, from professional lawyers, accountants, and bureaucrats to artists, dancers, musicians, lab technicians, clerical workers, and scientists. Neither union can build an effective political subject identity on the sole basis of the labor process—that is, on the basis of a common identity as a specific kind of worker. Therefore, the union must build identity on slightly different grounds, especially with regard to the activists themselves, who must build an identity on the grounds of being activists in their union, in a circular process. This perhaps explains the individual self-making through the powerful concept of *militancia*.

Second, for unionists the classic capital-labor-state triangle collapses because the state is also their employer. On the one hand, their conditions of employment make union activism easier than in the private sector: a large proportion of them have secure jobs, their legal rights to engage in union activity are on the whole respected by their employer, and under the Kirchner regimes they were an important source of political support for the government. On the other hand, the union cannot seek state mediation or support in difficult negotiations with management, so it is perhaps even more likely than usual for unions to become very identified with the employers. Indeed, although counterintuitive, it might be more necessary to explain ATE's ability to resist than UPCN's decision to ally itself with an "officialist" position.

The organizational ecology therefore structures the demands that this part of the labor movement can make, and one of the most important effects has been that unions became not only about the structural conflict between labor and management but also about defending the organization as a value in and of itself. This is one explanation for the social labor involved in collective self-making as a union. It is particularly explicit in the UPCN school, where unionists justify such a strategy by saying, following Perón, that an organization must negotiate from a position of power and therefore the labor they undertake to defend themselves as a union is necessary to attain that position. ATE activists want to constitute their union as a *factor de presión*, so their actions focus on protest and campaigning activities but also—and probably more important—on assemblies. The latter are really about constructing a horizontal politics and what ATE activists envisage as a truly democratic mode of existence within their organization. The two approaches conflicted seriously in the 1990s when UPCN defended its own people and ATE became a *factor de presión* from the outside. Individuals from both organizations claim that anything at all that was rescued from the situation was due to their union's actions.

The focus on the organization as institution can be problematic because both unions can turn in on themselves to preserve themselves as movement and expend much of their energy on discussions and debates about how best to organize. Thus, they run the risk of losing sight of a broader imagined telos beyond union strength itself, however that might be defined. Yet I think that it would be misguided to dismiss this by arguing that it is merely political ideology (ATE) or what one would expect from a bureaucratized and compromised labor movement (UPCN). Both criticisms rely on an assumption that the explanation for social movements need not really go very far "beyond grievance" (Shah 2013), that is, beyond collective interest rationally assessed, clearly articulated, and then (somehow automatically) deeply felt. Such a position requires little to no consideration of the means to act, yet in fact organization itself is probably crucial to getting to the point where it is possible collectively to feel not only grievances but also positive values and desires for transformation. Only through organization can those grievances, values, and desires be experienced, articulated, and maintained in a praxis that has power and longevity. Put differently, without organization, political struggle cannot take place, no matter how deeply felt or rationally chosen a set of political opinions might be.

What the activists of ATE and UPCN teach us is that political organization of this kind consists at least in part of a set of ethical projects of self-making, both individual and collective. These are the everyday practices of active citizenship in this context: they are the grounds of union power as political actors and interlocutors with government and employers. These practices of citizenship then shape the conditions of possibility for citizenship for formal-sector workers in Argentina beyond the union sphere, affecting the distribution of their social, cultural, and economic rights and their ability to make claims on the grounds of rights or other political discourses; their ability to participate collectively in government and the ways that they do so; and their subjective positioning as individual political actors who are part of distinct political communities. As much as it is a political project, their citizenship is thus revealed as a multifaceted ethical project of self-making and action on the world.

NOTES

INTRODUCTION

1. Britos is director of the Escuela Político Sindical (Political Unionist School) of Unión Argentina de Trabajadores Rurales y Estibadores (Argentine Union of Rural Workers and Stevedores, UATRE). He has been a Peronist activist since 1947.

2. A pro-Macri position would highlight contrasting aspects of the Kirchner regimes: irresponsible economic policies leading to severe inflation and dangerously dwindling national reserves, overly restrictive controls on imports and the purchase of dollars, corruption at the highest levels of government, insular and unnecessarily combative foreign policy, and failure to act on drug-trafficking problems in the country. The results of the second round of voting indicate a country split down the middle, and the impression I have from the last few years is of increased polarization, in part fueled by a virulent anti-Cristina media. See Lazar (2016a).

3. Peronism is the political movement founded by Juan Domingo Perón in the 1940s when he became minister for labor and then, from 1946 to 1955, president of Argentina. In 1955, he was deposed by military coup, and his supporters entered a period of clandestine resistance, demanding his return from exile, which was achieved in 1973. Shortly thereafter, he became president again but died in 1974; his third wife and vice president was deposed in 1976 by one of the most brutal military regimes in the region. After the return to democracy in 1982, the next Peronist regime was that of Carlos Menem, in 1989–99, followed by the 2001 economic crisis during the Kirchner regimes of 2003–15. The political party founded by Perón—the Partido Justicialista (the Justicialist Party) —and the Peronist movement are not necessarily coextensive. Perón attracted followers from an extremely wide political spectrum, from leftist Marxist guerrillas to anticommunist death-squad members. This very brief description of Peronism does not give a sense of its complexities as an identity and way of life for its adherents, not just as a political orientation. In this book I explore that complex picture for one group of Peronists (the UPCN unionists), but there are many studies of Peronism across different periods of its history. For some of the best, see Auyero (2001), D. James (1988b), Karush and Chamosa (2010), Levitsky (2003a), Torre (1998, 2002, 2012), Martuccelli and Svampa (1997), Munck, Galitelli, and Falcon (1987), Halperin Donghi (2012); Elena (2011).

4. This makes it more like the social movement unionism discussed by Moody (1997) and Waterman (1993) and relates it to both the history of anarcho-syndicalism prominent in Argentina since the early twentieth century and the consciously horizontal and

autonomous social movement activism of post-2001 Argentina, discussed by scholars such as Marina Sitrin (2006, 2012) and Ana Dinerstein (2003, 2014).

5. Within more economically focused anthropology and sociology, there is a distinguished ethnographic literature on trade unions, but it has largely focused on the Global North (e.g., Collins 2012; Durrenberger 2007; Zlolniski 2010; Durrenberger and Erem 2005; Fantasia and Voss 2004; Kasmir 2005; Lopez 2004; Mollona 2009; Johnston 1994; Moody 1997; Fantasia 1988). With a few exceptions, such as De Neve (2008), Donham (2011), and Werbner (2014), anthropologists have rarely directly engaged with trade unions in the Global South; and much of the anthropological work on organized labor in the Global South has been tied to questions of the globalization of the world economy (e.g., Collins 2007; De Neve 2008; Otañez 2010; Zlolniski 2010) or industrial employment patterns (Parry 2013).

6. On governance, see Ong (1996, 2003); Holston (2008); Blom Hansen and Stepputat (2001); Fassin (2015); Rose (1999); Nguyen (2010). On care of the self, see, for example, Faubion (2011); Cook (2010); Rose (1989).

7. For example, see Atzeni and Ghigliani (2007); Dinerstein (2003); Sitrin (2012); Alcaniz and Scheier (2007); G. Álvarez (2015); Mauro and Rossi (2015); Fernández Álvarez (2015); Schamber (2008).

8. For excellent recent surveys of sociological approaches to social movements, see Cox and Flesher Fominaya (2013); Tilly and Wood (2012); Walder (2009). Anthropological studies of social movements include Nash (2005); Juris (2008, 2012); Graeber (2009, 2013); Razsa and Kurnik (2012); Maeckelbergh (2009); Dave (2012); Escobar (2009). Also see the collections edited by Werbner, Webb, and Spellman-Poots (2014); and Juris and Khasnabish (2013).

9. On resource mobilization theory, see Jenkins (1983); on New Social Movements theory, see Cohen (1985); Melucci (1989); Touraine (1988). The political opportunities approach is most closely associated with Charles Tilly (e.g., 1978, 1993; Tilly and Tarrow 2006), but also see Jasper (2012) for an excellent survey. Examples of the framing approach are discussed in Johnston and Noakes (2005); and see Ullrich, Daphi, and Baumgarten (2014) for a critique of these and a more general overview of the role of culture in sociological theories of social movements.

10. For example, see Jean Cohen's (1985) description of the New Social Movements theorists; and Escobar and Alvarez (1992). But see Cox and Flesher Fominaya's (2013) discussion of how the NSM paradigm has itself been understood in an unsubtle way.

11. The canonical example of this is, of course, May 1968 in France, but even that was as powerful as it was in large part because the student protests in Paris were allied to a nationwide general strike led by the unions. Other key movements and events at this time were the Tlatelolco massacre of October 1968 in Mexico City, the 1960s counterculture movement in the United States, the US civil rights movement, the second wave of feminism in the United States and Europe, the UK "winter of discontent" in 1978–79, and the growth of indigenous movements in the Americas during the 1970s.

12. They must define themselves in this way because Peronism is so defining of twentieth-century activism in Argentina.

13. The danger is, as Erica Lagalisse cautions, that this may herald "a change on the Left whereby the economic reductionism that romanticised the working class is in some ways replaced by an ethnic reductionism that romanticises the indigenous as the new revolu-

tionary subject" (2013: 132). She also notes that both of these reductionisms marginalize gender. My study attempts to counter the reductionism that Lagalisse warns of, without falling prey to the temptation to romanticize them.

14. These include studies of squatters' groups in Madrid (Corsín Jiménez and Estalella 2013), anarchists in Slovenia (Razsa and Kurnik 2012; Razsa 2015), migrant workers' tenant groups in Berlin (Bojadzijev 2014), drug users in New York (Zigon 2014), and the Gezi Park protests in Istanbul (Tugal 2013); and on the urban commons, see Casas-Cortés, Cobarrubias, and Pickles (2014).

15. This was the economic reductionism that Lagalisse decried. Feminists had, of course, long been pointing out the importance of gender, and indigenous peoples had been mobilizing to protect their specific interests for centuries.

16. This includes Moody (1997); Johnston (1994); Fantasia and Voss (2004); Lopez (2004); Mollona (2009, 2015); Collins (2012). An example of the slipping out of view is, ironically, David Harvey's book *Rebel Cities* (2012), in which he produces a brilliant Marxian discussion of capitalist accumulation by dispossession in the cities. Although his class analysis is excellent, almost none of the rights to the city movements he describes are based on labor.

17. See Kalb (2014) for a discussion of the idea of the "global middle class."

18. My thanks to Jeff Juris for pointing this out and ensuring that I acknowledge it explicitly.

19. For example, see Laidlaw (2002, 2014); Lambek (2010); Robbins (2004, 2013); Faubion (2011); Zigon (2008). But note also a broader anthropology of morality and ethics that focuses on the circulation and power of moral concepts in political life (e.g., Fassin 2012, 2013; Englund 2008; Werbner 2014). One strong tradition of the study of public ethics can be located in legal anthropology, which Pnina Werbner (2014) traces back to Max Gluckman's work, and then through to more contemporary anthropologies of human rights (e.g., Wilson 1997; Cowan, Dembour, and Wilson 2001).

20. For example, see Forbess and Michelutti (2013); Carsten (2013, 2014); Eriksen (2010); Herzfeld (2007); Alonso (1994); Delaney (1995); Wade (2005); Stoler (2002); Bear (2007).

CHAPTER 1

1. Most of the employees of the national state—that is, ministries, decentralized organisms, etc.—are based in the Federal Capital; but this sectional office also represents those who are employed by the national state but based in different parts of the country. The other sectional offices are territorial and group together employees of the relevant provincial or municipal state, such as the sectional office for the province of Buenos Aires, Santa Fe, Rosario, etc. However, they represent only employees of their provincial government, not employees of the federal government based in that province.

2. He was president of the party in the city of Buenos Aires in 2011–14, then became first vice president.

3. Individuals also pay 1.5 percent of their salary for each dependent member of the health insurance plan. Ley de Obras Sociales, Law for Health Insurance Plans, no. 23.660, 1989; also Law 25.239, 1999, which modified employer's contribution. See http://infoleg .mecon.gov.ar/infolegInternet/anexos/0-4999/62/texact.htm.

4. Information in this paragraph is gleaned from conversations with UPCN leaders and cross-checked with the texts of laws available on the government website. It represents an ideal, since union finances are an enormously contested area. Many Argentines think that unions raise money by corrupt means or through direct support from the government in return for labor peace. For example, some accuse unions of diverting money from the health insurance organizations. Also, the Solidarity Fund has probably at times been a means for government to channel money to supportive unions or withhold money to punish recalcitrant unionists. See Balinotti (2012).

5. Ley de Asociaciones Sindicales, no. 23.551, 1988, http://www.infoleg.gov.ar/infoleg Internet/anexos/20000-24999/20993/texact.htm.

6. The literature on anthropology of the state is too numerous to list here, but important volumes and survey articles include Aretxaga (2003); Das and Poole (2004); Steinmetz (1999); Trouillot (2001); Blom Hansen and Stepputat (2001); Sharma and Gupta (2006).

7. SUTECBA changed its name in the mid-1990s to stress its claim to be the only union operating for municipal employees. Previously, it had been called UOEM (Unión de Obreros y Empleados Municipales; Union of Municipal Workers and Employees).

8. In 2008, ATE-Capital had a total of 18,925 affiliates, 73.4 percent of whom were employees of the national government; 25.6 percent, employees of CABA; and 1.2 percent, employees of the Buenos Aires provincial government. The CABA employees in the health sector made up 55 percent of ATE-Capital affiliates employed by CABA (a proportional reduction from 2000, when the health sector contained 90 percent of ATE affiliates in CABA) (Pereira et al. 2009).

9. Very little of this was articulated to me explicitly by ATE informants, who most often stressed the unity and coherence of their political program, with the exception of one interviewee. I have pulled together this narrative on the basis of this interview and conversations with local academic observers of ATE, as well as my sense of tensions within the organization between my two main research visits in 2009 and 2012. In the intervening time a substantial change in the leadership had occurred. Returning to my 2009 interview transcripts, I can see some underlying elements of the *kirchnerista*-oppositional tension then, but I had arrived just after the death of a key general secretary, Leopoldo González, who had been closely allied with Pablo Micheli (and Víctor de Gennaro). The adjunct secretary who became general secretary on González's death, Rodolfo Arrechea, was for some people a bit too *kirchnerista*, and he was off the scene by the time I made another visit in September 2011. When I conducted interviews in 2012, some people who had been quite prominent in some departments of ATE-Capital were no longer there, and when I asked why not, I was given quite evasive answers. By 2013, the cracks were beginning to show more obviously, and some informants discussed the divisions within ATE with me off the record.

10. SINEP is the name for the national system agreed in the collective bargaining agreement of 2006. Prior to 2006, the system was called SINAPA.

11. See Unión Personal, accessed 5 February 2015, https://www.unionpersonal.com.ar /modulos/institucional/.

12. The remaining 2 percent consists of other smaller but institution-specific unions, which do not have representation on the *paritarias*. These figures from UPCN delegates were fairly consistent.

13. This is possibly because for UPCN, contracted workers are those in the *planta transitoria* under Resolution 48, whereas ATE will also represent those on other kinds of self-

employed contracts. Since these latter groups fall outside the collective bargaining agreement, they cannot be represented by UPCN, although in practice they often actually speak up for them and negotiate with their employers on their behalf.

14. See "Images of State Employees—Slideshow," accessed 15 September 2016, www .sianlazar.net.

15. These figures are necessarily extremely rough because of the fluctuation in currency values, both at the official and unofficial peso-dollar exchange rates. They have been calculated at 8 pesos/dollar for the unofficial rate (the *dolar blue*), which was the figure during the first part of July 2013, and 5.5 pesos/dollar for the official rate—the rate at 23 July 2013.

16. See Lazar (2012) for further discussion of this issue.

17. See Collins (2012); Fantasia and Voss (2004); Johnston (1994); and Mollona (2009) for discussions of social movement unionism (also known as community unionism) and business unionism in the United States and Brazil.

18. See Calello and Parcero (2008); and Senén González and Bosoer (2012) for a discussion of this history.

19. All translations are mine unless otherwise noted.

20. For a more or less definitive history of the first Peronist government, see Torre (2002); and Torre and Pastoriza (2002). On housing, see Aboy (2007).

21. For studies of the relation between Peronism and the popular sectors outside the organized working class, see Martuccelli and Svampa (1997); Karush and Chamosa (2010); Levitsky (2003b); Auyero (2001); Adamovsky (2012).

22. See McGuire (1997); Torre (1998); Senén González and Bosoer (2012); and D. James (1988b) for different perspectives on Peronist unionism during this time.

23. UPCN's position on participation in the normalizing commissions can be found on its website, http://www.upcndigital.org/capital/institucional/historia. UPCN argues that the commissions were part of the democratizing process.

24. Perón converted the already existing Liga de Empleados Públicos (League of Public Employees) into UPCN. The league had been founded in 1918 as a mutual association representing those employees at middle-senior levels of hierarchy in the state (Armelino 2012).

25. This figure includes workers in informal employment outside the informal sector, which constituted 17.9 percent of nonagricultural employment, while employment in the informal sector constituted 32.1 percent of nonagricultural employment. The ILO cautions that most employment in the agricultural sector is likely to be informal (International Labour Office 2013: 3).

26. See "Trade Unions" (2014) concerning higher rates of unionization in the public sector in Europe. For the United Kingdom, public-sector union membership is 56 percent, while in the private sector membership is 14 percent. See "United Kingdom: Key Facts" (2014). For the United States, the database prepared by Hirsch and Macpherson (2003) shows 35.7 percent union membership in the public sector, contrasted with 6.6 percent in the private sector in 2014. Database available at http://www.unionstats.com.

CHAPTER 2

1. It is also a very Peronist list. Two people picked Peronism itself, while "loyalty" is a word very closely related to Peronist belonging (Balbì 2007; Lazar 2013). Three chose *militancia*, also very connected to Peronist political activity and to political activism more generally.

2. While *militancia* refers to active participation, a comparative indication of the prevalence of collective mobilization in Argentina may be gleaned by looking at figures of party political membership for the two main national parties, bearing in mind that many people in Argentina belong to social or political organizations without being a registered member of a political party. In December 2012, the PJ had 3.6 million members, or 12.3 percent of the electorate, and the UCR had 2.2 million members, 7.7 percent of the electorate (Cámara Nacional Electoral 2012). Absolute PJ membership figures have remained relatively stable over the last twenty years: in 1993, the figure was 3.85 million, which was at the time 18 percent of the electorate (Levitsky 2003a). This is high, as can be seen by examining figures for the United Kingdom, which estimate that only around 1 percent of the electorate is a member of one of the three main political parties. For the purposes of comparison, in the United Kingdom, by August 2015, the Labour Party was estimated to have around 270,000 members, and Conservative Party membership as of December 2013 was around 149,800 (Keen 2015). The UK population as of December 2011 was 63.2 million (see http://www.ons.gov.uk/ons/key-figures/index.html#Population and Migration), and Argentina's, 41.7 million (see http://data.worldbank.org/country /argentina).

3. I use "militancy" interchangeably with "activism" in this book. However, I translate *militante* as "activist" because the word "militant" in English implies extremity of belief rather than just the strong commitment to political activity that is usually meant when the word is used in Argentina.

4. The Radical party (Unión Cívica Radical; Radical Civic Union) is the second main national political party in Argentina. It was founded in 1891 so predates the Peronist movement. It was the party of the progressive president of the 1930s, Hipólito Yrigoyen, and is associated with the liberal middle classes.

5. The *montoneros* was a left-wing Peronist guerrilla group that began in the early 1970s. Perón expelled it from the PJ in May 1974, as he turned for support to the right wing of his movement, which included the unions and the right-wing death squads organized by López Vega and known as the AAA or Triple A (Alianza AntiComunista Argentina; Argentine Anticommunist Alliance). When Perón died, his successor, Isabel Perón, relied even more on López Vega and the AAA. Terrorist activities by the *montoneros* and the AAA destabilized the country during 1975–76, and *montonero* activity in particular provided the excuse for the military coup of March 1976.

6. Much of Cristina's political support base lies not only in youth activist movements like La Cámpora but also in popular associations in urban neighborhoods, such as the cooperative movement.

7. *El eternauta* is a mix of the words for "eternal" and "astronaut." It was a comic strip that began in the late 1950s and took on a strongly political (leftist) tone from about 1969.

8. This kind of position is related to the "theory of the two demons," which emerged in the 1980s, and is the argument that both the military and the guerrilla forces were vio-

lent and damaging. The implication is that there is a quantitative and qualitative equivalence between the military regimes and the guerrilla forces. Although the *montoneros* are generally accepted to be the very extreme edge of 1970s *militancia*, leftist *militancia* is in some instances and for some audiences tarnished by association. In fact, the majority of those persecuted by the military regimes were simply union delegates rather than guerrillas, and the *montoneros* were mostly defeated by mid-1976; but at times the polarized state of contemporary political argument obscures such distinctions.

9. Names in this chapter are pseudonyms unless I give both first name and surname.

10. According to the Truth Commission, around 11 percent of the victims of the 1976–83 dictatorship were aged between eleven and twenty (Nunca Mas 1984).

11. At the time of the interview in 2009, Lozano was a Congress deputy for Buenos Aires para Todos (2007–11) and ally of Proyecto Sur. He then broke from Proyecto Sur and in 2011 was elected deputy for the alliance Frente Amplio Progresista (Broad Progressive Front). In 2015 he formed the Frente Popular (Popular Front) with Victor de Gennaro and stood for election as deputy for the city of Buenos Aires.

12. And one assumes, although he didn't say so explicitly, he encouraged them to vote for the PJ.

13. See note on terms and translations in Rabinow (1997).

14. For example, see "Empleada publica," YouTube, uploaded by Daniel Gardia, 28 April 2008, http://www.youtube.com/watch?v=Xl49AYEJiqE.

15. This is also a language of *contención*, or containment, in the psychotherapeutic and political sense, the other organizing value of this book.

16. This is of course not so different for most religious communities (see Lazar 2008).

17. I would describe the sociability of both male and female union leaders as avuncular. The female equivalent (meaning "auntlike") is *materteral* according to the *Oxford English Dictionary*, but this term is little used in either everyday or even academic language. Elana Shever (2012) describes the incorporation of new recruits to the Cutral Có company town of oil workers in Neuquén as the creation of avuncular relationships.

18. According to *Oxford English Dictionary* (2014) online, "vocation" is "the action on the part of God of calling a person to exercise some special function, especially of a spiritual nature, or to fill a certain position; divine influence or guidance towards a definite (esp. religious) career; the fact of being so called or directed towards a special work in life; natural tendency to, or fitness for, such work."

19. I am aware that someone convinced of the need for change but not convinced of the need for collective organization would probably not be a trade union delegate and therefore would not feature in my sample of research participants.

CHAPTER 3

1. Although he did not say so specifically, this was most likely because the uncle had been exiled to Europe as a result of his political activities.

2. For lyrics and audio clips, see Instituto Nacional Juan Domingo Perón de Estudios e Investigaciones Históricas, Sociales y Políticas, 2013, http://www.jdperon.gov.ar/1945/10/marcha-peronista/.

3. Available at El Historiador, 9 March 1956, http://www.elhistoriador.com.ar/documentos/revolucion_libertadora/decreto_4161.php.

4. FREPASO (Frente por un Pais Solidario; Front for a Country in Solidarity) was a progressive coalition formed in 1994 out of groups of dissident PJ members (in the Frente Grande; Grand Front) and other leftist parties and individuals. It was relatively successful in elections in Buenos Aires in particular but dissolved in 2001.

5. Rucci was secretary of the CGT during 1970–73 and famously loyal to Juan Perón. He was assassinated in September 1973. At the time it was not clear who had shot him, but the *montonero* leadership later admitted that at least one group of *montoneros* had been behind the murder.

6. Among the many works of fiction and testimonial to explore experiences of the Dirty War, see *The Little School* by Alicia Partnoy, *The Kiss of the Spider Woman* by Manuel Puig, *Purgatory* by Tomás Eloy Martinez, and the plays and writings of Ariel Dorfman. For English-language academic literature on memory, experience, and the Dirty War, see Taylor (2003); Robben (2007); DuBois (2005); Jelin (2003).

7. See H.I.J.O.S., accessed 30 January 2015, www.hijos.org.ar (click on "Quienes Somos" and then "Historia").

8. This kind of exchange of activism for money was something that Peronists also worried about in the mid-1990s (Martuccelli and Svampa 1997: 149).

9. Colored dye was sometimes added to the water to be able subsequently identify who had been present at a given demonstration.

10. This is not to say that this operates purely at the level of discourse; there are plenty of ways that the Kirchner governments can be considered post-neoliberal (Grugel and Riggirozzi 2012). This is, as one would expect, a topic of much discussion and disagreement (e.g., see Svampa 2014).

11. This was an important aspect of Aristotle's definition of virtue. Richard Kraut (2014) suggests that this is significant because it was Aristotle's "decisive rejection of the thesis, found throughout Plato's early dialogues, that virtue is nothing but a kind of knowledge and vice nothing but a lack of knowledge."

CHAPTER 4

1. Due to the H1N1 epidemic in July 2009, the school was closed for a few weeks, so I was unable to attend the latter part of the course, which included these events.

2. Omar Auton, the first director of Unión Personal and chief negotiator on these matters in the 1990s, explained to me his perspective on the complexities of how the health insurance organization (*obra social*) was established. He said that initially health services for public-sector administrators were organized separately in each ministry. In the early 1990s, they were brought together into two systems, one created by law that covered health workers and the Ministry of Labor and the others created by decree. ATE and UPCN had representation in each of these systems, but when in 1993 the two were combined into one, ATE "retired" (this term skates over what was a complex political argument and power struggle). The next development was to bring the newly unified institution into the legal framework for *obras sociales*, so in 1995 *se sindicalizó*—it was unionized and brought under UPCN's control. The alternative would have been to fully privatize it, according to Auton. UP and UPCN are completely separate institutions, with separate bank accounts, but UPCN runs UP, and UPCN members gain greater discounts on UP services than those who are only affiliates of UP and not UPCN. UPCN activists are very clear that their control of UP constitutes an important source of power

for their organization—as well as a significant responsibility. ATE activists say that it is a business, a means to gain money for the union at best, and for the individual leaders at worst; and this is widely thought to be the case for many of the other union-controlled *obras sociales*. Many commentators and ordinary people consider the union control of *obras sociales* to be the single biggest source of corruption within unions and their leadership, since *obras sociales* generate millions of dollars of income each year. Hence Auton's emphasis that they are separate institutions.

The *obra social* for municipal employees is not regulated by the legal system (the Ley de Obras Sociales) but run by the CABA government with SUTECBA. Municipal employees have to belong to it—much to the chagrin of many, as it is not thought to be well run—whereas in those *obras sociales* regulated by the Ley de Obras Sociales, there is space for workers to choose any *obra social* from within that system—after one year in their own *obra social*.

3. This section is adapted from Lazar (2015). The fact that UPCN strongly self-identifies as verticalist makes it stand out from many trade unions, even those whom more radical actors consider to be verticals. In an Anglo-American context, for example, this is not considered to be a virtue, and unionists are more likely to talk of their "democratic centralism" (Jeff Juris, pers. comm., 2015).

4. Although there is a common assumption that populism consists of a situation where elites simply manipulate the masses (Conniff 1999; Panizza 2000; Szusterman 2000; Tamarin 1985) and that it therefore lacks philosophical content, in fact, Perón's organizational philosophy is remarkably thorough and even sophisticated. It was extremely important for a number of key figures in the UPCN hierarchy, who talked explicitly about the direct influence that Perón's works had on them and encouraged me to read his books *Conducción política* and *La comunidad organizada* or to watch some of his speeches on YouTube.

5. Viewing participation as more important than representation is arguably also the case in many other spaces where ordinary people debate politics. One can see this especially with regard to views of those democratic institutions populated by politicians as corrupt or incompletely democratic: frequently, more local and participatory forms of political organization are imagined to be more democratic than representative institutions designed in the liberal mould (Gutmann 2002; Lazar 2008; Shah 2007).

6. He is probably making reference here to the Oesterheld quote, as Alicia Kirchner had done.

7. The use of the word *mochila* here evokes school, and clearly these workshop sessions should be linked to the kinds of self-fashioning as citizenship that take place there (for Argentina, cf. Dussel 2005).

CHAPTER 5

1. All names in this chapter are pseudonyms.
2. A portion of this section is adapted from Lazar (2013).
3. Compare the quotes in Chapter 3 where Peronism is also called a *sentimiento* in this way.
4. See Lazar (2013) for a discussion of containment as the diversion of political agency and organization away from movements that seek to resolve contradictions between labor and capital/employer on a structural level.

5. Argentina is second only to the United States in the number of psychoanalysts affiliated with the International Psychoanalytic Association, and second only to France in the size of its community of Lacanian psychoanalysts. Note that Argentina's population is around one-eighth that of the United States and less than two-thirds that of France (Bass 2006: 434).

6. The discount is 40–50 percent, depending on the program for which they are registered. See Unión Personal, accessed 21 November 2016, https://www.unionpersonal.com .ar/modulos/planes/plan.php?plan=classic,.

7. This last is quite common to most of the wealthiest unions, which run hotels, traditionally located in the beach resort of Mar del Plata. The union-run hotels boomed in the 1950s and gave members of the Argentine working class their first ever access to a vacation. UPCN's recreational centers are the remnants of this mid-twentieth-century trend.

8. This helped to some extent to protect workers' rights during periods of military dictatorship, including that of 1976–83: although workers' representation was brutally suppressed or very tightly controlled by the regime, a number of agreements negotiated prior to 1976 nominally remained in force until renegotiated in the late 1980s. The provision was derogated in 2000 but reestablished in 2004 (Cardoso and Gindin 2009).

9. Respectively, Comisión Condiciones y Medio Ambiente de Trabajo, Comisión de Igualdad de Oportunidades y Trato, Fondo de Capacitación y Recalificación Laboral, and Comisiones Paritarias de Interpretación y Carrera Centrales.

10. This refers to a situation, for example, where payment is not registered for pension contributions, jobs are not stable, and there are no benefits such as sick pay. See Lazar (2012).

11. For example, in the United States significant parts of the civil service are explicitly political appointments; in the United Kingdom, connections to particular schools and universities are extremely important in civil service recruitment; in France, civil servants can explicitly be recruited only from a few elite institutions. As Bourdieu's work reminds us, a person's ability to enter and subsequently succeed in those institutions (schools, universities, grandes écoles) is heavily influenced by family and class background (e.g., Bourdieu and Passeron 1977).

12. When singing the marcha peronista, it is usual to raise your right arm, with the upper arm at shoulder height, the elbow bent, and the palm facing you, and beat the back of your hand out away from you in time to the song.

13. Artfully? Possibly, because Lionel's advocacy of Néstor was not usually especially passionate, although he thought Néstor had been a good president and done some very important things for Argentina. People agreed that the video was moving. Perhaps Lionel had got caught up in the moment.

14. From the album Yo nunca me metí en la política, 2010.

CHAPTER 6

1. The Malbrán ATE junta interna led a very celebrated and ultimately successful two hundred–day strike and occupation in 1996–97 at the height of Menem's state reforms to protest the firing of some of their number.

2. A portion of this section is adapted from Lazar (2015).

3. They mobilized to ensure that people were placed in the correct category for their contracts.

4. This section is adapted from Lazar (2014).

5. See, for example, Hardt and Negri (2000, 2005, 2009); Escobar (2009); Juris (2008); Harvey (2012); Chatterjee (2006); Melucci (1989); Alvarez , Dagnino, and Escobar (1998).

6. I am grateful to Rupert Stasch for prompting me to consider this implication of my ethnography.

7. The Cordobazo was a series of street demonstrations and strikes in Cordoba against the military leadership of Onganía and associated very strongly with oppositional union-ist currents. See Brennan (1993). For an excellent discussion of the mobilization of 17 October, see D. James (1988a).

8. This was posted when this book was under review.

9. On Alfonsín, see Colloni (2009); on Kirchner, see "Cientos de miles de personas" (2010). There are also multiple YouTube clips of the two wakes.

10. See https://sianlazar.wordpress.com/video-clips/ for video clips and photos taken from marches, although these also give only a very partial sense of the experience of a demonstration.

11. The juxtaposition of Ross and Deleuze and Guattari is taken—with permission—from a lecture given by Christos Lynteris on 27 February 2013. Unfortunately, the lecture remains unpublished.

12. Deleuze and Guattari are at pains to stress that we should "never believe that a smooth space will suffice to save us" (2004: 500).

13. For example, see "El bombo legüero," *Nuestras Raíces* (blog), http://folkloreargentino .blogspot.com/2007/05/el-bombo-legero.html; Raices del Folklore, http://www.raices delfolklore.com.ar/tradiciones-y-costumbres/instrumentos-musicales/463-el-bombo -legueero.html; and "El bombo Santiagueño," *blogdelnoa* (blog), http://www.blogdelnoa .com.ar/santiago-del-estero/bombo-santiagueno/, all accessed 19 September 2013.

CONCLUSION

1. This might bring an additional dimension to discussions of ethical action within anthropology, which have to date often taken place as a debate between ethics as societal structure or social mores and ethics as action. Hannah Arendt has been an important influence on the proponents of especially the latter side of this debate (Lambek 2010).

2. Gramsci said, "The philosophy of *praxis* [is] the result and the crowning point of all previous history. Out of the critique of Hegelianism arose modern idealism and the philosophy of *praxis*. Hegelian immanentism becomes historicism, but it is absolute historicism only with the philosophy of *praxis*—absolute historicism or absolute humanism" (1998: 766). The "absolute historicism" is highlighted in what I think is the most barebones definition of praxis as "human activity in its material context" (Flynn 2013), from Jean-Paul Sartre, but Gramsci was also pointing to a metacritique of idealist philosophy, which was further developed by György Lukács and the Frankfurt school (Feenberg 2014).

REFERENCES

Aboy, Rosa. 2007. "'The Right to a Home': Public Housing in Post–World War II Buenos Aires." *Journal of Urban History* 33 (3): 493–518.

Adamovsky, Ezequiel. 2012. *Historia de las clases populares en la Argentina: Desde 1880 hasta 2003*. Buenos Aires: Editoral Sudamericana.

Adelman, Jeremy. 1992. "Reflections on Argentine Labour and the Rise of Perón." *Bulletin of Latin American Research* 11 (3): 243–59.

Albro, Robert. 2000. "The Populist Chola: Cultural Mediation and the Political Imagination in Quillacollo, Bolivia." *Journal of Latin American Anthropology* 5 (2): 30–88.

Alcaniz, Isabella, and Melissa Scheier. 2007. "New Social Movements with Old Party Politics: The MTL *Piqueteros* and the Communist Party in Argentina." *Latin American Perspectives* 34 (2): 157–71.

Alonso, Ana Maria. 1994. "The Politics of Space, Time and Substance: State Formation, Nationalism, and Ethnicity." *Annual Review of Anthropology* 23 (1): 379–405.

Álvarez, Gonzalo Pérez. 2015. "Continuity and Rupture in the Labor and *Piquetero* Movements in Argentine Patagonia, 1990–2011." *Latin American Perspectives* 42 (2): 42–59.

Álvarez, Lucía. 2015. "No Fue Magia. El PRO al balotaje." *Revista Anfibia*. http://www.revistaanfibia.com/cronica/nofuemagia/.

Alvarez, Sonia E., Evelina Dagnino, and Arturo Escobar, eds. 1998. *Cultures of Politics, Politics of Cultures: Revisioning Latin American Social Movements*. Boulder, CO: Westview Press.

Amato, Fernando, and Christian Boyanovsky Bazán. 2012. *Setentistas: De la plata a la casa rosada*. Buenos Aires: Penguin Random House Grupo Editorial Argentina.

Anderson, Benedict R. 2005. *Under Three Flags: Anarchism and the Anti-colonial Imagination*. London: Verso.

Anguita, Eduardo, and Martìn Caparrós. 1997–2001. *La voluntad: Una historia de la militancia revolucionaria en la Argentina*. 3 vols. Buenos Aires: Grupo Editorial Norma.

Archetti, Eduardo P. 1999. *Masculinities: Football, Polo and the Tango in Argentina, Global Issues*. Oxford: Berg.

Arendt, Hannah. 1998. *The Human Condition*. 2nd ed. Chicago: University of Chicago Press.

Aretxaga, Begoña. 2003. "Maddening States." *Annual Review of Anthropology* 32:393–410.

Arias, Cora Cecilia, Nicolás Diana Menéndez, and Paula Dinorah Salgado. 2015. "The Double Confrontation of Grassroots Unionism in Argentina: Union Democratization and Defense of Working Conditions." *Latin American Perspectives* 42 (2): 12–29.

Aristotle. 1988. *Ethics*. London: Penguin.

———. 1992. *The Politics*. London: Penguin.

Armelino, Martín. 2005. "Resistencia sin integración: Protesta, propuesta y movimiento en la acción colectiva sindical de los noventa: El caso de la CTA." In *Tomar la palabra: Estudios sobre protesta social y acción colectiva en la Argentina contemporánea*, edited by Federico Schuster, Francisco Naishtat, Gabriel Nardacchione, and Sebastián Pereyra, 275–312. Buenos Aires: Prometeo Libros.

———. 2015. "Reformas de mercado y reacciones sindicales en Argentina: Una revisión desde la experiencia de los trabajadores públicos." *Desarrollo Económico* 55 (216): 245–78.

Atzeni, Maurizio, and Pablo Ghigliani. 2007. "Labour Process and Decision-Making in Factories under Workers' Self-Management: Empirical Evidence from Argentina." *Work, Employment & Society* 21 (4): 653–71.

———. 2009. "Labour Movement in Argentina since 1945: The Limits of Trade Union Reformism." In *Trade Unionism since 1945: Towards a Global History*, vol. 2, *The Americas, Asia and Australia*, edited by Craig Phelan, 223–48. Bern: Peter Lang.

Austin, J. L. 1962. *How to Do Things with Words*. William James Lectures. Oxford: Clarendon Press.

Auyero, Javier. 2001. *Poor People's Politics: Peronist Survival Networks and the Legacy of Evita*. Durham, NC: Duke University Press.

———. 2003. *Contentious Lives: Two Argentine Women, Two Protests, and the Quest for Recognition*. Durham, NC: Duke University Press.

———. 2007. *Routine Politics and Violence in Argentina: The Gray Zone of State Power*. Cambridge: Cambridge University Press.

Auyero, Javier, and Débora Alejandra Swistun. 2009. *Flammable: Environmental Suffering in an Argentine Shantytown*. Oxford: Oxford University Press.

Badiou, Alain. 2005. *Being and Event*. London: Continuum.

Bailey, Frederick G. 1969. *Stratagems and Spoils: A Social Anthropology of Politics*. Oxford: Blackwell.

Balbì, Fernando. 2007. *De leales, desleales y traidores: Valor moral y conceptión de política en el peronismo*. Buenos Aires: Editorial Antropofagia.

Balinotti, Nicolás. 2012. "Moyano promueve juicios al estado por los fondos de las obras sociales." *La Nacion*, 5 February.

Barth, Fredrik. 1965. *Political Leadership among Swat Pathans*. London: Athlone.

Bass, Jeffrey. 2006. "In Exile from the Self: National Belonging and Psychoanalysis in Buenos Aires." *Ethos* 34 (4): 433–55.

Bear, Laura. 2007. *Lines of the Nation: Indian Railway Workers, Bureaucracy, and the Intimate Historical Self*. New York: Columbia University Press.

Benegas, Diego. 2013. "Trabajar el barrio: El escrache como intervención cultural." *Acta Sociologica* 60 (January–April): 79–101.

Bion, Wilfred. 1959. "Attacks on Linking." *International Journal of Psychoanalysis* 40: 308–15.

Blaser, Mario. 2010. *Storytelling Globalization from the Chaco and Beyond*. Durham, NC: Duke University Press.

Blom Hansen, Thomas, and Finn Stepputat, eds. 2001. *States of Imagination: Ethnographic Explorations of the Postcolonial State*. Durham, NC: Duke University Press.

Blondet, Cecilia. 2002. "The 'Devil's Deal': Women's Political Participation and Authoritarianism in Peru." In *Gender Justice, Development and Rights*, edited by Maxine Molyneux and Shahra Razavi, 277–305. Oxford: Oxford University Press.

Blustein, Paul. 2005. *And the Money Kept Rolling In (and Out): The World Bank, Wall Street, the IMF and the Bankrupting of Argentina*. New York: PublicAffairs.

Bojadzijev, Manuela. 2014. "Urban Struggles, Frontiers of Capital, and Migration in the Current Global Crisis: A Perspective from Berlin." Paper presented at EASA Congress, Tallinn.

Bourdieu, Pierre. 1977. *Outline of a Theory of Practice*. Translated by Richard Nice. Cambridge: Cambridge University Press.

Bourdieu, Pierre, and Jean-Claude Passeron. 1977. *Reproduction in Education, Society, and Culture*. Translated by Richard Nice. London: Sage.

Brennan, James. 1993. "Working Class Protest, Popular Revolt, and Urban Insurrection in Argentina: The 1969 'Cordobazo.'" *Journal of Social History* 27:477–98.

Brysk, A. 1994. *The Politics of Human Rights in Argentina: Protest, Change, and Democratization*. Stanford, CA: Stanford University Press.

Butler, Judith. 1990. *Gender Trouble: Feminism and the Subversion of Identity*. London: Routledge.

Calello, Osvaldo, and Daniel Parcero. 2008. *Historia de ATE: Los pioneros: Sus uchas, sus esperanzas*. Vol. 1, *1925–1932*. Buenos Aires: CTA Ediciones.

Callon, Michel. 2007. "What Does It Mean to Say That Economics Is Performative?" In *Do Economists Make Markets? On the Performativity of Economics*, edited by Donald A. MacKenzie, Fabian Muniesa, and Lucia Siu, 311–57. Princeton, NJ: Princeton University Press.

Cámara Nacional Electoral. 2012. "Estadística de afiliados." http://www.pjn.gov.ar/02 _Central/ViewDoc.Asp?Doc=62430&CI=INDEX100.

Camusso, Marcelo, and Maria Eugenia Santiago. 2008. "De la esfera militar al plano político: La Escuela Superior Peronista." Paper presented at Primer Congreso de estudios sobre el peronismo: La primera década. http://redesperonismo.com.ar/archivos/CD1 /PP/camusso.pdf.

Canelo, Brenda. 2013. *Fronteras internas: Migración y disputas espaciales en la ciudad de Buenos Aires*. Buenos Aires: Antropofagia.

Carbonella, August, and Sharryn Kasmir. 2014. "Introduction: Toward a Global Anthropology of Labor." In *Blood and Fire: A Global Anthropology of Labor*, edited by Sharryn Kasmir and August Carbonella, 1–29. New York: Berghahn Books.

Cardoso, Adalberto, and Julian Gindin. 2009. "Industrial Relations and Collective Bargaining: Argentina, Brazil and Mexico Compared." Geneva: International Labour Office. http://www.ilo.org/public/libdoc/ilo/2009/109B09_212_engl.pdf.

Carerra, Nicolás Iñigo, María Isabel Grau, and Analía Martí. 2006. *Agustín Tosco: La clase revolucionaria*. Buenos Aires: Ediciones Madres de Plaza de Mayo.

Carsten, Janet. 2000. *Cultures of Relatedness: New Approaches to the Study of Kinship*. Cambridge: Cambridge University Press.

———. 2004. *After Kinship*. Cambridge: Cambridge University Press.

———. 2013. "Introduction: Blood Will Out." *Journal of the Royal Anthropological Institute* 19:S1–S23.

———. 2014. *Natural Politics: Substance, Kinship, Worldview*. Presented at CUSAS Seminar, 31 May. http://cambridgesocialanthropology.blogspot.co.uk/2014/08/cusas -seminar-with-prof-janet-carsten.html.

Casas-Cortés, Maribel, Sebastian Cobarrubias, and John Pickles. 2014. "The Commons." In *A Companion to Urban Anthropology*, edited by Donald Nonini, 449–69. Oxford: Wiley-Blackwell.

Castells, Manuel. 1983. *The City and the Grassroots: A Cross-cultural Theory of Urban Social Movements*. London: Edward Arnold.

Certeau, Michel de. 1984. *The Practice of Everyday Life*. Berkeley: University of California Press.

Chatterjee, Partha. 2006. *The Politics of the Governed: Reflections on Popular Politics in Most of the World*. Leonard Hastings Schoff Lectures. New York: Columbia University Press.

"Cientos de miles de personas despidieron a Néstor Kirchner en la Casa Rosada." 2010. *La Nacion*, 29 October. http://www.lanacion.com.ar/1319326-cientos-de-miles-de-perso nas-despidieron-a-nestor-kirchner-en-la-casa-rosada.

Cohen, Jean L. 1985. "Strategy or Identity: New Theoretical Paradigms and Contemporary Social Movements." *Social Research* 52 (4): 663–716.

Cohen, Michael, and Margarita Gutman, eds. 2002. *Argentina in Collapse? The Americas Debate*. New York: New School University.

Collins, Jane. 2007. "The Rise of a Global Garment Industry and the Reimagination of Worker Solidarity." *Critique of Anthropology* 27 (4): 395–409.

———. 2012. "Theorizing Wisconsin's 2011 Protests: Community-Based Unionism Confronts Accumulation by Dispossession." *American Ethnologist* 39 (1): 6–20.

Colloni, Stella. 2009. "Conmovedor y multitudinario funeral del ex presidente argentino Raúl Alfonsín." *La Jornada*, 3 April. http://www.jornada.unam.mx/2009/04/03 /mundo/030n2mun.

Conniff, Michael, ed. 1999. *Populism in Latin America*. Tuscaloosa: University of Alabama Press.

Cook, Joanna. 2010. *Meditation in Modern Buddhism: Renunciation and Change in Thai Monastic Life*. Cambridge: Cambridge University Press.

Corsín Jiménez, Alberto, and Adolfo Estalella. 2013. "The Atmospheric Person: Value, Experiment, and 'Making Neighbors' in Madrid's Popular Assemblies." *HAU: Journal of Ethnographic Theory* 3 (2): 119–39.

Cowan, Jane K., Marie-Benedicte Dembour, and Richard Wilson, eds. 2001. *Culture and Rights: Anthropological Perspectives*. Cambridge: Cambridge University Press.

Cox, Laurence, and Cristina Flesher Fominaya. 2013. "European Social Movements and Social Theory: A Richer Narrative?" In *Understanding European Movements: New Social Movements, Global Justice Struggles, Anti-austerity Protest*, edited by Cristina Flesher Fominaya and Laurence Cox, 7–29. London: Routledge.

DaMatta, Roberto. 1991. *Carnivals, Rogues, and Heroes: An Interpretation of the Brazilian Dilemma*. Translated by John Drury. Notre Dame, IN: University of Notre Dame Press.

Das, Veena, and Deborah Poole, eds. 2004. *Anthropology in the Margins of the State*. Santa Fe, NM: SAR Press.

Dave, Naisargi. 2012. *Queer Activism in India: A Story in the Anthropology of Ethics*. Durham, NC: Duke University Press.

De La Cadena, Marisol. 2010. "Indigenous Cosmopolitics in the Andes: Conceptual Reflections beyond 'Politics.'" *Cultural Anthropology* 25 (2): 334–70.

Delaney, Carol. 1995. "Father State, Motherland, and the Birth of Modern Turkey." In

Naturalizing Power: Essays in Feminist Cultural Analysis, edited by Silvia Yanagisako and Carol Delaney, 177–200. Milton Park, UK: Taylor and Francis.

Del Campo, Hugo. 2005. *Sindicalismo y peronismo: Los comienzos de un vínculo perdurable.* Buenos Aires: Siglo Veintiuno.

Deleuze, Gilles, and Felix Guattari. 2004. *A Thousand Plateaus.* London: Bloomsbury Academic.

De Neve, Geert. 2008. "Global Garment Chains, Local Labour Activism: New Challenges to Trade Union and NGO Activism in the Tiruppur Garment Cluster, South India." In *Research in Economic Anthropology*, vol. 28, *Hidden Hands in the Market: Ethnographies of Fair Trade, Ethical Consumption, and Corporate Social Responsibility*, edited by Geert De Neve, Peter Luetchford, Jeffrey Pratt, and Donald C. Wood, 213–40. Bingley, UK: Emerald Insight.

Di Marco, Laura. 2012. *La Cámpora: Historia secreta de los herederos de Néstor y Cristina Kirchner.* Buenos Aires: Editorial Sudamericana.

Dinerstein, Ana C. 2003. "¡Que se vayan todos! Popular Insurrection and the Asambleas Barriales in Argentina." *Bulletin of Latin American Research* 22 (2): 187–200.

———. 2014. *The Politics of Autonomy in Latin America: The Art of Organising Hope.* London: Palgrave.

Donham, Donald. 2011. *Violence in a Time of Liberation: Murder and Ethnicity at a South African Gold Mine, 1994.* Durham, NC: Duke University Press.

Douglas, Hazel. 2007. *Containment and Reciprocity: Integrating Psychoanalytic Theory and Child Development Research for Work with Children.* London: Routledge.

Doyon, Louise. 2006. *Perón y los trabajadores: Los orígenes del sindicalismo peronista, 1943–1955.* Buenos Aires: Siglo Veintiuno.

DuBois, Lindsay. 2005. *The Politics of the Past in an Argentine Working-Class Neighbourhood.* Toronto: University of Toronto Press.

Durkheim, Émile. (1915) 1965. *The Elementary Forms of the Religious Life.* Translated by Joseph Ward Swain. Reprint, London: Free Press.

Durrenberger, E. Paul. 2007. "The Anthropology of Organized Labor in the United States." *Annual Review of Anthropology* 36 (1): 73–88.

Durrenberger, E. Paul, and Suzan Erem. 2005. *Class Acts: An Anthropology of Urban Workers and Their Union.* Boulder, CO: Paradigm.

Dussel, Ines. 2005. "When Appearances Are Not Deceptive: A Comparative History of School Uniforms in Argentina and the United States (Nineteenth–Twentieth Centuries)." *Paedagogica Historica* 41 (1–2): 179–95.

Elena, Eduardo. 2011. *Dignifying Argentina: Peronism, Citizenship, and Mass Consumption.* Pittsburgh: University of Pittsburgh Press.

Englund, Harri. 2008. "Extreme Poverty and Existential Obligations: Beyond Morality in the Anthropology of Africa?" *Social Analysis* 52 (3): 33–50.

Equipo Estudios Laborales. 2010. *Informe: Los conflictos laborales in el trienio 2006–2008.* Buenos Aires: Ministerio de Trabajo, Empleo y Seguridad Social. http://www.trabajo.gov.ar/left/estadisticas/descargas/conlab/Conflicto_Laboral_2006_2009.pdf.

Eriksen, Thomas Hylland. 2010. *Ethnicity and Nationalism: Anthropological Perspectives.* 3rd ed. London: Pluto Press.

Escobar, Arturo. 2009. *Territories of Difference: Place, Movements, Life, "Redes."* Durham, NC: Duke University Press.

———. 2010. "Latin America at a Crossroads." *Cultural Studies* 24 (1): 1–65.

Escobar, Arturo, and Sonia E. Alvarez, eds. 1992. *The Making of Social Movements in Latin America: Identity, Strategy, and Democracy.* Boulder, CO: Westview Press.

Etchemendy, Sebastián. 2001. "Constructing Reform Coalitions: The Politics of Compensations in Argentina's Economic Liberalization." *Latin American Politics and Society* 43 (3): 1–36.

———. 2005. "Old Actors in New Markets: Transforming the Populist/Industrial Coalition in Argentina, 1989–2001." In *Argentine Democracy: The Politics of Institutional Weakness,* edited by Steven Levitsky and Maria Victoria Murillo, 62–87. University Park: Pennsylvania State University Press.

———. 2013. "La 'doble alianza' gobierno-sindicatos en el kirchnerismo (2003–2012): Origenes, evidencias y perspectivas." In *Instituciones gubernamentales y actores de la política argentina,* edited by Carlos H. Acuña. Buenos Aires: SXXI.

Etchemendy, Sebastián, and Ruth Berins Collier. 2007. "Down but Not Out: Union Resurgence and Segmented Neocorporatism in Argentina (2003–2007)." *Politics & Society* 35 (3): 363–401.

Evans-Pritchard, Edward. 1940. *The Nuer.* Oxford: Clarendon Press.

Fairbrother, Peter. 2008. "Social Movement Unionism or Trade Unions as Social Movements." *Employee Responsibilities and Rights Journal* 20 (3): 213–20.

Fantasia, Rick. 1988. *Cultures of Solidarity: Consciousness, Action, and Contemporary American Workers.* Berkeley: University of California Press.

Fantasia, Rick, and Kim Voss. 2004. *Hard Work: Remaking the American Labor Movement.* Berkeley: University of California Press.

Fassin, Didier. 2012. *Humanitarian Reason: A Moral History of the Present Times.* Berkeley: University of California Press.

———. 2013. "On Resentment and *Ressentiment*: The Politics and Ethics of Moral Emotions." *Current Anthropology* 54 (3): 249–67.

———. 2014. "The Ethical Turn in Anthropology: Promises and Uncertainties." *HAU: Journal of Ethnographic Theory* 4 (1): 7.

———. 2015. *At the Heart of the State: The Moral World of Institutions.* London: Pluto Press.

Faubion, James D. 2011. *An Anthropology of Ethics.* Cambridge: Cambridge University Press.

Faulk, Karen. 2008. "If They Touch One of Us, They Touch All of Us: Cooperativism as a Counterlogic to Neoliberal Capitalism." *Anthropological Quarterly* 81 (3): 579–614.

———. 2012. *In the Wake of Neoliberalism: Citizenship and Human Rights in Argentina.* Stanford, CA: Stanford University Press.

Feenberg, Andrew. 2014. *The Philosophy of Praxis: Marx, Lukács, and the Frankfurt School.* London: Verso.

Ferguson, James. 1990. *The Anti-politics Machine: "Development," Depoliticisation and Bureaucratic Power in Lesotho.* Cambridge: Cambridge University Press.

———. 2015. *Give a Man a Fish: Reflections on the New Politics of Distribution.* Durham, NC: Duke University Press.

Fernández Álvarez, María Inés, ed. 2015. *Hacer juntos(as): Din'amicas, contornos y relieves de la política colectiva.* Buenos Aires: Editorial Biblios.

Figari, Carlos. 2005. "*Ocupar, resistir, producir y educar*": *Fábricas y empresas recuperadas en la ciudad de Buenos Aires.* LabourAgain Publications. http://www.iisg.nl/labouragain/documents/figari.pdf.

Flesher Fominaya, Cristina. 2014. "Movement Culture as Habit(us): Resistance to Change in the Routinized Practices of Resistance." In *Conceputalizing Culture in Social Movement Research*, edited by Britta Baumgarten, Priska Daphi, and Peter Ullrich, 186–205. Houndmills, Basingstoke, UK: Palgrave Macmillan.

Flynn, Thomas. 2013. "Jean-Paul Sartre." In *The Stanford Encyclopedia of Philosophy* (Fall 2013 ed.), edited by Edward N. Zalta. http://plato.stanford.edu/archives/fall2013/entries/sartre/.

Forbess, Alice, and Lucia Michelutti. 2013. "From the Mouth of God: Divine Kinship and Popular Democratic Politics." *Focaal* 2013 (67): 3–18.

Fortes, Meyer. 1949. *The Web of Kinship among the Tallensi: The Second Part of an Analysis of the Social Structure of a Trans-Volta Tribe.* London: Oxford University Press, for the International African Institute.

Fortes, Meyer, and Edward Evans-Pritchard, eds. 1940. *African Political Systems.* London: Oxford University Press, for the International African Institute.

Foucault, Michel. 1988. "Technologies of the Self." In *Technologies of the Self: A Seminar with Michel Foucault*, edited by Luther Martin, 16–49. London: Tavistock.

———. 1990. *The History of Sexuality.* Vol. 3, *The Care of the Self.* London: Penguin.

———. 1992. *The History of Sexuality.* Vol. 2, *The Use of Pleasure.* Translated by Robert Hurley. London: Penguin.

Freire, Paulo. 1996. *Pedagogy of the Oppressed.* London: Penguin.

Gay, Robert. 1998. "Rethinking Clientelism: Demands, Discourses and Practices in Contemporary Brazil." *European Review of Latin American and Caribbean Studies* 65:7–24.

Germani, Gino. (1956) 2006. "La integracion de las masas a la vida politica y el totalitarismo." In *Gino Germani: La renovacion intelectual de la sociologia*, edited by Alejandro Blanco, 201–21. Reprint, Bernal: Universidad Nacional de Quilmes Editorial.

Giroux, Henry. 2005. *Schooling and the Struggle for Public Life: Democracy's Promise and Education's Challenge.* 2nd ed. Boulder, CO: Paradigm.

Glaser, Barney G., and Anselm L. Strauss. 1967. *The Discovery of Grounded Theory: Strategies for Qualitative Research.* Hawthorne, NY: Aldine de Gruyter.

Gluckman, Max. 1965. *The Ideas in Barotse Jurisprudence.* New Haven, CT: Yale University Press.

Graeber, David. 2009. *Direct Action: An Ethnography.* Edinburgh: AK Press.

———. 2013. *The Democracy Project: A History, a Crisis, a Movement.* London: Random House.

Gramsci, Antonio. 1998. *Selections from the Prison Notebooks.* London: Laurence and Wishart.

Grassi, Estela. 2003. *Políticas y problemas sociales en la sociedad neoliberal: La otra década infame.* Buenos Aires: Espacio.

Grugel, Jean, and Pía Riggirozzi. 2012. "Post-neoliberalism in Latin America: Rebuilding and Reclaiming the State after Crisis." *Development and Change* 43 (1): 1–21.

Guano, Emanuela. 2002. "Spectacles of Modernity: Transnational Imagination and Local Hegemonies in Neoliberal Buenos Aires." *Cultural Anthropology* 17 (2): 181–209.

———. 2003. "A Color for the Modern Nation: The Discourse on Class, Race, and Education in the Porteño Middle Class." *Journal of Latin American Anthropology* 8 (1): 148–71.

Guevara, Che. 1965. *El socialismo y el hombre en Cuba.* https://www.marxists.org/espanol/guevara/65-socyh.htm.

Guglielmucci, Ana. 2013. *La consagración de la memoria: Una etnografía acerca de la institucionalización del recuerdo sobre los crímenes del terrorismo de estado en la Argentina*. Buenos Aires: Antropofagia.

Gutmann, Matthew. 2002. *The Romance of Democracy: Compliant Defiance in Contemporary Mexico*. Berkeley: University of California Press.

Guyer, Jane I. 2007. "Prophecy and the Near Future: Thoughts on Macroeconomic, Evangelical, and Punctuated Time." *American Ethnologist* 34 (3): 409–21.

Haidar, Julieta. 2015. "Interpreting Argentine Business Unionism." *Latin American Perspectives* 42 (2): 60–73.

Halperin Donghi, Tulio. 2012. *La larga agonia de la argentina peronista*. Buenos Aires: Ariel.

Hardt, Michael, and Antonio Negri. 2000. *Empire*. Cambridge, MA: Harvard University Press.

———. 2005. *Multitude*. London: Hamish Hamilton.

———. 2009. *Commonwealth*. Cambridge, MA: Belknap Press.

Harris, Olivia. 2004. "Braudel: Historical Time and the Horror of Discontinuity." *History Workshop Journal* 57:161–74.

Harvey, David. 2012. *Rebel Cities: From the Right to the City to the Urban Revolution*. London: Verso.

Herzfeld, Michael. 2007. "Global Kinship: Anthropology and the Politics of Knowing." *Anthropological Quarterly* 80 (2): 313–23.

Heywood, Paolo. 2015. "Making a Difference: Ethics, Activism, and Anthropological Theory." PhD diss., University of Cambridge.

Hinshelwood, R. D. 1989. *A Dictionary of Kleinian Thought*. London: Free Association Books.

Hirsch, Barry T., and David A. Macpherson. 2003. "Union Membership and Coverage Database from the Current Population Survey: Note." *Industrial and Labor Relations Review* 56 (2): 349–54.

Holston, James. 2008. *Insurgent Citizenship: Disjunctions of Democracy and Modernity in Brazil*. Princeton, NJ: Princeton University Press.

Holston, James, and Arjun Appadurai, eds. 1999. *Cities and Citizenship*. Durham, NC: Duke University Press.

Horowitz, Joel. 1990. *Argentine Unions, the State and the Rise of Peron, 1930–1945*. Berkeley: University of California Press.

Howell, Signe. 2006. *Kinning of Foreigners: Transnational Adoption in a Global Perspective*. Oxford: Berghahn Books.

International Labour Office. 2013. "Women and Men in the Informal Economy: A Statistical Picture." 2nd ed. Geneva: International Labour Office. http://wiego.org/publications/women-and-men-informal-economy-statistical-picture-2nd-edition.

Issa, Daniela. 2007. "Praxis of Empowerment: *Mística* and Mobilization in Brazil's Landless Rural Workers' Movement." *Latin American Perspectives* 34 (2): 124–38.

James, Daniel. 1988a. "October 17th and 18th, 1945: Mass Protest, Peronism and the Argentine Working Class." *Journal of Social History* 21 (3): 441–61.

———. 1988b. *Resistance and Integration: Peronism and the Argentine Working Class, 1946–1976*. Cambridge: Cambridge University Press.

———. 2000. *Doña María's Story: Life History, Memory, and Political Identity*. Durham, NC: Duke University Press.

Jasper, James. 2012. "Introduction: From Political Opportunity Structures to Strategic Interaction." In *Contention in Context: Political Opportunities and the Emergence of Protest*, edited by Jeff Goodwin and James Jasper, 1–36. Stanford, CA: Stanford University Press.

Jelin, Elizabeth. 2003. *State Repression and the Labors of Memory*. Minneapolis: University of Minnesota Press.

Jelin, Elizabeth, and Eric Hershberg. 1996. *Constructing Democracy: Human Rights, Citizenship, and Society in Latin America*. Oxford: Westview Press.

Jenkins, J. Craig. 1983. "Resource Mobilization Theory and the Study of Social Movements." *Annual Review of Sociology* 9 (1): 527–53.

Johnston, Hank, and John A. Noakes, eds. 2005. *Frames of Protest: Social Movements and the Framing Perspective*. Lanham, MD: Rowman and Littlefield.

Johnston, P. 1994. *Success While Others Fail: Social Movement Unionism and the Public Workplace*. Ithaca, NY: ILR Press.

Juris, Jeffrey S. 2008. *Networking Futures: The Movements against Corporate Globalization*. Durham, NC: Duke University Press.

———. 2012. "Reflections on #Occupy Everywhere: Social Media, Public Space, and Emerging Logics of Aggregation." *American Ethnologist* 39 (2): 259–79.

———. 2014. "Embodying Protest: Culture and Performance within Social Movements." In *Conceptualizing Culture in Social Movement Research*, edited by Britta Baumgarten, Priska Daphi, and Peter Ullrich, 227–49. Houndmills, Basingstoke, UK: Palgrave Macmillan.

Juris, Jeffrey S., and A. Khasnabish. 2013. *Insurgent Encounters: Transnational Activism, Ethnography, and the Political*. Durham, NC: Duke University Press.

Kaiser, Susana. 2002. "*Escraches*: Demonstrations, Communication and Political Memory in Post-dictatorial Argentina." *Media, Culture & Society* 24 (4): 499–516.

———. 2011. "Memory Inventory: The Production and Consumption of Memory Goods in Argentina." In *Accounting for Violence: Marketing Memory in Latin America*, edited by Ksenija Bilbija and Leigh Payne, 313–38. Durham, NC: Duke University Press.

Kalb, Don. 2014. "Class." In *A Companion to Urban Anthropology*, edited by Donald Nonini, 157–76. Oxford: Wiley-Blackwell.

———. 2015. "Introduction: Class and the New Anthropological Holism." In *Anthropologies of Class*, edited by James Carrier and Don Kalb, 5–33. Cambridge: Cambridge University Press.

Karush, Matthew, and Oscar Chamosa, eds. 2010. *The New Cultural History of Peronism*. Durham, NC: Duke University Press.

Kasmir, Sharryn. 2005. "Activism and Class Identity: The Saturn Auto Factory Case." In *Social Movements: An Anthropological Reader*, edited by June Nash, 78–96. Oxford: Blackwell.

Keane, W. 2016. *Ethical Life: Its Natural and Social Histories*. Princeton, NJ: Princeton University Press.

Keen, Richard. 2015. "Membership of UK Political Parties." Briefing paper SN05125, House of Commons Library, 11 August. http://www.parliament.uk/briefing-papers/sn05125.pdf.

Klein, Naomi. 2014. *This Changes Everything: Capitalism vs. the Climate*. London: Allen Lane.

Kraut, Richard. 2014. "Aristotle's *Ethics*." In *The Stanford Encyclopedia of Philoso-*

phy (Spring 2016 ed.), edited by Edward N. Zalta. http://plato.stanford.edu/archives/spr2016/entries/aristotle-ethics/.

Laclau, Ernesto. 2005. *On Populist Reason*. London: Verso.

Lagalisse, Erica. 2013. "Gossip as Direct Action." In *Contesting Publics: Feminism, Activism, Ethnography*, edited by Sally Cole and Lynne Phillips, 112–37. London: Pluto Press.

Laidlaw, James. 2002. "For an Anthropology of Ethics and Freedom." *Journal of the Royal Anthropological Institute* 8 (2): 311–32.

———. 2014. *The Subject of Virtue: An Anthropology of Ethics and Freedom*. Cambridge: Cambridge University Press.

Lambek, Michael. 2010. *Ordinary Ethics: Anthropology, Language, and Action*. New York: Fordham University Press.

Lazar, Sian. 2008. *El Alto, Rebel City: Self and Citizenship in Andean Bolivia*. Durham, NC: Duke University Press.

———. 2010. "Schooling and Critical Citizenship: Pedagogies of Political Agency in El Alto, Bolivia." *Anthropology and Education Quarterly* 41 (2): 181–205.

———. 2012. "A Desire to Formalize Work? Comparing Trade Union Strategies in Bolivia and Argentina." *Anthropology of Work Review* 33 (1): 15–24.

———. 2013. "Citizenship, Political Agency and Technologies of the Self in Argentine Trade Unions." *Critique of Anthropology* 33 (1): 110–28.

———. 2014. "Historical Narrative, Mundane Political Time, and Revolutionary Moments: Coexisting Temporalities in the Lived Experience of Social Movements." *Journal of the Royal Anthropological Institute* 20:91–108.

———. 2015. "Of Autocracy and Democracy, or Discipline and Anarchy: When Organizational Structure Meets Political Ideology in Argentinean Public Sector Trade Unions." *PoLAR* 38 (2): 279–99.

———. 2016a. "'The Happiness Revolution': Argentina and the End of Post-neoliberalism?" *FocaalBlog*. http://www.focaalblog.com/2016/03/17/sian-lazar-the-happiness-revolution-argentina-and-the-end-of-post-neoliberalism.

———. 2016b. "Notions of Work, Patrimony and Production in the Life of the Colón Opera House." *Journal of Latin American and Caribbean Anthropology* 21 (2): 231–53.

Lessa, Francesca, and Cara Levey. 2015. "From Blanket Impunity to Judicial Opening(s): H.I.J.O.S. and Memory Making in Postdictatorship Argentina (2005–2012)." *Latin American Perspectives* 42 (3): 207–25.

Levitsky, Steven. 2003a. "From Labor Politics to Machine Politics: The Transformation of Party-Union Linkages in Argentine Peronism, 1983–1999." *Latin American Research Review* 38 (3): 3–36.

———. 2003b. *Transforming Labor-Based Parties in Latin America: Argentine Peronism in Comparative Perspective*: New York: Cambridge University Press.

Licht, Silvia. 2009. *Agustín Tosco (1930/1975): Sindicalismo clasista, socialismo y peronismo revolucionario*. Buenos Aires: Editorial Biblos.

Lopez, S. H. 2004. *Reorganizing the Rust Belt: An Inside Study of the American Labor Movement*. Berkeley: University of California Press.

Maeckelbergh, Marianne. 2009. *The Will of the Many: How the Alterglobalisation Movement Is Changing the Face of Democracy*. London: Pluto Press.

Malikail, Joseph. 2003. "Moral Character: Hexis, Habitus and 'Habit.'" *Minerva—An Internet Journal of Philosophy* 7:1–22.

Manzano, Virginia. 2013. *La política en movimiento: Movilizaciones colectivas y políticas estatales en la vida del Gran Buenos Aires*. Rosario, Argentina: Prohistoria.

Marcuse, Herbert. 1969. *An Essay on Liberation*. https://www.marxists.org/reference /archive/marcuse/works/1969/essay-liberation.pdf.

Marshall, Adriana, and Laura Perelman. 2004. *Sindicalización: Incentivos en la normativa sociolaboral*. Vol. 4, *Cuadernos del ides*. Buenos Aires: IDES.

Martuccelli, Danilo, and Maristella Svampa. 1997. *La plaza vacìa: Las transformaciones del peronismo*. Buenos Aires: Editorial Losada.

Marx, Karl. 1845. *Theses on Feuerbach*. https://www.marxists.org/archive/marx/works /1845/theses/theses.htm.

Mason, Alfredo. 2007. *Sindicalismo y dictadura: Una historia poco contada (1976–1983)*. Buenos Aires: Editorial Biblos.

Mattingly, Cheryl. 2014. "Moral Deliberation and the Agentive Self in Laidlaw's Ethics." *HAU: Journal of Ethnographic Theory* 4 (1): 473–86.

Mauro, Sebastián, and Federico M. Rossi. 2015. "The Movement of Popular and Neighborhood Assemblies in the City of Buenos Aires, 2002–2011." *Latin American Perspectives* 42 (2): 107–24.

Mauss, Marcel. 1973. "Techniques of the Body." *Economy and Society* 2 (1): 70–88.

McGuire, James. 1997. *Peronism without Perón: Unions, Parties, and Democracy in Argentina*. Stanford, CA: Stanford University Press.

Melucci, Alberto. 1989. *Nomads of the Present: Social Movements and Individual Needs in Contemporary Society*. Philadelphia: Temple University Press.

Mollona, Massimiliano. 2009. "Community Unionism versus Business Unionism: The Return of the Moral Economy in Trade Union Studies." *American Ethnologist* 36 (4): 651–66.

———. 2015. "Anthropology and Class: A View from a Brazilian Barrio." In *Anthropologies of Class: Power, Practice, and Inequality*, edited by James Carrier and Don Kalb, 149–63. Cambridge: Cambridge University Press.

Molyneux, Maxine. 2000. *Women's Movements in International Perspective: Latin America and Beyond*. Houndmills, Basingstoke, UK: Palgrave Macmillan.

Moody, Kim. 1997. "Towards an International Social-Movement Unionism." *New Left Review* 225 (September–October): 52–72.

Munck, Ronaldo, Ricardo Galitelli, and Ricardo Falcon. 1987. *Argentina from Anarchism to Peronism: Workers, Unions and Politics 1855–1985*. London: Zed Books.

Murmis, Miguel, and Juan Carlos Portantiero. 1972. *Estudios sobre los orígenes del peronismo*. Buenos Aires: Siglo Veintiuno.

Nash, June, ed. 2005. *Social Movements: An Anthropological Reader*. Oxford: Blackwell.

———. 2014. "Reassessing the Culture Concept in the Analysis of Global Social Movements: An Anthropological Perspective." In *Conceptualizing Culture in Social Movement Research*, edited by Britta Baumgarten, Priska Daphi, and Peter Ullrich, 67–87. Houndmills, Basingstoke, UK: Palgrave Macmillan.

Natanson, José. 2012. *¿Porqué los jóvenes están volviendo a la política? De los indignados a la Cámpora*. Buenos Aires: Debate.

Nguyen, Vinh-Kim. 2010. *The Republic of Therapy: Triage and Sovereignty in West Africa's Time of AIDS*. Durham, NC: Duke University Press.

Nouzeilles, Gabriela, and Graciela R. Montaldo. 2002. *The Argentina Reader: History, Culture, Politics*. Durham, NC: Duke University Press.

Nunca Más. 1984. "Part II: The Victims." http://www.desaparecidos.org/nuncamas/web/english/library/nevagain/nevagain_210.htm (English) or http://www.desaparecidos.org/nuncamas/web/index2.htm (Spanish).

Ong, Aihwa. 1996. "Cultural Citizenship as Subject-Making: Immigrants Negotiate Racial and Cultural Boundaries in the United States [and Comments and Reply]." *Current Anthropology* 37 (5): 737–62.

———. 2003. *Buddha Is Hiding: Refugees, Citizenship, the New America.* California Series in Public Anthropology. Berkeley: University of California Press.

Osterweil, Michal. 2014. "Social Movements." In *A Companion to Urban Anthropology*, edited by Donald Nonini, 470–85. Oxford: Wiley-Blackwell.

Otañez, Marty. 2010. "The Tobacco Trap: Obstacles to Trade Unionism in Malawi." In *Anthropology of Labor Unions*, edited by E. Paul Durrenberger and Karaleah Reichart, 189–210. Denver: University of Colorado Press.

Panizza, Francisco. 2000. "New Wine in Old Bottles? Old and New Populism in Latin America." *Bulletin of Latin American Research* 19:145–47.

———. 2005. *Populism and the Mirror of Democracy.* London: Verso.

Parry, Jonathan. 2013. "Company and Contract Labour in a Central Indian Steel Plant." *Economy and Society* 42 (3): 348–74.

Pereira, Fabián, Gustavo Martinez, Mónica Maidana, and Pablo Sanseverino. 2009. "ATE Capital en el siglo XXI: Nueve años de crecimiento sostenido. Informe de la secretaria de organización." Unpublished manuscript.

Perón, Juan Domingo. 1971. *Conducción política.* Buenos Aires: Editorial Freeland.

Phelan, Craig, ed. 2009. *Trade Unionism since 1945: Towards a Global History.* Vol. 2, *The Americas, Asia and Australia.* Bern: Peter Lang.

Plotkin, Mariano Ben. 2001. *Freud in the Pampas: The Emergence and Development of a Psychoanalytic Culture in Argentina.* Stanford, CA: Stanford University Press.

———. 2003. *Argentina on the Couch: Psychiatry, State, and Society, 1880 to the Present.* Albuquerque: University of New Mexico Press.

Polletta, Francesca. 2002. *Freedom Is an Endless Meeting: Democracy in American Social Movements.* Chicago: University of Chicago Press.

Pozzi, Pablo, and Fabio Nigra, eds. 2015. "Argentina a Decade after the Collapse Part 2: Old and New Social Movements." Special issue, *Latin American Perspectives* 42 (2).

Rabinow, Paul, ed. 1997. *The Essential Works of Foucault, 1954–1984.* Vol. 1, *Ethics, Subjectivity and Truth.* New York: New Press.

Razsa, Maple. 2013. "The Subjective Turn: The Radicalization of Personal Experience within Occupy Slovenia." *Cultural Anthropology Online.* https://culanth.org/fieldsights/74-the-subjective-turn-the-radicalization-of-personal-experience-within-occupy-slovenia.

———. 2015. *Bastards of Utopia: Living Radical Politics after Socialism.* Bloomington: Indiana University Press.

Razsa, Maple, and Andrej Kurnik. 2012. "The Occupy Movement in Žižek's hometown: Direct Democracy and a Politics of Becoming." *American Ethnologist* 39 (2): 238–58.

Robben, Antonius. 2007. *Political Violence and Trauma in Argentina.* Philadelphia: University of Pennsylvania Press.

Robbins, Joel. 2004. *Becoming Sinners: Christianity and Moral Torment in a Papua New Guinea Society.* San Diego: University of California Press.

————. 2013. "Beyond the Suffering Subject: Toward an Anthropology of the Good." *Journal of the Royal Anthropological Institute* 19 (3): 447–62.

Rose, Nikolas. 1989. *Governing the Soul: The Shaping of the Private Self.* London: Routledge.

————. 1999. *Powers of Freedom: Reframing Political Thought.* Cambridge: Cambridge University Press.

Ross, Kristin. 2008. *The Emergence of Social Space: Rimbaud and the Paris Commune.* London: Verso.

Sahlins, Marshall. 2013. *What Kinship Is—and Is Not.* Chicago: University of Chicago Press.

Schamber, Pablo. 2008. *De los dessechos a las mercancías: Una etnografía de los cartoneros.* Buenos Aires: Editorial SB.

Scolnik, Fernando. 2015. "Grassroots Labor Organizations in Metropolitan Buenos Aires, 2003–2007." *Latin American Perspectives* 42 (2): 30–41.

Senén González, Cecilia, David Trajtemberg, and Barbara Medwid. 2009. "La expansión de la afiliación sindical: Análisis del módulo de relaciones laborales de la EIL." In *Trabajo, ocupación y empleo: Estudios laborales 2008*, edited by Ministerio de Trabajo Gobierno de Argentina, 13–34. Buenos Aires: Ministerio de Trabajo, Empleo y Seguridad Social.

Senén González, Santiago, and Fabián Bosoer. 2012. *La lucha continúa . . . 200 años de historia sindical en la Argentina.* Buenos Aires: Vergara.

Seveso, César. 2010. "Political Emotions and the Origins of the Peronist Resistance." In *The New Cultural History of Peronism: Power and Identity in Mid-Twentieth-Century Argentina*, edited by Matthew Karush and Oscar Chamosa, 239–69. Durham, NC: Duke University Press.

Shah, Alpa. 2007. "Keeping the State Away: Democracy, Politics and Imaginations of the State in India's Jharkhand." *Journal of the Royal Anthropological Institute* 13 (1): 129–45.

————. 2013. "The Intimacy of Insurgency: Beyond Coercion, Greed or Grievance in Maoist India." *Economy and Society* 42 (3): 480–506.

Sharma, Aradhana, and Akhil Gupta, eds. 2006. *The Anthropology of the State: A Reader.* Oxford: Blackwell.

Shever, Elana. 2012. *Resources for Reform: Oil and Neoliberalism in Argentina.* Stanford, CA: Stanford University Press.

Silver, Beverly. 2003. *Forces of Labor: Workers' Movements and Globalization since 1870.* Cambridge: Cambridge University Press.

Sitrin, Marina, ed. 2006. *Horizontalism: Voices of Popular Power in Argentina.* Oakland, CA: AK Press.

————. 2012. *Everyday Revolutions: Horizontalism and Autonomy in Argentina.* London: Zed Books.

Standing, Guy. 1989. "Global Feminisation through Flexible Labour." *World Development* 17 (7): 1077–95.

————. 2011. *The Precariat: The New Dangerous Class.* London: Bloomsbury.

Steinmetz, George, ed. 1999. *State/Culture: State Formation after the Cultural Turn.* Ithaca, NY: Cornell University Press.

Stoler, Ann Laura. 2002. *Carnal Knowledge and Imperial Power: Race and the Intimate in Colonial Rule.* Berkeley: University of California Press.

Suriano, Juan. 2010. *Paradoxes of Utopia: Anarchist Culture and Politics in Buenos Aires, 1890–1910.* Oakland, CA: AK Press.

Sutton, Barbara. 2010. *Bodies in Crisis: Culture, Violence, and Women's Resistance in Neoliberal Argentina.* New Brunswick, NJ: Rutgers University Press.

Svampa, Maristella. 2014. *Maldesarrollo: La Argentina del extractivismo y del despojo.* Buenos Aires: Ediciones Katz.

Svampa, Maristella, and Claudio Pandolfi. 2004. Las vías de la criminalización de la protesta en Argentina. *Observatorio Social de América Latina* 5:285–96.

Szusterman, Celia. 2000. "Carlos Saúl Menem: Variations on the Theme of Populism." *Bulletin of Latin American Research* 19:193–206.

Tamarin, David. 1985. *The Argentine Labor Movement, 1930–1945: A Study in the Origins of Peronism.* Albuquerque: University of New Mexico Press.

Tate, Winifred. 2007. *Counting the Dead: The Culture and Politics of Human Rights Activism in Colombia.* Berkeley: University of California Press.

Taylor, Diana. 2003. *The Archive and the Repertoire: Performing Cultural Memory in the Americas.* Durham, NC: Duke University Press.

Tilly, Charles. 1978. *From Mobilization to Revolution.* London: Addison-Wesley.

———. 1993. "Contentious Repertoires in Great Britain, 1758–1834." *Social Science History* 17 (2): 253–80.

Tilly, Charles, and Sidney Tarrow. 2006. *Contentious Politics.* Oxford: Oxford University Press.

Tilly, Charles, and Lesley Wood. 2012. *Social Movements, 1768–2012.* Boulder, CO: Paradigm.

Torre, Juan Carlos. 1990. *La vieja guardia sindical y Perón: Sobre los orígenes del peronismo.* Buenos Aires: Editorial Sudamericana-Instituto Torcuato di Tella.

———. 1998. "The Ambivalent Giant: The Peronist Labor Movement, 1945–1995." In *Peronism and Argentina,* edited by James Brennan, 125–40. Wilmington, DE: Scholarly Resources.

———, ed. 2002. *Los años peronistas (1943–1955).* Edited by Juan Suriano. Nueva Historia Argentina. Buenos Aires: Sudamericana.

———. 2012. *Ensayos sobre movimiento obrero y peronismo.* Buenos Aires: Siglo Veintiuno.

Torre, Juan Carlos, and Eliza Pastoriza. 2002. "La democratización del bienestar." In *Los años peronistas (1943–1955),* edited by Juan Carlos Torre, 257–312. Buenos Aires: Editorial Sudamericana.

Touraine, Alain. 1988. *The Return of the Actor: Social Theory in Post-industrial Society.* Minneapolis: University of Minnesota Press.

"Trade Unions." 2014. European Trade Union Institute. http://www.worker-participation.eu/National-Industrial-Relations/Across-Europe/Trade-Unions2.

Trouillot, Michel-Rolph. 2001. "The Anthropology of the State in the Age of Globalization." *Current Anthropology* 42 (1): 125–38.

Tugal, Cihan. 2013. "Commentary: 'Resistance Everywhere': The Gezi Revolt in Global Perspective." *New Perspectives on Turkey* 49:157–72.

Turner, Lowell, and Richard W. Hurd. 2001. "Building Social Movement Unionism: The Transformation of the American Labor Movement." Cornell University ILR School, DigitalCommons@ILR. http://digitalcommons.ilr.cornell.edu/articles/313.

Turner, Victor. 1969. *The Ritual Process: Structure and Anti-structure.* London: Routledge.

Ullrich, Peter, Priska Daphi, and Britta Baumgarten. 2014. "Protest and Culture: Concepts and Approaches in Social Movement Research—an Introduction." In *Conceptualizing Culture in Social Movement Research*, edited by Britta Baumgarten, Priska Daphi, and Peter Ullrich, 1–22. Hpundmills, Basingstoke, UK: Palgrave Macmillan.

Usami, Koichi. 2004. "Transformation and Continuity of the Argentine Welfare State: Evaluating Social Security Reform in the 1990s." *Developing Economies* 42 (2): 217–40.

Wade, Peter. 2005. "Rethinking Mestizaje: Ideology and Lived Experience." *Journal of Latin American Studies* 37 (2): 239–57.

Walder, Andrew G. 2009. "Political Sociology and Social Movements." *Annual Review of Sociology* 35 (1): 393–412.

Waterman, Peter. 1993. "Social-Movement Unionism: A New Union Model for a New World Order?" *Review (Fernand Braudel Center)* 16 (3): 245–78.

Weber, Max. 1968. *Economy and Society: An Outline of Interpretive Sociology.* New York: Bedminster Press.

Werbner, Pnina. 2014. "'The Duty to Act Fairly': Ethics, Legal Anthropology, and Labor Justice in the Manual Workers Union of Botswana." *Comparative Studies in Society and History* 56 (2): 479–507.

Werbner, Pnina, Martin Webb, and Kathryn Spellman-Poots, eds. 2014. *The Political Aesthetics of Global Protest: The Arab Spring and Beyond.* Edinburgh: Edinburgh University Press.

Wilson, Richard, ed. 1997. *Human Rights, Culture and Context: Anthropological Perspectives.* London: Pluto Press.

Wolanski, Sandra. 2015. "La familia telefónica: Sobre las relaciones de parentesco en la política sindical." *Cuadernos de Antropología Social* 42:91–107.

Zigon, Jarrett. 2008. *Morality: An Anthropological Perspective.* Oxford: Berg.

———. 2014. "An Ethics of Dwelling and a Politics of World-Building: A Critical Response to Ordinary Ethics." *Journal of the Royal Anthropological Institute* 20 (4): 746–64.

Zlolniski, Christian. 2010. "Economic Globalization and Changing Capital-Labor Relations in Baja California's Fresh-Produce Industry." In *Anthropology of Labor Unions*, edited by E. Paul Durrenberger and Karaleah Reichart, 157–88. Denver: University of Colorado Press.

Zorzoli, Luciana. 2015. "Trade Unions under Reform: Neoliberal Transformations from Dictatorship to Democracy in Argentina." Paper presented at the Latin American Anthropology Seminar Series Senate House, London, 12 February.

INDEX

Page numbers in italic indicate material in figures.